TRENDS
& ISSUES
IN POSTSECONDARY ENGLISH STUDIES

2000 EDITION

NATIONAL COUNCIL OF TEACHERS OF ENGLISH
1111 W. KENYON ROAD, URBANA, ILLINOIS 61801-1096

Staff Editor: Bonny Graham
Interior Design: Tom Kovacs for TGK Design; Carlton Bruett
Cover Design: Carlton Bruett

NCTE Stock Number: 55154-3050
ISSN 1527-4241

42671847

TRENDS AND ISSUES

Keeping track of the myriad issues in education can be a daunting task for those educators already stretched to fit thirty hours into a twenty-four-hour day. In an effort to inform and support English educators, the National Council of Teachers of English annually offers this volume featuring current trends and issues deemed vital to the professional conversation by our membership at large. Whether specialists or generalists, teachers know that no single "trend" or "issue" could touch the interests and concerns of all members of NCTE; with these books—one for each section of the Council: Elementary, Secondary, Postsecondary—we aim to chronicle developments in the teaching and learning of English language arts.

The wealth of NCTE publications from which to draw the materials for *Trends and Issues* proves a double-edged sword. Publishing thirteen journals (bimonthly and quarterly) and twenty to twenty-five books annually provides ample content, yet what to include and what not? Of course, timeliness and pertinence to the issues of the day help shape the book, and, more important, we aim to meet our primary goal: to answer the question, Is this valuable to our members? This edition of *Trends and Issues* offers readers a seat at the table, a chance to join the discussion. At the postsecondary level, the trends and issues cited for this year are "Race/Class/Gender Positions," "Technology," and "Writing Assessment." At the secondary level, members cited "The World Wide Web in the Classroom," "The Reemergence of Critical Literacy," and "Aesthetic Appreciation versus Critical Interrogation" as those topics of current relevance to them as English language arts professionals. At the elementary level, the trends and issues encompass "Writing and a Move to New Literacies," "Critical Literacy," and "Taking New Action."

We hope that you'll find this collection a valuable resource to be returned to often, one that facilitates professional development and reminds us that we all have a stake in the language arts profession.

NCTE invites you to send us those trends and issues in the English language arts that you feel are the most relevant to your teaching. Send your comments either to our Web site at www.ncte.org or e-mail directly to Paul Bodmer at pbodmer@ncte.org.

Paul Bodmer
Associate Executive Director

CONTENTS

III. TECHNOLOGY

INTRODUCTION

A fictionalized and often romanticized segment of U.S. history is the mountain man era of the early nineteenth century. Often based on the real-life adventures of actual fur traders and mountain men, most of these people would have been considered illiterate by today's standards, and possibly only signature literate in their own day. A common description of a good mountain man, however, is that he could "read" sign. If he could not read sign, he did not survive. Reading sign was a complex activity that included choosing the right river valley to follow (whether he stayed on the main river or chose a tributary) to reach his destination; knowing whether the clouds on the edge of the horizon meant a thundershower that would cause the creek he was camping by to rise; and constantly scanning the horizon for signs of other life that might be dangerous, friendly, or food. Just as the mountain man interpreted his environment in order to survive, we interpret language. If literacy in a larger sense is the skill to interpret, through our senses, the environment surrounding us, then literacy skills must be learned in order to survive in our environment.

Aiding literacy are the tools of that literacy, whether they be weather forecasting, telescopes, printed matter from printing presses, or the digitized images on a screen. Those who are allowed, or taught, to use the literacy tools of our society become the leaders of the culture and the possessors of the literacy. This is simply common sense. What is important is how the tools are made available. If we allow only a small percentage of our population to attend school and learn to read (males of the upper class, for instance), then our literacy and culture will be controlled by those few. Cynthia Selfe tells us in her 1998 Conference on College Composition and Communication chair's address that the same argument is being made with regard to digital literacy. It is imperative, she says, that we pay attention to whatever tools of literacy are part of our culture, because enfranchising some people and disenfranchising others from those tools create the culture we may or may not want to have.

The idea that literacy is defined by who has access to that literacy ties together the three sections of this volume of *Trends and Issues*. The thread is most obvious in the first section, Race/Class/Gender Positions, and in the third, Technology. The middle section, Assessment, also addresses this issue, in that how we assess literacy tools determines who shall possess the tools.

The strength of the articles and book chapters collected here is that all are solidly grounded in the belief that what we do matters as we work to create a profession that enfranchises and enlightens the whole world we work in.

1 RACE/CLASS/GENDER POSITIONS

NCTE publications for 1999 included a wide variety of articles and books that explored the effects of positioning due to race, class, and gender. The following pieces were chosen because they each offer a lens through which we can view how we learn, live, and grow, and therefore how we must research, write, and teach, based on the positions we hold.

The June 1999 *College Composition and Communication (CCC)* is rich with articles about gender, class, and race positions. In fact, three of the pieces included in this publication come from that issue. Victor Villanueva's CCCC chair's address, "On the Rhetoric and Precedents of Racism," leads this publication as it frames and questions our deliberate, even if unintentional, focusing of our lenses. In "Feminism in Composition: Inclusion, Metonymy, and Disruption," Joy Ritchie and Kathleen Boardman explore the different but converging narratives of feminism in composition as scholars broke into the field, figured out how to work alongside the established gender assumptions, and opened the conversation for a variety of voices.

Julie Lindquist expands the topic of positioning to the issue of class in "Class Ethos and the Politics of Inquiry: What the Barroom Can Teach Us about the Classroom." She uses her experiences as a bartender in a neighborhood bar to explore how that community is both like and different from the academic community of the classroom. The final selection for this section returns to the June *CCC*, showcasing Jacqueline Jones Royster and Jean C. Williams's essay "History in the Spaces Left: African American Presence and Narratives of Composition Studies." Building on William Cook's CCCC chair's address from 1992, they explore the consequences of the authority vested in the standard text and how that authority, deliberately or not, excludes others from the conversation.

The articles chosen for this volume focus on the need to look more closely at the consequences of not paying attention to or acknowledging the lenses through which we perceive and do our work. As Royster and Williams remind us, "The privilege of primacy . . . sets in motion a struggle between these 'prime' narratives and other narrative views . . . for agency and authority" (p. 90). In many ways, it is the subtexts of these articles that speak to the larger need to be aware.

1 On the Rhetoric and Precedents of Racism

Victor Villanueva

Una Historia

The scene is Peru. It's the end of the 15th century. Father Valverde, a Franciscan, is speaking to the Incan philosopher-rhetorician about the ways of the world. The Franciscan intends to be instructive, to attempt to raise the indigenous from its ignorance. But the Incan doesn't recognize the developmental mindset and enters into dialectical interplay. Having heard of how things work according to Father Valverde, the Incan responds:

> You listed five preeminent men whom I ought to know. The first is God, three and one, which are four, whom you call the creator of the universe. Is he perhaps our Pachacamac and Viracocha? The second claims to be the father of all men, on whom they piled their sins. The third you call Jesus Christ, the only one not to cast sins on that first man, but he was killed. The fourth you call pope. The fifth, Carlos, according to you, is the most powerful monarch of the universe and supreme over all. However, you affirm this without taking account of other monarchs. But if this Carlos is prince and lord of all the world, why does he need the pope to grant him concessions and donations to make war on us and usurp our kingdoms? And if he needs the pope, then is not the pope the greater lord and most powerful prince of all the world, instead of Carlos? Also you say that I am obliged to pay tribute to Carlos and not to others, but since you

Reprinted from *College Composition and Communication*, June 1999.

give no reason for this tribute, I feel no obligation to pay it. If it is right to give tribute and service at all, it ought to be given to God, the man who was Father of all, then to Jesus Christ who never piled on his sins, and finally to the pope. . . . But if I ought not give tribute to this man, even less ought I give it to Carlos, who was never lord of these regions and whom I have never seen.

The record of this meeting at Atahualpa notes that,

> The Spaniards, unable to endure this *prolixity of argumentation*, jumped from their seats and attacked the Indians and grabbed hold of their gold and silver jewels and precious stones. (Dussel 53)

A little later, 1524, a little further north, Mexico. Twelve recently arrived Spanish Franciscan missionaries have agreed to a dialogue with the indigenous people of the region. The Aztecan delegation consists of a group of *tlamatinime*, or philosophers. Somewhere between the ages of six and nine, young Aztecs (which might have included women) left their families to join the *Calmécac* community. There, they received a rigorous education based on discussions with teachers, or wise ones (*Huebuetlatoli*). The discussions will allow the young Aztecs to acquire the wisdom already known (*momachtique*), a wisdom which is to be rendered in the adequate word (*in quali tlatolli*). This, then, was the Aztecan trivium, displayed in the rhetoric called the flower-and-song (*in xochitl in cuicatl*) (Dussel 95–97).

The *tlamatinime* address the missionaries in the manner of the flower-and-song, in what could be read as a five-part rhetorical rendition. First, there is a salutation and introduction:

> Our much esteemed lords: What travail have you passed through to arrive here. Here, before you, we ignorant people contemplate you.
>   What shall we say? What *should we direct to your ears*? Are we anything by chance? We are only a vulgar people.

The *proemium*-like intro done, the *tlamatinime* turn to the matter at hand, an attempt to enter into a dialogue concerning the doctrine that the missionaries had brought. The Aztecan flower-and-song enters into a context-setting that is like the classical Roman *narratio*:

> Through the interpreter we will respond by returning the-nourishment-and-the-word to the lord-of-the-intimate-which-surrounds-us. For his sake, we place ourselves in danger. . . . Perhaps our actions will result in our perdition or destruction, but where are we to go? We are common mortals. *Let us now then die; let us now perish since our gods have already died.* But calm your heart-of-flesh, lords, for

we will break with the customary for a moment and open for you a
little bit the *secret*, the ark of the lord, our God.

Next, *dispositio*:

You have said the *we do not know* the lord-of-the-intimate-which-
surrounds-us, the one from whom the-heavens-and-the-earth come.
You have said that our gods were not *true* gods.

We respond that we are perturbed and hurt by what you say, because
our progenitors never spoke this way.

Refutatio takes the form of three topics not unlike Aristotle's: authority,
ideology as worldview, and antiquity. The first is authority:

Our progenitors passed on the *norm of life* they held as *true* and the
doctrine that we should worship and honor the gods.

Such doctrine is consistent with the Aztecan worldview:

They taught . . . that these gods give us life and have gained us for
themselves . . . in the beginning. These gods provide us with suste-
nance, drink and food including corn, beans, goose feet (*bledos*), and
chia, all of which conserve life. We pray to these gods for the water
and rain needed for crops. These gods are happy . . . *where they exist*,
in the place of *Tlalocan*, where there is neither hunger, nor sickness,
nor poverty.

Then the appeal to antiquity:

And in what form, when, where were these gods first invoked?. . .
This occurred a very long time ago in Tula, Huapalcalco, Xuchatla-
pan, Tlamohuanchan, Yohuallican, and Teotihuacan. These gods have
established their dominion over the entire universe (*cemanauac*).

Conclusio
Are we now to destroy the ancient *norm of our life?*—the *norm of
life* for the Chichimecas, the Toltexs, the Acolhuas, and the Tec-
panecas? We *know* to whom we owe our birth and our lives.
  We refuse to be tranquil or to believe as truth what you say, even
if this offends you.
  We lay out our reasons to you, lords, who govern and sustain the
whole world (*cemanáualt*). Since we have handed over all our power
to you, if *we abide here, we will remain only prisoners*. Our final
response is do with us as you please. (Dussel 112–14)

No multiculturalism there, no cultural hybrid possible, though some try hard
now to reclaim the Incan or Aztecan, try hard to be more than the
Eurocentric *criollo* of Latin America.

Algunas Ideas

As academics and teachers we become accustomed to juggling dozens of constraints at a time. We adjust to the multidimensional nature of our jobs. But just for a little while we'd like to focus on one aspect of our careers, work one thing through. Except for the occasional sabbatical leave some of us are granted in our jobs, however, the best we can usually do is set priorities. It's something of the too-much-to juggle mindset, I would say, that gives rise to multiculturalism. So many inequities, so much rampant bigotry leveled at so many things. None of it should be ignored. But if we're to set priorities, I would ask that we return to the question of racism, the "absent presence" in our discourse (Prendergast). Although gays and lesbians are subject to more acts of hate in this country right now than any other group, the attacks are most often leveled at gays and lesbians of color (Martínez 134). Women of color carry a double yoke, to use Buchi Emecheta's words, being women and being of color. And it's a secret to no one that the greatest number of poor are people of color. This is not to say that the eradication of racism—even if possible—would mean the eradication of bigotry and inequity. It is to say that as priorities go, racism seems to have the greatest depth of trouble, cuts across most other bigotries, is imbricated with most other bigotries, and also stands alone, has the greatest number of layers. According to Mike Davis:

> No matter how important feminist consciousness must be . . . , racism remains the divisive issue within class and gender [and sexual orientation]. . . . The real weak link in the domestic base of American imperialism is a Black and Hispanic working class, fifty million strong. This is the nation within a nation, society within a society, that alone possesses the numerical and positional strength to undermine the American empire from within. (299, 313–14)

The numbers have risen since Davis wrote this in 1984. And he failed to mention the Asian Americans and Pacific Islanders, the amazing percentages that don't succeed and the others who are "model minorities" rather than simply assimilated. Or the American Indians. Racism continues to be among the most compelling problems we face. Part of the reason why this is so is because we're still unclear about what we're dealing with, so we must thereby be unclear about how to deal with it.

Part of that insecurity about what it is we face when we talk or write about racism can be seen in our references to "race and ethnicity." I've used the term myself, to distinguish what we are biologically from how we're treated or regarded, to point to the ways in which racism doesn't always effect those who are visibly different from the majority. But referring to ethnicity is tricky, carries connotations that don't necessarily apply to people of color in the U.S.

Ethnicity grows out of a consciousness of an older, less sustainable racism. The concept of ethnicity first evolved in response to Social Darwinism, traveling through the 1920s to the 1960s, at which time class and colonialist concerns came to the fore (Omi and Winant, Grosfoguel, Negrón-Muntaner, Georas). Since the 1960s, the talk of colonialism has taken a new turn, and the realization that racism remains even when there is class ascension has made for something of a separation between discussions of class and of color. So ethnicity is back, now decidedly associated with race. And with ethnicity comes the concept that was historically a subset of ethnicity, *cultural pluralism* (Omi and Winant 12).

Ethnicity received its most complete treatment in Nathan Glazer and Daniel P. Moynihan's *Beyond the Melting Pot: The Negroes, Puerto Ricans, Jews, Italians, and Irish of New York City*, first published in 1963, with a second edition in 1970. Glazer and Moynihan describe a process that sounds much like hybridity, a postcolonial term enjoying currency. Ethnic groups do not necessarily assimilate, say Glazer and Moynihan:

> Ethnic groups . . . even after distinctive language, customs, and culture are lost . . . are continually recreated by new experiences in America. The mere existence of a name itself is perhaps sufficient to form group character in new situations, for the name associates an individual, who actually can be anything, with a certain past, country, or race.

So something new emerges in the acculturation process—neither fish nor fowl, a new language and culture with ties to something older. And this new thing is an *interest group*. Glazer and Moynihan continue:

> But as a matter of fact, someone who is Irish or Jewish or Italian generally has other traits than the mere existence of the name that associates him with other people attached to the group. A man is connected to his group by ties of family and friendship. But he is also connected by ties of *interests*. The ethnic groups in New York are also *interest groups*. (qtd. in Omi and Winant 18)

From this it wasn't much of a leap to the bootstraps mentality, with Glazer and Moynihan writing in *1975* that "ethnic groups bring different norms to bear on common circumstances with consequent different levels of success—hence *group* differences in status," so that any group that fails does so by virtue of flaws in the group's "norms," as in the stereotypical contention that the dropout rate among Chicanos and Latinos are so high because Latino culture does not prize education like other groups do (qtd. in Omi and Winant 21).

Because this country has always consisted of many groupings (even before the first Europeans), the notion of ethnicity rings true. And because so many ethnicities still feel attachments to their ancestry, even if only as nostalgia, the concept of a cultural plurality sounds right. Ethnicity and the cultural plurality suggested by multiculturalism appeal to common sense in ways that can address racism—and sometimes they do, maybe often—but without tugging at its hegemony with the kind force so many of us would wish.

Racism runs deep. Consider some of the litany of the 1980s with which E. San Juan opens his book on *Racial Formations/Critical Transformations*:

> Vigilante gunman Bernard Goetz catapulted into a folk hero for shooting down four black youths in a New York subway. Fear of Willy Horton, a black inmate helped elect a president. . . . Antibusing attacks in the early eighties in most big cities. The 1982 murder of Chinese American Vincent Chin mistaken by unemployed Detroit autoworkers for a Japanese. . . . The election to the Louisiana legislature of Republican David Duke, former head of the Ku Klux Klan. (1)

And also:

- We watched the 1992 beating of Rodney King, watched Alicia Soltero Vásquez being beaten by Border Patrolmen.
- San Francisco, 1997. Two young Latino children are found completely covered in flour. They wanted their skin to be white enough to go to school, they say.
- Oxnard, 1995, Mexican and Chicana women working at a Nabisco plant are denied toilet breaks. They are told to wear diapers during their shift.
- Rohnert Park, 1997. Police kill a Chinese engineer, father of three, who had come home drunk and angry after having put up with racist insults at a bar. He's loud. A neighbor calls the police. Still drunk, he grabs a one-eighth inch thick stick, brandishes it. He's shot. His wife, a nurse, is disallowed to administer care. He's handcuffed. Dies while awaiting an ambulance. The reason for shooting him? The police were afraid he would use martial arts with that one-eighth inch stick (Martinez 10–11)

We know that incidents like these are ubiquitous. And we know they're on our campuses—at the University of Nevada, at Miami University of Ohio, at my own campus. Everywhere.

Multiculturalism hasn't improved things much, not even at the sites where students are exposed to such things. Maybe the relatively low numbers of people of color on our campuses or in our journals—or the high numbers at community colleges with disproportionately few of color among the faculty—reinforce racist conceptions. The disproportionately few people of color in front of the classrooms or in our publications, given the ubiquity of the bootstrap mentality, reifies the conception that people of color don't do better because they don't try harder, that most are content to feed off the State. The only apparent generalized acknowledgement of racism as structural comes by way of the perception of a reverse discrimination.

Yet the numbers underscore that there is no reversal. Latinos have the highest poverty rates from all Americans—24%, with Navajo close behind, followed by African Americans (Martínez 7). And there's no use blaming insufficiency in English, as Latinos and Navajo lose their native tongues, the Navajo struggling to hold on to their Dine' language (Veltman, DeGroat).

Among Latinos, 64% are native to the U.S. Half of all Latinos never complete high school, the highest percentage for all groups (Dept. of Health). Although segregation by race is no longer legal, there is an economic segregation, a white and middle-class flight from inner cities that relegates African American and Latino students to schools that lack a strong tax base and are thereby poorly funded (Martínez 7). While Latinos make up over 12% of the public school population, less than 4% of faculty or administration are Latina or Latino, and less than 1% of those who sit on school boards as voting members are Latina or Latino.

Of course, some do make it to higher education. Twenty percent of those who receive Associate Degrees are of color. Of that 20%, Latinas and Latinos account for 6%. Those rates are relatively the same through Bachelors and Masters degrees. At the doctoral level, Asian Americans earn about 4.5% of all PhDs, African Americans 3%, Latinos 2%, American Indians, about .3%, and white folks who are not Latina or Latino 61% (the remaining 27% going to foreign nationals) (37, 39). In English Language and Literature for 1995, Latinos and Latinas received 26 PhDs—not 26% but 26: 8 for Latinos and 18 for Latinas—African Americans 37, Asian Americans 35, American Indians 7. White folks who were not Latino received 1,268—of which 743 were awarded to women (US Dept. of Education). That's 1,268 white to 26 Latino or Latina PhDs in English. I have so little patience with reverse discrimination.

These numbers could still be broken down by field within English, but there are no clear numbers that include race breakdowns. If CCCC membership demographics can tell us much, though, the numbers aren't encouraging, with a 92% white membership, 5% African American, 1.4% Chicanos or Latino, 1% Asian American, and 0.5% Native American/ American Indian. And there is only the most infinitesimal amount of representation in our journals, with *TETYC* giving the most attention to race issues of the three journals searched (*TETYC, CCC,* and *College English*), with none in a search by article titles looking at issues concerning Latinas or Latinos—not even to address the English-Only movement.

Even though members of CCCC and NCTE have tended to treat its members of color with respect and have advanced our numbers into positions of leadership regularly, and even though both NCTE and CCCC will soon be entering into a membership campaign that should increase the pool of people of color, I believe that our best recruiting tool for those graduate students of color, the undergraduates of color, the students who have vaulted the fault line and are in college at all will not be the pictures of people of color in the *Council Chronicle* or in the convention program books or even at our wonderful conventions—since all of those media mainly reach the already-subscribed; rather, it will be through our journals, the journals on library shelves or online, with people of color writing frankly, sympathetically about matters concerning racism, and all of us writing about what matters to those students of color. That's what will attract people of color in sufficient numbers to begin to affect racism. We can do better than 7% among our teachers and scholars of color, better than a representation that is statistically insignificant in our journals.

Cuentos

A number of graduate students of color in English at my campus write an article for the school newspaper which gains a full-page spread. Its title, "Black Masks, White Masks," parodies a famous book on colonialism and race by Frantz Fanon. The grad students write that they no longer wish to be reduced to wearing white masks if they are to succeed in the university, that the denial of their being of color affords them nothing but their silencing. Among their examples of the racism they feel, they write of a Halloween party in which one of their fellows appeared in blackface (Dunn et al. 6).

A meeting of grad students and department faculty. Tempers run hot. Blackface says he never meant to offend. He was paying homage to the great jazz and blues musicians of the past, playing Muddy Waters tunes. He would have been born in the 1970s, maybe unaware of a dark history of such homages.

> *Holiday Inn*: Bing Crosby in blackface, singing "Who was it set the darkies free? Abraham. Abraham." Mr. Crosby surely didn't mean to offend. But that was then, you might have said before this little *cuentito*.

Stunned silence. A student of color leaves.

A large-seeming fellow, red hair, small, blue eyes, always earnest, always speaking with broad gestures from large, thick hands, all befreckled, always the one to find contradictions. He stands. Says that as he sees it, this thing about silencing doesn't wash, that those complaining about it are the very ones who are always speaking up in classes, and that (without a breath) he can't think of a one from among the faculty present who doesn't speak of multiculturalism, that the damned text used in the first-year composition program is really an Ethnic Studies book, for gosh sake (or words to that effect). (The book is Ronald Takaki's *A Different Mirror*, "a history of multicultural America," according to the subtitle, its author, "a professor in the Ethnic Studies Department" at his university.) All are effectively silenced for a dramatically long moment.

Then, from behind the semi-circle of chairs, a South Asian woman stands. She self-identifies as a person of color, as one of those colonized by another's empire, British accent to her speech, dark brown skin, large black eyes that seem to well with tears, thick black mane framing her small face. She's clearly agitated. Breaks the silence. She speaks about the difference between speaking and being heard, that if one is constantly speaking but is never heard, never truly heard, there is, in effect, silence, a silencing. She says that speaking of ethnic studies or multiculturalism is less the issue than how racism seems always to be an appendage to a classroom curriculum, something loosely attached to a course but not quite integral, even when race is the issue.

She, two Latinas, and one African American woman had attended, then boycotted a graduate seminar on Feminist Theory a few semesters before. Expecting that the most common and longest form of oppression in human history, gender discrimination, would serve as a bond that would tie them to the other class members and the professor, these four women were surprised, then hurt, then angered, at their silencing by their sisters. One of

the Latinas does her presentation in Spanish, says "Nobody listens anyway."
No one commented, or even acknowledged not knowing what she had said.
The African American woman posted a message on an African American
listserv warning others not to apply to the school, that it was too deeply
racist.

A poem by Puerto Rican poet Victor Hernández Cruz:

Anonymous

And if I lived in those olden times
With a funny name like Choicer or
Henry Howard, Earl of Surrey, what chimes!
I would spend my time in search of rhymes
Make sure the measurement termination surprise
In the court of kings snapping till woo sunrise
Plus always be using the words *alas* and *hath*
And not even knowing that that was my path
Just think on the Lower East Side of Manhattan
I would have been like living in satin
Alas! The projects hath not covered the river
Thou see-est vision to make thee quiver
Hath I been delivered to that "wildernesse"
So past
I would have been the last one in the
Dance to go
Taking note the minuet so slow
All admire my taste
Within thou *mambo* of much more haste.

One of my daughters had had enough with the teacher who singled her
and her girlfriends out, except the Latina girlfriend from Venezuela, who
bore European features and a French and German name, never called out
even though she did in fact cut up with the others when they were cuttin'
up. My daughter had shaken her booty at the teacher after a disciplining of
one sort or another. The teacher: "That might be okay in your culture, but not
in mine." I don't think multiculturalism took.

A meeting with that teacher and the principal. After explanations, I break
into a lecture about racism. I do that. Often. From the Principal: "We had
some problems with that at the beginning of the year, but we took care of
them." And I want to know how he solved the problem of our nation "at the
beginning of the year."

A joke to some and not to others tells about an immigration official who
detains the Puerto Rican at the border. "But I'm Puerto Rican," says the

detained citizen. "I don't care what kind of Mexican you are," says the official.

A poem by Sandra María Esteves:

From Fanon

We are a multitude of contradictions
reflecting our history
oppressed
controlled
once free folk
remnants of that time interacting in our souls

Our kindred was the earth
polarity with the land
respected it
called it mother
were sustained and strengthened by it

The european thru power and fear became our master
his greed welcomed by our ignorance
tyranny persisting
our screams passing unfulfilled

As slaves we lost identity
assimilating our master's values
overwhelming us to become integrated shadows
unrefined and dependent

We flee escaping, becoming clowns in an alien circus
performing predictably
mimicking strange values
reflecting what was inflicted

Now the oppressor has an international program
and we sit precariously within the monster's mechanism
internalizing anguish from comrades
planning and preparing a course of action.

On Breaking Precedents

I have failed some tests, have had a fellow worker bleed in green and red over a paper I had wished to submit for publication, have gotten the maybe-you-could-consider-submitting-this-essay-somewhere-else letter from journal editors. That's just part of the job. But I have only once felt insulted. Some years have passed, and I have forgotten the editor who had written my rejection letter; I've even forgotten the journal, I realize as I write this. But I still bear a grudge. The essay challenged the idea of a postcolonialism, invoking Frantz Fanon. The Rejecter said he saw no reason to resurrect Fanon. The essay also cited Aristotle and Cicero. Their resurrection went unquestioned. Rejecter also said that he feared that in bringing in Fanon, I risked essentializing. *Essentialism*, as I understand the term, is the "belief in real, true human essences, existing outside of or impervious to social and historical context" (Omi and Winant 187). But I had argued in that piece, as I have always argued, that race in America is a result of colonialism, that "racial discrimination and racial prejudice are phenomena of colonialism," to use John Rex's words (75). This is historical, not merely a matter of physiognomy. How was I essentializing?

In the years that have followed that infuriating letter, I have seen my concern of that essay echoed, seen a rekindled interest in Fanon grow and grow, and have heard how others of color have been insulted by a particular use of the word *essentializing*. Henry Louis Gates in an essay titled "On the Rhetoric of Racism in the Profession," for example, writes that

> Long after white literature has been canonized, and recanonized, our attempts to define a black American canon—foregrounded on its own against a white backdrop—are often decried as racist, separatist, nationalist, or "essentialist" (my favorite term of all). (25)

And so maybe that was the problem, that I had been read as taking on an old, 1960s type of argument for nationalism among people of color in bringing up Fanon's rendering of internal colonialism.

Now as I try to think of how this profession can improve on its multiculturalism, do more than assuring that people of color are represented in our materials, more than assuring that people of color are read and heard in numbers more in keeping with the emerging demographics of the nation and the world, I remain tied to the belief that we must break from the colonial discourse that binds us all. What I mean is that there are attitudes from those we have revered over the centuries which we inherit, that are woven into the discourse that we inherit. I believe this happens. But even if not, consider the legacy.

Among all that is worthwhile in the intellectual discourse we inherit from the colonizers of the United States, there is also a developmental and racist discourse. Here is how Kant, in 1784, answers the question as to "What is Enlightenment?"

> Enlightenment (*Aufklärung*) is the exit of humanity by itself from a state of culpable immaturity (*verschuldeten Unmündigkeit*). . . .

> Laziness and cowardliness are the causes which bind the great part of humanity in this frivolous state of immaturity. (qtd. in Dussel 20)

For Hegel,

> Universal history goes from East to West. Europe is absolutely the *end of universal history*. Asia is the beginning.
>
> Africa is in general a closed land, and it maintains this fundamental character. It is characteristic of the blacks that their consciousness has not yet even arrived at the intuition of any objectivity . . . He is a human being in the rough.
>
> This mode of being of the Africans explains the fact that it is extraordinarily easy to make them fanatics. The Reign of the Spirit is among them so poor and the Spirit in itself so intense . . . that a representation that is inculcated in them suffices them not to respect anything and to destroy everything.

And as for Spain, Hegel continues:

> Here one meets the lands of Morocco, Fas (not Fez), Algeria, Tunis, Tripoli. One can say that this part does not properly belong to Africa, but more to Spain, with which it forms a common basin. De Pradt says for this reason that when one is in Spain one is already in Africa. This part of the world . . . forms a niche which is limited to sharing the destiny of the great ones, a destiny which is decided in other parts. It is not called upon to acquire its own proper figure. (qtd. in Dussel 21–24)

This is the legacy of racism. And how is it passed on? The Naturalization Act of 1790—1790!—denying rights of full citizenship to nonwhites (Takaki, "Reflections"). The Chinese Exclusion Act of 1882. The 1928 Congressional Hearings on Western Hemisphere Immigration:

> Their minds run to nothing higher than animal functions—eat, sleep, and sexual debauchery. In every huddle of Mexican shacks one meets the same idleness, hordes of hungry dogs, and filthy children with faces plastered with flies, disease, lice, human filth, stench, promiscuous fornication, bastardly, lounging, apathetic peons and lazy squaws, beans and dried fruit, liquor, general squalor, and envy and hatred of the gringo. These people sleep by day and prowl by night like coyotes, stealing anything they can get their hands on, no matter how useless to them it may be. Nothing left outside is safe unless padlocked or chained down. Yet there are Americans clamoring for more of these human swine to be brought over from Mexico. (Estrada et al. 116)

And after the slurs run through the mind, there comes the question as to how this is an issue of immigration to the Western Hemisphere as a whole, rather than simply to one country of the Western Hemisphere. To understand that, we would need to recognize the discourse of diplomacy toward our neighbors to the South since the time of John Quincy Adams, summed up in a 1920s lecture to new envoys to Central and South America:

> If the United States has received but little gratitude, this is only to be expected in a world where gratitude is rarely accorded to the teacher, the doctor, or the policeman, and we have been all three. But it may be that in time they will come to see the United States with different eyes, and have for her something of the respect and affections with which a man regards the instructor of his youth and a child looks upon the parent who has molded his character. (Schoultz 386)

Or George Bush referring to Daniel Omega's presence at a meeting as like an unwelcome dog at a garden party (Schoultz vii, 386). And after the summer hurricanes hit Central America during the summer of '98, we all heard Bush's pleas for aid for Honduras, since if such were not granted, those people might come here.

From Kant to our current politicians, from the exclusion of somehow "essentialized" notions of race to ongoing English-Only laws and the end of Affirmative Action, we are steeped in racism. And we are steeped in a colonial discourse, one which continues to operate from a developmental rather than dialectical model—despite our best efforts.

If Latin America is like a child to the U.S., the U.S. continues to act as the colonial offspring of Europe. Here's an analogy from diplomacy. Historian Lars Schoultz writes:

> When a State Department official begins a meeting with the comment "we have a problem with the government of Peru," in less than a second the other participants instinctively turn to a mental picture of a foreign state that is quite different from the one that would have been evoked if the convening official had said, in contrast "we have a problem with the government of France."
>
> What exactly is the difference? To begin, Peru is in Latin America, the "other" America; France is in northwestern Europe, the cradle of the dominant North American culture. Peru is poor; France is rich. Peru is weak; France has nuclear weapons. Peru has Incan ruins . . .; France has ancient ruins too, but it also has the Louvre. Peru makes pisco; France makes claret. Peru is not so firmly democratic; France is. Peru is a Rio Treaty ally, which, as alliances go, is something of a charade; France is a NATO ally, which is a very serious alliance. In most of our history, Peru has not mattered much in international relations; France has mattered a lot. . . . U.S. policy toward

Peru is *fundamentally* unlike U.S. policy toward France, despite the
fact that both policies are driven by self-interest. (xvi–xvii)

Now, imagine the phrase "there is a Mexican philosopher" and compare it
to "there is a French philosopher." Which carries the greater weight? The
analogy holds.

I began this essay with a reference to the logic of the Incas and the
rhetorical training and rhetoric of the Aztecs prior to the European conquest.
The source was a series of lectures delivered in Europe by an Argentine
philosopher who resides in Mexico City, Enrique Dussel. Apart from a
couple of dozen students in one seminar I've taught, I don't believe there are
many in this country who know him or his work or the ways he might
inform our concern with rhetoric or with liberatory pedagogy. His work
mainly concerns the Philosophy of Liberation, and a good deal of it is in
translation. We don't look to the South. Freire came to our attention only
after he became a member of the faculty at Harvard. We tend to get our
Great Thinkers from Europe, and too often only after our literary brothers and
sisters, themselves too many and too often still quite literally an English
colony, have discovered them. I'm not saying we shouldn't. I am grateful for
habitus and hegemony as concepts that came from Europe. I have a great
affection for the rhetoricians of Greece and Rome. But we must break from
the colonial mindset and learn from the thinkers from our own hemisphere
as well. There is, for example, a community college with a long record of
trying to break through structural racism (now facing bureaucratic problems),
Hostos Community College. Do we know who the school is named after?
Do we know about his educational philosophy? He was a Puerto Rican
philosopher, Eugenio María Hostos. Freire refers to many of the European
thinkers, but he also refers to others. Do we know them? Might not knowing
them be of some worth?

Break precedent! We are so locked into the colonial mindset that we are
now turning to the ex-colonials of Europe to learn something about our own
people of color. There again, I'm grateful for the insights. But what are the ex-
colonials of the U.S. saying, the ex-colonials of our hemisphere, now caught
in neocolonial dependency? In this essay, for example, I have called on the
research of a number of Puerto Ricans, a Filipino, a number of Chicanas and
Chicanos, an American Indian, African Americans, as well as an Argentine
from Mexico—ex-colonials and contemporary colonials of the United States,
writing and researching on their colonial relations to the United States. What
we know are the writers. And they have a great deal to say that we should
hear. But the Grand Theorists, to our mind, must be of "the continent" (as if

the Americas weren't). At Hunter College in New York there is a Center for
Puerto Rican Studies. What is being said there, not by postcolonials but by
still-colonials? Some Puerto Ricans, for instance, are arguing for *jaiba*
politics, a strategy of mimicry and parody that might have application in the
classroom, a way to think our ways through the contradiction of a political
sensibility in the composition classroom and instruction in academic
discourse (Grosfoguel, Negrón-Muntaner, Georas 26–33). I haven't studied
the concept of *jaiba* further or its possible application in composition studies
yet. But I am hoping more of us will.

We shouldn't ignore the concepts that come of the ex-colonies of Europe,
nor should we ignore European attempts to think its ways through bigotries
of all sorts, since the problems of racism and hatred are Europe's also—but
we also should not ignore the concepts that come of members of the interior
colonies like Puerto Rico and the American Indian nations, the internal
colonies of the formerly colonized as in America's people of color, the
neocolonies of Latin America.

From Sandra María Esteves:

Here

I am two parts/a person
boricua/spic
past and present
alive and oppressed
given a cultural beauty
. . . and robbed of a cultural identity

I speak the alien tongue
in sweet boriqueño thoughts
know love mixed with pain
have tasted spit on ghetto stairways
. . . here, it must be changed
we must change it.

Works Cited

Cruz, Victor Hernández, "Anonymous." *Puerto Rican Writers At Home in the USA:
    An Anthology.* Faythe Turner, Ed., Seattle: Open Hand P, 1991. 119.
Davis, Mike. "The Political Economy of Late Imperial America." *New Left Review*
    143 (1984): 6–38.
De Groat, Jennie. Personal Communication, 21 Nov. 1998.

Department of Health and Human Services. Hispanic Customer Service Demographics, *http://www.lhhslgovlheolhisp.html*, 4 October 98.

Dunn, Cataya, Azfar Hussan, Abraham Tarango, Sumatay Sivamohan. "Black
Masks, White Masks" *The Daily Evergreen*, 23 April 1998, 6.

Dussel, Enrique. *The Invention of the Americas: Eclipse of "the Other" and the
Myth of Modernity.* Trans. Michael D. Barber. New York: Continuum, 1995.

Emecheta, Buchi. *Double Yoke.* New York: Braziller, 1982.

Esteves, Sandra María. "From Fanon." Turner 186–87.

———. "Here." Turner 181.

Estrada, Leonardo F., F. Chris Garcia, Reynal do Flores Macias, and Lionel Mal-
donado. "Chicanos in the United States: A History of Exploitation and Resistance." *Daedalus* 2 (1981): 103–31.

Fanon, Frantz. *Black Skin, White Masks.* Trans. by Charles Lam Markmann. New
York: Grove, 1967.

Gates, Henry Louis, Jr. "On the Rhetoric of Racism in the Profession." *Literature,
Language, and Politics.* Ed. Betty Jean Craige. Athens: U of Georgia P, 1988.
20–26.

Glazer, Nathaniel and Daniel P. Moynihan. *Beyond the Melting Pot: The Negroes,
Puerto Ricans, Jews, Italians, and Irish of New York City.* Cambridge: MIT P, 1970.

Grosfoguel, Ramón, Frances Negrón-Muntaner, and Chloé S. Georas. "Beyond
Nationalist and Colonialist Discourses: The *Jaiba* Politics of the Puerto-Rican
Ethno Nation," *Puerto Rican Jam: Rethinking Colonialism and Nationalism.*
Grosfoguel et al., eds. Minneapolis: U of Minnesota P, 1997. 1–36.

Martinez, Elizabeth. *De Colores Means All of Us: Latino Views for a Multi-Colored
Century.* Cambridge: South End, 1998.

Omi, Michael and Howard Winant. *Racial Formation in the United States: From
the 1960s to the 1990s.* New York: Routledge, 1994.

Prendergast, Catherine. "Race: The Absent Presence in Composition Studies." *CCC*
50 (1998): 35–53.

President's Advisory Commission on Educational Excellence for Hispanic Americans. *Our Nation on the Fault Line: Hispanic American Education.* Washington, DC: USIA, September 1996.

Rex, John. *Race, Colonialism and the City.* London: Routledge, 1973.

San Juan, E. *Racial Formations/Critical Transformations: Articulations of Power in
Ethnic and Racial Studies in the United States.* Atlantic Highlands: Humanities P, 1992.

Schoultz, Lars. *Beneath the United States: A History of U.S. Policy Toward Latin
America.* Cambridge: Harvard UP, 1998.

Takaki, Ronald. *A Different Mirror: A History of Multicutural America.* Boston:
Little, 1993.

———. "Reflections on Racial Patterns in America." *From Different Shores.* Ed.
Ronald Takaki. New York: Oxford UP, 1987.

Turner, Paythe, ed. *Puerto Rican Writers At Home in the USA: An Anthology.* Seattle: Open Hand P, 1991.

U.S. Department of Education, National Center for Educational Statistics, Integrated Postsecondary Education Data System. "Completions Survey." Washington: US. Department of Education. April 1997.

Veltman, Calvin. "Anglicization in the United States: Language Environment and Language Practice of American Adolescents." *International Journal of Social Languages* 44 (1983): 99–114.

2 Feminism in Composition: Inclusion, Metonymy, and Disruption

Joy Ritchie and Kathleen Boardman

At a time when composition is engaged in clarifying its theoretical, political, and pedagogical histories, it is appropriate to construct a story of feminism's involvement in the disciplinary conversations. Despite the recent burgeoning of feminist perspectives in our discipline, it is not easy to delineate how feminism has functioned over the past three decades to shape and critique our understandings of the gendered nature of writing, teaching, and institutions. Although some accounts suggest that feminism, until recently, has been absent or at least late-blooming in the field, we find a more complex relationship in our rereading of essays and books in composition written from a feminist perspective—in particular, the many accounts of personal experience in the field written by feminists and by women since the 1970s. In this essay we look, and look again, at the few articles and notes that appeared in CCC, *College English*, and *English Journal* in the early 1970s. We also focus on feminist retrospective accounts—re-visions of composition written since the mid-1980s.

In writing this brief critical historical survey, we have found ourselves working from various impulses. First, we want to document and celebrate the vitality of feminism in composition, from its early manifestations in the small scattering of essays published in the 1970s (some of them frequently cited, others forgotten) to the explosion of feminist theory and well-documented feminist practice of the last decade. We wish to point out that much early feminist work in composition is not documented in our official publications, having occurred in informal conversations, in classrooms, and

Reprinted from *College Composition and Communication*, June 1999.

in committee meetings. At the same time, we want to suggest ways to examine and theorize experiential accounts—both published and unpublished—of feminism in composition. We must also consider seriously the causes and consequences of the delay in feminism's emergence in the published forums of our discipline and the extent to which feminism, despite its recent vitality, has remained contained or marginalized in composition. Finally, we hope to speculate on the positive and negative potential of inclusive, metonymic, and disruptive strategies for feminism's contribution to composition's narratives.

In the past decade, feminists have been visibly active in our discipline. They have examined the subjectivity of the gendered student and the position of women writers in the profession. Questioning assumptions about genre, form, and style, they have provided an impetus to seek alternative writing practices. Feminist perspectives have produced analyses of the gendered nature of the classroom, the feminization of English teaching, the working conditions for female teachers, and the implications of feminist theory for scholarship. Feminist scholars like Andrea Lunsford and Cheryl Glenn have begun rewriting the rhetorical tradition by reclaiming, refiguring, and regendering "Rhetorica." They are also critiquing earlier constructions of history and scholarship in composition. And from a different direction, scholars are drawing upon feminist, African American, lesbian, Native American, and class-based examinations of difference in order to complicate definitions of diversity within composition. Two recent essay collections, Susan Jarratt and Lynn Worsham's *Feminism and Composition Studies: In Other Words*, and Louise Phelps and Janet Emig's *Feminine Principles and Women's Experience in American Composition and Rhetoric*, especially highlight the strength of feminism(s) in composition and show how important feminism has been in shaping women's definitions of themselves, their work, and their commitment to pursuing questions of equity in the field.

Yet in the 1970s, while the work of composition as an emerging discipline was occurring right next door to, down the hall from, or in the basement under the work of feminist linguists and literary scholars, composition's official published discussions were largely silent on issues of gender. There is little explicit evidence of systematic theorizing about gender from the 1950s to the late 1980s. As late as 1988, Elizabeth Flynn could write, "For the most part . . . the fields of feminist studies and composition studies have not engaged each other in a serious or systematic way" (425). Indeed, when we began this study, we framed it as a paradox: prior to the mid-1980s, feminism seemed absent from composition but present among compositionists. From those early investigations we pulled one useful reminder: that the connections of composition and feminism have not been an inevitable result of the presence of so many women in the field. But subsequent conversations with a number of longtime teachers and scholars, who spoke to us about their own feminist beliefs and activities in composition dating back to the *1960s*, reminded us that the near-absence of feminism from our publications does not constitute absence from the field.

The absence-presence binary also did not help us explain our own history as feminists in composition. As secondary English teachers, teaching women's literature and applying our feminist perspectives to high school courses in the 1970s, we moved into graduate courses and tenure track jobs in composition in the late 1980s and 1990s. Reflecting on our own experience, we recognized that much of the creative feminist energy in composition's history is not visible in the publications we searched: it appeared in informal conversations, in basement classrooms, and in committees on which women served. This energy might be viewed as ephemeral, yet we can testify, along with others, that it created solidarity among women, influenced students and colleagues, and helped form an epistemology on which later feminist work could grow. Sharon Crowley reminds us further that composition allowed and acknowledged women's participation in teaching and scholarship before many other disciplines began to do so—as we see from the important work of Josephine Miles, Winifred Horner, Ann Berthoff, Janet Emig and others. Still, Theresa Enos' collection of anecdotes from women in the field over the last several decades cautions us that the job conditions and security for many of these practitioners were terrible.

Crowley's and Enos' different perspectives point again to a history of women and feminism in composition that cannot be constructed in a tidy narrative. In the documents and accounts we have read and heard, we find three overlapping tropes that shed light on the roles feminism has played in composition and in the strategies women have used to gain a place in its conversations: (1) Following the pattern of developing feminist thought in the 1970s and 1980s, many early feminist accounts in composition sought inclusion and equality for women. (2) More recent accounts like those of Louise Phelps and Janet Emig posit feminism as a "subterranean" unspoken presence (xv), and Susan Jarratt and Laura Brady suggest the *metonymy* or contiguity of feminism and composition. (3) Also developing during this time has been what feminist postmodernists define as *disruption* and critique of

hegemonic narratives—resistance, interruption, and finally redirection of ·
composition's business as usual.

   While it's tempting to posit this as a linear, evolutionary set of tropes—that
women have grown out of and into as we've matured theoretically—we find
it too restrictive to do so. These narratives coexist and have multiple
functions, often depending on the historical or theoretical context in which
they are read. For example, some early attempts at inclusion, based on
experiential accounts, function also as disruptive narratives, and a number of
very recent accounts might be characterized as primarily metonymic
narratives. Furthermore, each of these tropes has both advantages and
disadvantages for feminism in composition: for example, a narrative aimed
at *including* women may also function to *contain* feminism within narrow
boundaries. We also emphasize that we are not interested in categorizing
narratives (and narrators) as "inclusionist," "disruptionist," and so on. Rather
we hope to tease out the tropes, show how these narratives can be reread in
multiple ways, and suggest how each one enacts one or more
epistemological positions with respect to women's experience, identity, and
difference.

   As we reread for these rhetorical strategies, we find that the conceptions
of experience in each of these sets of narratives also require examination.
Most of the feminist writing in composition is grounded in accounts of
personal experience. For example, many women have told powerful stories
of their first recognition of their marginality in a field they had previously
thought of as theirs. We must beware of reading these moving accounts too
transparently and untheoretically. In her essay "Experience," Joan W. Scott
offers a useful caution:

> When experience is taken as the origin of knowledge, the vision of
> the individual subject (the person who had the experience or the his-
> torian who recounts it) becomes the bedrock of evidence upon which
> explanation is built. Questions about the constructed nature of expe-
> rience, about how subjects are constituted as different in the first
> place, about how one's vision is structured—about language (or dis-
> course) and history—are left aside. (25)

Scott reminds us that narratives of experience should be encountered not as
uncontested truth but as catalysts for further analysis of the conditions that
shape experience.

   We want to be clear about our view of experience: we are not dismissing
such accounts but only suggesting ways to read and listen to them. The
problem is not that these narratives are personal or that they are experiential,

but that they are often untheorized. In understanding both the value and the limitations of feminist uses of experience in our field, we have found the work of Scott and of Rosemary Hennessy particularly useful. Both address "experience" as a construct and show ways to continue to value women's experiences as sources of knowledge; but they also suggest ways to theorize experience to make it a more critical rhetorical tool. Scott advises us to keep in mind that "experience is at once always already an interpretation and is in need of interpretation. What counts as experience is neither self-evident nor straightforward; it is always contested, always therefore political" (37). Hennessy views experience as a critical tool for examining the values and ideologies used to construct women's experiences, but she adds an important qualification for ensuring that women's experience is not narrowly read. Any critical theorizing of women's experience must be undertaken in the context of a continual "re-contextualization of the relationship between personal and group history and political priorities" (Minnie Bruce Pratt, qtd in Hennessy 99) and in relation to the "counterhegemonic discourses" of others (99). We have found that by attending to certain feminist tropes in our discipline, we can not only begin to tease out the relationships between composition and feminism, but also gain a better sense of the important dialectical relationships between experience and theory.

Adding Women: Narratives Aimed at Inclusion

Correcting the long absence of women from intellectual and political landscapes, inserting women's perspectives into contexts dominated by patriarchy, and giving women equal status with men have constituted one of the central feminist projects—that of inclusion. This effort to add women has been criticized retrospectively as ineffective because it arises from Enlightenment conceptions of individual autonomy and the unquestioned "truth" of individual experience. Discussions of inclusion of women as women may reinforce essentialist or biological definitions of gender, and they often neglect to theorize the discourses that keep women and minorities marginalized. Most critically, many attempts to include women in the conversations of the field have in fact added only white, middle-class, heterosexual women. Despite these criticisms, we need to reread these attempts from their cultural context and for their first steps toward gender awareness. As Suzanne Clark reminds us, "feminists challenging a certain kind of feminism in composition represent a luxury: women now have a sufficient number to play out [their] anxieties of influence" (94). Our analyses need to take into account cultural and historical contexts out of which women were working that made these assumptions viable at the time.

Some of the first published evidence of the initiative to add women to the conversation came in NCTE publications aimed primarily at secondary teachers. The March 1972 *English Journal* printed "The Undiscovered," Robert A. Bennett's NCTE presidential address of the previous November. In highlighting "the undiscovered human resources of our professional organization" (352), Bennett includes girls and women among "those peoples of American society who have not yet been allowed to make their fullest contribution":

> The talents of the great number of women teachers who are today still nonmembers of the Council or who are inactive in Council affairs, provide another undiscovered resource. As a professional organization, we must reach out to these women and encourage them . . . to become full partners in our common effort. (353)

After urging the organization to examine wage and promotion policies, document discriminatory practices, and work for recognition of women in curriculum and pedagogy, Bennett declares, "NCTE must take a stand for recognition of the contribution of women to society and to our profession. We have not done it. Let's get at it" (353).

Two months later, *English Journal* carried a short "Open Letter from Janet Emig, Chairwoman, NCTE Committee on the Role and Image of Women," asking the membership to nominate committee members and to send information about any "instances of discrimination against women in the profession, either in the form of a brief narrative or, if you are the woman involved, as a signed or as an anonymous case history" (710). A direct result of NCTE's new commitment to include women, Emig's committee was soliciting stories that would potentially disrupt business-as-usual in the profession, (a practice that Theresa Enos repeated more than 20 years later for *Gender Roles and Faculty Lives in Rhetoric and Composition*). The CCCC Committee on the Status of Women also continues to solicit narratives, in various forums, in order to ascertain more clearly the status of women in the field.

While a review of *CCC* from the late 1960s through the late 1980s uncovers few essays or other documents that would indicate a gendered feminist consciousness in composition, two landmark special issues of *College English*, in 1971 and 1972, report on the newly formed MLA Commission on the Status of Women in the Profession and document courses designed by feminists in English to reshape the curriculum from the standpoint of women students. The narratives in these special issues set the pattern for the impulse a decade or more later in composition to add women to its perspectives. Arising from the writers' own consciousness-raising experiences, the narratives articulate the potential for student and teacher subjectivities that are not neutral or universal but uniquely influenced by the textual, social, and political context of gender. Florence Howe's impassioned 1971 essay, in which she inserts her own personal account of discrimination, reports the inequities in women's status she uncovered as chair of the MLA commission. In addition to these first attempts to address women's low status in the profession, Howe and Elaine Showalter both illustrate their efforts to rectify the lack of women's texts and perspectives in English courses. Showalter describes her newly organized course, "The Educated Woman in Literature," in practical terms, and Howe presents a writing course she designed to help women alter their self-image "from centuries of *belief* in their inferiority, as well as from male-dominated and controlled institutions" (863). A second special issue of *College English* (October 1972) contains important essays concerning women's inclusion in the discipline of English, among them Tillie Olsen's "Women Who are Writers in Our Century: One Out of Twelve" and Adrienne Rich's "When We Dead Awaken: Writing as Re-vision." Each of these essays seeks to insert women—their perspectives, their writing, their lived experiences—into a discipline from which they had been excluded.

In "Taking Women Students Seriously," her important 1978 essay emphasizing the necessity of including women's perspectives in education, Adrienne Rich described how the experience of changing from one teaching context to another allowed her to translate the critical questions she asked as a writing instructor of minority students into parallel questions she needed to ask about women students:

> How does a woman gain a sense of her *self* in a system . . . which devalues work done by women, denies the importance of female experience, and is physically violent toward women? . . . How do we, as women, teach women students a canon of literature which has consistently excluded or depreciated female experience? (239)

These early essays set a pattern for subsequent inclusive questions that women in composition began asking. Beginning by describing their own consciousness-raising experiences in their essays, the writers moved on to document the concrete changes in teaching and critical perspectives they advocated. What are women's experiences in classrooms, in institutions? How do women use language? How are women writers different from male writers? Questions like these included women in ways that had not been possible in a "gender-blind" field of composition; they set the stage for writers in the 1980s like Pamela Annas and Elizabeth Flynn to engage them further in work that again sought women's inclusion in the field and sparked feminist discussions for a newer generation of women.[1]

In the late 70s, the trope of inclusion appeared in essays applying feminist language research to composition by investigating claims made by Robin Lakoff in her 1975 *Language and Woman's Place*—that women, by using a ladylike middle-class language, contributed to their own oppression. Lakoff's argument reflected the "dominance" approach to women's language use that was prominent among feminists of the 70s: attributing gender differences in language mainly to social oppression of women. Joan Bolker's 1979 *College English* article, "Teaching Griselda to Write," is a practitioner's account of her experience struggling with the absence of voice and authority in the work of "good-girl" student writers. The many citations of this short article in the past 19 years suggest that it has resonated with feminists in composition. In 1978, two articles examining women's "different" style appeared in *CCC*. In "The Feminine Style: Theory and Fact," Mary P. Hiatt discusses her study of the stylistic features of women's and men's writing. She reports "clear evidence of a feminine style . . . [that] is in fact rather different from the common assumptions about it" (226). Contrary to Lakoff's generalizations about women's oral language, women's written style, according to Hiatt, has "no excesses of length or complexity or emotion" (226). In "Women in a Double-Bind: Hazards of the Argumentative Edge," Sheila Ortiz Taylor draws composition instructors' attention to the "invisible, though real, disadvantage" that women students face in writing courses because "both the methods and the goals of such classes are alien to them" (385). She argues that the competitive, impersonal style of traditional argument alienates women; she urges instructors to validate "conversational tone, dramatic technique, and intimate reader involvement" (389).

Among the first composition articles to train the spotlight on women's language experiences, these essays highlight deficiency. (Ironically, as in Lakoff's book, an essentialized "woman" is both *included* and *found lacking*.) Bolker, Taylor, and Hiatt respond differently to the idea that women students must have special problems because a feminine style represents deficiency. Taylor uses the language of victimization to describe the woman student: "She must feel that something is wrong with her, a self-destructive disapproval common enough in women . . . of course, much of the damage has been done by the time our students reach us. They have been taught a special language" (385). But Taylor adds that a feminine style of argument is only "deficient" because society has refused to validate it. Bolker believes that with more self-esteem and voice, the good girl can be a contender in the arena of the dominant discourse. Hiatt implies that readers need to be more discerning about the gender differences they *think* they see. None of these articles is heavily theorized; with the possible exception of Hiatt's, they arise from and return directly to classroom experience. Because they do not attend closely to larger systemic issues of power and discourse, these studies also make it possible for feminist concerns to be contained, encapsulated, or dismissed as "women's issues." Yet essays like these deserve credit for challenging the field's gender-blindness by insisting that women be included in narratives of classroom writing practices. They have contributed to a sense of intuitive connection between composition and those who ask, at least implicitly, "What difference might it make if the student (or teacher) is female?"

Making Intuitive Connections: Narratives of Metonymic Relationship

In their introduction to *Teaching Writing: Pedagogy, Gender, and Equity*, one of the first books to connect writing and feminism in composition, Cynthia Caywood and Gillian Overing say that despite the absence of explicit discussion, they had experienced as practitioners an "intuitive understanding" of a "fundamental connection" between feminism and revisionist writing theory. While highlighting an absence of attention to gender, they also posit a more complicated reading of this absence by pointing to the nearly parallel lives of composition and feminist theory. According to this story, the two have run for years in the same direction, along close trajectories; to bring the fields together it is necessary only to notice the shared goals and common directions, and to make connections more visible and explicit. Caywood and Overing ask, "At what point did our parallel interests in feminism and revisionist writing theory converge?" (xi). More recently Susan Jarratt, Laura Brady, Janet Emig, and Louise Phelps have suggested that the boundaries have been permeable between feminist work in literary studies, the social sciences, and composition. This resonates with our own sense, as practitioners in the 70s, that boundaries between feminism and composition were often marked by unarticulated overlaps and crossovers. This permeability may have been partly the result of the interdisciplinary nature of composition, which drew for its theoretical substance from linguistics, cognitive and developmental psychology, and literary criticism. But while this intuitive connection may have created alliances among women in composition and feminists in other fields, it may also have delayed the emergence of feminist theory and continued its marginalization in the field.

Various factors account for the intuitive sense of connection that many of us have experienced and narrated. First, emerging pedagogical theories spoke a language that resonated with feminism's concerns of the time: coming to voice and consciousness, illuminating experience and its relationship to individual identity, playing the believing game rather than the doubting game, collaborating rather than competing, subverting hierarchy in the classroom. These watchwords characterized composition's link to liberal political and social agendas shared by feminist scholars in other disciplines and aimed at challenging established traditions, epistemologies, and practices of the academy.[2] Sharon Crowley explicitly connects Dewey's progressivism with Janet Emig's development of "process pedagogies," arguing that this link between progressivism and process pedagogies was vitally important in reconceptualizing composition "as an art rather than a course," and "because its theorists discovered a way to talk about student writing that authorized teachers to think of themselves as researchers" (17). This reconceptualization resonated for feminists theoretically and politically.

Secondly, at that time many women in the profession were doing double-duty as composition and literature teachers. Among the *College English* authors represented in the special issues we have pointed out, Florence Howe taught composition and wrote about how her course focused on women, and Adrienne Rich taught writing with Mina Shaughnessy in the SEEK program at CCNY. Many feminist composition instructors, coming from literary critical backgrounds, continued reading in their fields and appropriating whatever feminist approaches seemed useful—much as compositionists of the 80s and 90s have appropriated the work of Belenky, Clinchy, Goldberger, and Tarule and poststructuralist feminists.

The material conditions surrounding women in composition have also contributed to a felt sense of the feminist connections to our work. Composition was and still is constructed as women's work, and the majority of workers were women; many of us teaching writing or working on composition degrees during the 70s and 80s were newly arrived from secondary teaching. Surrounded by colleagues with similar career patterns, we entered conversations that enacted an interplay between our lives and our professional work. The drawbacks of the "feminization" of the field were not theorized until several years later.

Finally, as the field developed in the 1970s, although journal editors and the professional hierarchy were primarily male, the names of women were also moving into prominent places: Mina Shaughnessy, Janet Emig, Ann Berthoff, Sondra Perl, Anne Gere, Lillian Bridwell-Bowles, and others were writing many of the important articles and books we studied. Many feminists refer with appreciation to the "foremothers," first for their presence as models, and secondly for their ideas which, though not articulated in terms of gender, are often read, in retrospect, as consistent with feminist practice. In many cases, these ideas have to do with nurturing, collaboration, revisioning, and decentering.

Some retrospective accounts use theory to make the composition-feminism connections less intuitive, more explicit. Turning from foremothers to "midwives," Carolyn Ericksen Hill uses feminist theory to read composition history through the gendering of practices, of theories, and of the field itself.[3] She reads the label "midwives" back onto male composition theorists active in the 60s and early 70s: Peter Elbow, Ken Macrorie, John Schultz, and William Coles, Jr. Without necessarily claiming them as feminists, she can, with the aid of postmodern theory, gender their approach as feminine and place their work in a certain feminist context: they helped "birth" the experiential self. The expressivist/nurturing feminist connection has often been made in passing, but Hill's label "midwives" claims these key composition figures for feminist theorizing—and also marginalizes them. In the 1990s, Hill argues, these four "expressivist" figures have been pushed to the edge of a newly theorized and professionalized field; their gender-blindness and humanistic model of the autonomous self have had to make way for gender difference and shifting subject positions, powerful constructs for feminist analysis. Hill sees in the compartmentalization—rather than dynamic rereading—of the four men's so-called expressivism a parallel with the "othering" of "woman," and of feminism, that continues to occur.

The rereading of "foremothers"—or even "midwives"—as feminist precursors may also be problematic if it ignores context and complexity, as we see from a few examples of foremothers who resist labeling. In the late 1970s, Ann Berthoff roundly rejected the gendering of logic and the either/or-ism of all discussions of women's ways of knowing; she reaffirmed this rejection at the 1998 CCCC convention. Still, the foremother figures can both exemplify and disrupt the notion of the feminization of the field. As foremothers they are both marginalized and typically characterized as nurturers. But insofar as they are envisioned as foremothers, as founders, they are not feminized but rather constructed in a traditionally masculine position.

Evidence that stories of connection continue to resonate with us may be found in Jan Zlotnik Schmidt's introduction to *Women/Writing/Teaching*, a 1998 collection of essays by women writers and teachers. Schmidt emphasizes the importance of women's experience in making writing-teaching connections and expresses her hope that readers will also "explore their own life stories, their development of selfhood, their multiple identities as writers, teachers, and writing teachers" (xii). Retrospective narratives that create foremothers, midwives, connections, and nurturing community in composition's history foreground the double potential of the metonymic relationship between feminism and composition. This intuitive connection helps to create a sense of solidarity and vitality. But it may also reinforce the very structures that keep feminist perspectives contained in a separate, benign category rather than giving feminist analysis a central place, or at least keeping it insistently, vocally disruptive of the discipline's metanarratives. For example, some feminist practitioners have told powerful stories about replacing hierarchical, agonistic classroom environments with decentered, nurturing classrooms based on an ethic of care. But, as Eileen Schell argues, "femin*in*ist pedagogy, although compelling, may reinforce rather than critique or transform patriarchal structures by reinscribing what Magda Lewis calls the 'woman as caretaker ideology'" ("The Cost" 74, our italics).

Granting feminism's intuitive connections with a discipline that challenged current-traditional conceptions of language and introduced new decentered writing pedagogics, it is also important to recognize that some feminist agendas were more likely to disrupt than to aid composition's early progress toward full disciplinary status. Composition needed to build institutional legitimacy in the traditional academy; a fundamental feminist goal was to disrupt rather than extend patriarchal discourses and their assumptions about knowledge. Composition sought a single theory of the writing process and the writing subject; feminist theorists challenged notions of a singular universal concept of truth. The trope of metonymy may have difficulty expanding to cover some of these adversarial relationships.

Feminist Disruptions

Composition has many narratives of feminist disruption which emphasize neither inclusion nor intuitive connection but rather represent some form of feminism (newly experienced or theorized) reaching back to reread and even reconfigure past experience and practice. We see increasing numbers of current feminists drawing on postmodern theories to analyze and critique the basic "process" narratives of composition's first 20 years, to raise questions about difference(s), and to critique disciplinary practices and structures that have shaped composition. Disruption is often linked to postmodern theories of power, discourse, and ideology rather than to consciousness-raising sessions, discussions of pedagogy, or attempts to create equitable and inclusive conditions for women. In order to intervene significantly in power structures that keep women subordinate, feminists investigate and uncover the contradictions in those dominant structures. The feminist narratives we have reread remind us, however, that efforts at inclusion, connection, and disruption often work synthetically rather than as adversaries or as unequal partners. As Theresa Enos says, her book's "most powerful use of 'data' is the narrative, in the stories that help us define our places in academia so that we can better trace our future" (1).

The explicit recognition of composition's lack of attention to women's material lives has led women in anger, frustration, and recognition to tell the stories of their coming to awareness. A classic feminist narrative of the early 70s is the story of a "good girl," silenced by her compulsion to please, whose recognition of her oppression releases an anger strong enough to overcome politeness and fear; thus she finds both her voice and an agenda for change. The consciousness-raising sessions of the late 60s and early 70s provided a model for this narrative, as did the two special women's issues of *College English*, 1971–72, that we have mentioned. In "When We Dead Awaken," Rich told her own story of frustration at the demands that she be good at all the roles women were supposed to play, while Howe, after narrating how she had acquiesced in years of inequitable treatment, wrote, "Eighteen months as commission Chairwoman [of the MLA Commission on the Status of Women] has eroded that wry smile. I feel now a growing anger as I come to realize that . . . I am not alone in my state" (849).

Many of today's feminist accounts of the 60s and 70s follow a similar pattern. Lynn Z. Bloom's essay, "Teaching College English as a Woman" (1992), is a scathing look at the bad old days in college English, when a woman in the field—whether student or teacher—would be exploited if she did not get angry and speak up. Bloom recalls a conversion experience when, as a part-time composition instructor, she finally was able to obtain office space: in a basement room full of desks, on the floor under the stairs, next to the kitty litter. Surveying these wretched conditions, she told herself,

"If I ever agree to do this again, I deserve what I get" (821). Separated by
more than 20 years, Bloom's and Howe's angry accounts illustrate what we
might call individual, liberal disruption: the idea that once a woman sees
clearly, her life is changed, and she is thus empowered to become effectively
active for change and reform. These accounts show the "revisioning" that
feminist thinking has enabled individual women to do. We read these
accounts as disruptive because in addition to realizing that the liberal
Enlightenment agenda hasn't included *her,* each of these women also
recognizes that she must take action to disrupt and change the structures that
have kept her subordinate.

Other women who are currently doing feminist work in composition
studies have provided similar testimonies of naive compliance, oppressed
silence, eventual recognition, and new outspokenness.[4] That we now have
so many such narratives may mean that women in composition today are
finally in a position to claim the authority of the autobiographical; it may
also mean that, largely due to feminist efforts, the conventions of scholarly
discourse have expanded to include the personal narrative as a way of
situating oneself in one's scholarship. But perhaps the personal testimony
remains an effective—and still necessary—tool of disruption. Many of these
stories are disruptive because they expose "the pattern of well-rewarded,
male supervision of under-rewarded, female workers" that has existed in
composition and "is entrenched in our whole culture" (Enos vii). The
disruption that is so central to the consciousness-raising narrative itself also
highlights gaps in our reading of our past and of business as usual. Rereading
the consciousness-raising essays that have recurred in composition over the
past 25 years can show us more sites where women have been silent but
where feminists want to rupture that silence.

Many narratives deal with experiences in teaching and department
politics, but a 1993 retrospective account by Nancy McCracken, Lois
Green, and Claudia Greenwood tells how they acquiesced as researchers
to a field characterized by "a persistent silence on the subject of gender" in
its "landmark research studies on writing development and writing
processes" (352). Now writing collaboratively, they return to studies of
teacher responses to student writing that they had published earlier (and
separately), reinterpreting those studies in terms of gender differences.
These authors emphasize that until the late 80s the climate in composition
studies had made it difficult to notice or report gender differences in
empirical studies: "None of us went looking for gender differences. When
the data began to speak of gender, we dared not listen" (356). They recount

their worries about being accused of biological determinism, about seeming to exclude men, about appearing unprofessional, and about calling attention to themselves as women. Now, they say, they feel empowered not only to note gender difference but to insist on it. Theirs is not a story of breaking silence by themselves. Instead, the current "research environment in which it is both important and safe to study the interplay between students' gender and their development as writers" (354) has made it possible to revise their findings. Their story is not about singular heroism but about collaboration, in a network of mutual support, in a research/scholarly environment that has made discursive structures more visible. Their story is not about going solo against a hostile discipline but about rereading the field and their own complicity. Their reading disrupts, among other things, their *own* research, by requiring that they return to it and revise it.

Some of the early disruptive narratives we have mentioned are reformist, and they may even be read as attempts at inclusion as well as disruption. Another form of disruptive narrative is less grounded in the impulse for individual disruption and change, but seeks wider consideration of difference. Such critiques often create conflict and may evoke more resistance because they demand changes in institutional and epistemological structures that conflict with composition's continuing need to establish legitimacy. They support the emergence of different perspectives rather than suppressing them. In these accounts difference is expanded from the single male/female binary to differences, taking into account multiple inflections of social class, sexual orientation, and race. For example, Harriet Malinowitz's study of lesbian and gay students in writing classes and Shirley Wilson Logan's writing on the confluence of race and gender in composition both attempt to expand our understanding of what differences can mean in composition classrooms. They articulate the connections among differences as well as show the privileging or erasure of some categories by others. Writing out of her own experience as a Chinese student speaking several languages, Min-Zhan Lu has drawn upon third-world and minority feminisms as well as other cultural theorists to disrupt composition teachers' view of the conflicts students face in negotiating the political, linguistic, and rhetorical "borderlands" between home and school. She reopens a debate about the processes of acculturation and accommodation at work in writing classrooms, particularly those that serve minority and immigrant students. In doing so, she rereads the work of Mina Shaughnessy, Thomas Farrell, Kenneth Bruffee, and others in light of current contexts in order to critique the wider public debates about literacy and to highlight the cultural conflicts and necessary resistances of today's students on the margins.

At times these disruptions can create tension and anger even among feminists, highlighting the way feminism itself is shaped by and embedded in existing hierarchical discourses. This conflict may seem to undermine any sense of solidarity that existed when feminism appeared in a more intuitive rather than carefully articulated and scrutinized form. But in fact, such conflict may produce one of feminism's most important benefits—the proliferation of differences. Nedra Reynolds argues: "Feminists daring to criticize other feminists have opened up spaces for analyzing difference; they interrupted the discourses of feminism in the singular to make possible feminism in the plural" (66). Other disruptive narratives of difference are only now emerging and await further exploration. Constructs like Gloria Anzaldua's *mestiza*, Trinh T. Minh-ha's subject-in-the-making, Donna Haraway's cyborg, and Judith Butler's performer of gender extend postmodern notions of difference in disruptive directions with their advocacy of multiplicity, fluidity, hybridity, and indeterminacy.

Feminists in composition in the past decade have used postmodern theories to reread the feminization and the femin*in*ization of composition as problematic and to seek to revise institutional frameworks. The preponderance of women in composition has not led inevitably to the triumph of feminist interests and values in the field. For example, Susan Miller tells the story of the "sad women in the basement" and describes feminization as the "female coding" of the "ideologically constructed identity for the teacher of composition" (123); it involves constructing composition as "women's work." Feminization refers to the gendering of the entire field of composition and of various activities that have taken place within it (nonhierarchical pedagogy, the writing process movement, "romantic" philosophies, nurturing of writers). For Miller, feminization points to the devaluation of the composition instructor, and the subordination of composition to literature, throughout the history of the field. For Rhonda Grego and Nancy Thompson, compositionists "still reside within our gendered roles," but we are not limited to a traditional "wifely" role because the field has lately been "developing terms and methods through which to name our work at least to ourselves, if not yet fully to the ruling apparatus of the academic system" (68). In *Gypsy Academics and Mother Teachers*, Eileen Schell combines materialist feminist and postmodern perspectives, labor and institutional history, and the personal narratives of women nontenure-track teachers to analyze the gendered division of labor in composition and to critique femin*in*ization—the coopting of the "ethic of care." She also provides strategies for coalition-building and tangible plans of action for reconceptualizing women's positions and reshaping institutional structures. Feminization narratives like these work disruptively in two directions: their analysis foregrounds the political position of composition within institutional structures, but it also highlights tensions within women's roles and interests in composition.

Finally, disruptive narratives in composition have begun to analyze the established narratives of the discipline and the agency of students and teachers constructed by those narratives. They explore the ideologies underlying the discourses where composition has been situated, including those espoused by feminists, to underscore the contradictions and dangers that those create for women as well as for the field in general. An early example is Susan Jarratt's rereading of Peter Elbow's work and of the tendency in feminism and expressivism to suppress conflict and promote consensus.[5] She argues that such a stance fails to arm women students and teachers with the tools to confront the power relations inherent in their positions. An important recent example of disruption is Nedra Reynolds' rereading of several major narratives in the field. Reynolds emphasizes that interruption—talking back, forcibly breaking into the prevailing discourse of a field—is a way to create agency: "Agency is not simply about finding one's own voice but also about intervening in discourses of the everyday [this would include personal experience narratives] and cultivating rhetorical tactics that make interruption and resistance an important part of any conversation" (59). She points out the tendency of "some of the most important voices in composition today . . . to ignore work in feminism that might complement or complicate their ideas" (66). She not only "interrupts" some of the major cultural studies theorists but also analyzes the conceptions of subjectivity and agency in the work of James Berlin, John Trimbur, and Lester Faigley. She criticizes the dominant narrative's tendency to compartmentalize interrupters and disrupters as "rude women," thereby denying them agency. As part of the evidence for her argument, she tells stories about a cultural studies conference where bell hooks and other women participants analyzed the "terror" of the typical "white supremacist hierarchy" (65). Reynolds urges women to develop strategies for interrupting dominant discourses in composition and challenges them to offer their students the means to resist rigid forms of discourse.

Conclusion: In Excess

These three different but also converging narratives of feminism suggest a rich tradition of feminist thought and activity in composition: pushing for admission, working intuitively alongside, and interrupting the conversation. We believe these three tropes may help us read and revise feminism's evolving place in the narratives of composition; they provide useful insight for feminists about existing tensions in the relationship of theory to experience and practice; and they point to strategies feminists may seek to promote or avoid in the future.

In composition's last three decades, the impulse has been toward legitimation, theory-building, and consolidation. The disruption and the assertion of difference that feminists and others represent have come slowly and with struggle; they have been delayed and even suppressed by the need to build a more unified disciplinary discourse. In several recent metanarratives that assess where composition has come from and where it is going, we find traces of these three lines of feminist thought that may help us see where feminism might most usefully lead composition and where they might go together. These recent commentaries demonstrate that tropes of inclusion and metonymic connection still define feminism's relationship to the field.

In *Fragments of Rationality*, Lester Faigley practices inclusion as he credits feminism for its efforts to theorize a postmodern subject with agency; he also cites the contributions of feminists in foregrounding important pedagogical and political questions. James Berlin's *Rhetorics, Poetics, Cultures* does not mention feminism, but this book, like Faigley's, does cite several postmodern feminists' efforts to theorize subjectivity and difference. In Joseph Harris' *A Teaching Subject: Composition Since 1966*, the connections between women practitioners, feminism, and "the teaching subject" are neither articulated nor connected; they remain an unspoken presence. Like Berlin, Sharon Crowley argues in *Composition in the University* that despite its progress over the past 30 years, composition has remained a conservative discipline, still trapped in current-traditionalism, still shackled to the service role of Freshman English, and still bound to the limitations of humanism in English departments. Unlike Berlin, she looks to feminist thought for its disruptive power, as one of several theoretical perspectives that might help dislodge composition from narrow disciplinary confines.

The representation of feminist perspectives in these recent commentaries suggests that in the future these relationships will persist—with unspoken alliances between feminist thought and composition, and inclusive reliance on postmodern feminism(s) where they advance the general argument. But it is to the disruptive strategy, framed in dialogue with inclusivity and metonymy, that we return. It is tempting to see disruption as the newest and best hope for feminism and to privilege theorizing as the most worthwhile activity for feminism and composition. But it's also clear that different emphases may be more effective as rhetorical contexts shift and historical moments change. While efforts at inclusion suffer from the limitations we've outlined, and untheorized or unarticulated practices also create risks of marginalization and erasure, disruptive strategies, by themselves, also have limitations. The history of feminism suggests that it is necessary to do more than interrupt a disciplinary conversation. Disruption may be only temporary, and as Reynolds and others point out, it's easy to push disrupters to the sidelines, to stop listening to them and to marginalize them once again. In addition, the task of disruption requires rhetorical skill. Those who interrupt may gain momentary attention, but those who can't sustain the conversation, hold up the argument, or tell an absorbing story will soon drop—or be dropped—from the discussion.

Certainly feminists in composition have provided the field with models for persuasive and beautiful writing that tells and disrupts stories of experience. (Lynn Worsham's "After Words: A Choice of Words Remains" is a recent example.) If theorizing and disruption are detached from lived experience and material history, they may remain irrelevant. And if disruption only fractures and doesn't again create connection, a sense of an even tentatively inclusive agenda, it will lack the vital energy and supportive alliances to sustain its own taxing work. Over the last 30 years, feminists have demonstrated that critique and disruption are never finished and that coalition-building and collaboration are vital for change.

Our rereading of 30 years of feminist writing suggests that in both early and more recent work, feminism has been most challenging and disruptive and also provided a sense of alliance and inclusion when it has maintained a dialogical relationship between theory and experience. Despite its short history, feminist work in composition can certainly provide many revitalizing demonstrations of this dialogical relationship as one of its contributions to academic feminism. Virtually all the feminist work we've reviewed and see emerging has, at least in part, claimed, interpreted, and revised accounts of experience and history: the personal history of one's life as a woman, the practice of the teacher, or the experience of the scholar. As Suzanne Clark points out, narratives of experience theorized become possible sites of

agency: "At the same time that stories of personal experience invoke and re-
cite determinant categories of identity . . . such stories also produce an excess
not easily retrofitted as the norm" (98). Rather than dismissing stories of
experience, Clark suggests that we look at them for what is "excessive," that is,
for parts of the narrative that do not fit our current explanations: "What
refuses, despite the sometimes daunting applications of straitjacket pseudo-
sciences, to be contained?" (98). One of feminism's most potentially powerful
tools is the deployment of what is excessive, what is other. Difference,
"otherness," disrupts, as Rosemary Hennessy argues, because the "gaps,
contradictions, *aporias*" that otherness creates force dominant perspectives
into crisis management to "seal over or manage the contradictions. . . . But
they also serve as the inaugural space for critique" (92).

   Many gaps remain for feminists to explore in composition and in its
relationship to English and the broader culture. Although researchers have
now examined from a feminist perspective the status of women in
composition and the feminized status of composition within English studies,
many women still teach composition in the "basement," and the wider
institutional, economic, and cultural conditions continue to create barriers
against improving their status. Although women and men in our field have
considered how class, gender and race may shape their pedagogy, we have
not thoroughly come to terms with students' or teachers' gendered, classed,
or raced position in the academy—or the continuing failure to provide a
viable education for many minority students or encouragement for minority
colleagues in our field. Although various critics have highlighted the gender
blindness of liberatory and critical pedagogics, we have not thoroughly
considered how such theories and pedagogics stop short of realizing their
goals where women students, minorities, and gay and lesbian students are
concerned. Although we have a body of metacommentary on research
methodologies and ethical representation of research subjects, we have only
begun to explore effective ways to connect our research to wider public
concerns and debates about literacy.

   Our own interest in diversity and multiplicity makes us curious about the
possible uses of "excess" as a trope for feminists in composition of the
present and future. Already we are exploring feminist or "diverse discourses,"
which are in excess of what a singular linear argument requires. We are
pushing for notions and accounts of agency that exceed limited ideas of the
determined subject. Might the re-visionary stories of the next generation refer
to greedy visions of *more* as well as angry recognitions of *lack*? Can we
envision narratives of a disruptive practice that overflows as well as

challenges? Excess might be proposed as inclusion with a difference: uncontained and without limits.

At this time when composition is reviewing its past and seeking to chart new directions, a glance beyond the academy suggests that political and economic conditions will create continuing intellectual and practical "straitjackets" in composition's next 50 years. The energy of feminists will be vital to the disruption of restrictive theory and practice. This energy will be important for sustaining coalitions for change; it is our best hope for inclusion and proliferation of difference, multiplicity, and uncontainable excess.

Notes

1. In two recent collections of essays on composition, Villanueva's *Cross-Talk in Comp Theory*, and Bloom, Daiker, and White's *Composition in the Twenty-First Century*, the only essay specifically from a feminist perspective is Flynn's 1988 "Composing as a Woman." The frequent inclusion of this essay suggests the impact it has had; the fact that it is the only one included suggests that, in some venues at least, it has been used to contain feminism at the same time.

2. For example, the February 1970 issue of *CCC* contains articles by Donald Murray and by William Coles articulating many of the crucial progressive assumptions emerging in composition: the value of individual students' writing as an articulation of agency and selfhood rather than merely as an object of diagnosis and correction. The *CCC* journals of that year also contain several proposals for alternative freshman English courses for minority students, and the October 1972 issue contains the CCCC Executive Committee's Resolution, "The Student's Right to His Own Language." Although they remain steadfastly gender-blind, essays like these attest to the profession's increasing attempts in the late 60s and 70s to redefine writing and writing instruction. These disciplinary calls for cultural diversity in the curriculum and for the students' rights to their own language caused a great deal of ferment in the profession and foregrounded issues of difference, yet they still did not open a discursive space for women to speak as women writers and teachers or to consider the gendered implications of Coles' goal for writing: "to allow the student to put himself together" (28).

3. Belenky, Clinchy, Goldberger, and Tarule are noted for their use of "midwife" in their discussion of educators who promote constructed knowledge. But the term was applied to writing instructors much earlier. In 1970, Stephen Judy wrote in *English Journal* (which he was later to edit): "We need to discard the structure of the composition teacher as one who passes on knowledge about writing, makes assignments, and corrects errors on themes. A more appropriate role can be described as that of coach or catalyst, or one that I prefer, that of midwife: one who assists in the process of bringing something forth but does not participate in the process himself" (217). This passage suggests possibilities for

metonymy: the masculine pronoun may simply illustrate composition's gender-blindness, but it may also be a trace of the gender-shifting that Hill does twenty years later. Judy adds, "It would be difficult for a midwife to do *her* job adequately if the expenant mother knew she were going to be graded on the re-sults. (217, italics ours).

4. Wendy Bishop, Lillian Bridwell-Bowles, Louise Phelps, and Nancy Sommers are just a few of the women who have written personal narratives that practice and reflect on disruption of a status quo. Jacqueline Jones Royster writes, "I have been compelled on too many occasions to count to sit as a well-mannered Other" (30). Theresa Enos' *Gender Roles and Faculty Lives in Rhetoric and Composition* contains a number of anonymous stories from women in composition, along with her narrative of her own experience as an "academically battered woman (ix). Gesa Kirsch's interviews with women in various academic disciplines explore their interpretations of their experiences as writers and raise "questions of gender and language, women's participation in public discourse, and womens 'ways of writing'" (xvii). A new collection, *Women/Writing/Teaching,* edited by Jan Zlotnik Schmidt presents ten previously published and ten new essays by women that examine their personal experiences as writers and teachers.

5. We could cite numerous other examples: Patricia Sullivan's rereading of Stephen North's *The Making of Knowledge in Composition;* Nancy Welch's use of feminist theory and her own experience to reread Lacan and other theorists and to disrupt composition's conceptualization of revision; and the important work of increasing numbers of feminists rereading and regendering the rhetorical tra-dition from Aspasia to Ida B. Wells, from Gertrude Buck to Toni Morrison.

Works Cited

Annas, Pamela J. "Style as Politics: A Feminist Approach to the Teaching of Writ-ing." *College English* 47 (1985): 360–71.

Belenky, Mary Field, Blythe McVicker Clinchy, Nancy Rule Goldberger, and Jill Mattuck Tarule. *Women's Ways of Knowing: The Development of Self, Voice, and Mind.* New York: Basic 1986.

Bennett, Robert A. "NCTE Presidential Address: The Undiscovered." *English Jour-nal* 61 (1972): 351–57.

Berlin, James. *Rhetorics, Poetics and Cultures: Refguring College English Studies.* Urbana: NCTE, 1996.

Berthoff, Ann E. "Rhetoric as Hermeneutic." *CCC* 42 (1991): 279–87.

Bishop, Wendy. "Learning Our Own Ways to Situate Composition and Feminist Studies in the English Department." *Journal of Advanced Composition* 10 (1990): 339–55.

Bloom, Lynn Z. "Teaching College English as a Woman." *College English* 54 (1992): 818–825.

Bloom, Lynn Z., Donald A. Daiker, and Edward M. White, eds. *Composition in the Twenty-First Century: Crisis and Change.* Carbondale: Southern Illinois UP. 1996.

Bolker, Joan. "Teaching Griselda to Write." *College English* 40 (1979): 906–08.

Brady, Laura. "The Reproduction of Othering." Jarratt and Worsham 21–44.

Bridwell-Bowles, Lillian. "Freedom, Form, Function: Varieties of Academic Discourse." *CCC* 46 (1995): 46–61.

Caywood, Cynthia, and Gillian Overing, eds. *Teaching Writing: Pedagogy, Gender, and Equity,* Albany: State U of New York P, 1987.

Clark, Suzanne. "Argument and Composition." Jarratt and Worsham 94–99.

Coles, William, Jr. "The Sense of Nonsense as a Design for Sequential Writing Assignments." *CCC* 21 (1970): 27–34.

Crowley, Sharon. *Composition in the University Historical and Polemical Essays.* Pittsburgh Series in Composition, Literacy, and Culture. Pittsburgh: U of Pittsburgh P, 1998.

Enos, Theresa. *Gender Roles and Faculty Lives in Rhetoric and Composition.* Carbondale: Southern Illinois UP, 1996.

Faigley, Lester. *Fragments of Rationality: Postmodernity and the Subject of Composition.* Pittsburgh Series in Composition, Literacy, and Culture. Pittsburgh, U of Pittsburgh P, 1992

Flynn, Elizabeth A. "Composing as a Woman." *CCC* 39 (1988): 423–35.

Fontaine, Sheryl I., and Susan Hunter, eds. *Writing Ourselves into the Story: Unheard Voices from Composition Studies.* Carbondale: Southern Illinois UP, 1993. 1–17.

Grego, Rhonda, and Nancy Thompson. "Repositioning Remediation: Renegotiating Composition's Work in the Academy." *CCC* 47 (1996): 62–84.

Harris, Joseph. *A Teaching Subject: Composition Since 1966.* Upper Saddle River: Prentice, 1997.

Hennessy, Rosemary. *Materialist Feminism and the Politics of Discourse.* Thinking Gender Series. New York: Routledge, 1992.

Hiatt, Mary R. "The Feminine Style: Theory and Fact." *CCC* 29 (1978): 222–26.

Hill, Carolyn Ericksen. *Writing from the Margins: Power and Pedagogy for Teachers of Composition.* New York: Oxford UP, 1990.

Howe, Florence. "A Report on Women and the Profession." *College English* 32 (1971): 847–54.

———. "Identify and Expression: A Writing Course for Women." *College English* 32 (1971): 863–871.

Jarratt, Susan C. "Feminism and Composition: The Case for Conflict." *Contending with Words: Composition and Rhetoric in a Postmodern Age.* Ed. Patricia Harkin and John Schilb. New York: MLA, 1991. 105–23.

Jarratt, Susan C., and Lynn Worsham, eds. *Feminism and Composition Studies: In Other Words,* New York: MLA, 1998.

Judy, Stephen. "The Search for Structures in the Teaching of Composition. *English Journal* 59 (1970): 213–218.

Kirsch, Gesa E. *Women Writing the Academy: Audience, Authority, and Transformation.* Studies in Writing and Rhetoric. Carbondale: Southern Illinois UP, 1992.

Kirsch, Gesa E., and Patricia A. Sullivan, eds. *Methods and Methodology in Composition Research.* Carbondale: Southern Illinois UP, 1992.

Lakoff, Robin. *Language and Woman's Place.* New York: Harper, 1975.

Logan, Shirley W., ed. *With Pen and Voice: The Rhetoric of Nineteenth Century African-American Women.* Carbondale: Southern Illinois UP, 1995.

Lu, Min-Zhan. "Conflict and Struggle: The Enemies or Preconditions of Basic Writing?" *College English* 54 (1992): 887–913.

———. "From Silence to Words: Writing as Struggle." Perl 165–176.

Malinowitz, Harriet. *Textual Orientations: Lesbian and Gay Students and the Making of Discourse Communities.* Portsmouth: Boynton, Heinemann, 1995.

McCracken, Nancy, Lois Green, and Claudia Greenwood. "Gender in Composition Research: A Strange Silence." Fontaine and Hunter 352–73.

Miller, Susan. *Textual Carnivals: The Politics of Composition.* Carbondale: Southern Illinois UP, 1991.

Murray, Donald M. "The Interior View: One Writer's Philosophy of Composition." *CCC* 21 (1970): 21–26.

Olsen, Tillie. "Women Who Are Writers in Our Century: One Out of Twelve." *College English* 34 (1972): 6–17.

"Open Letter from Janet Emig, Chairwoman, NCTE Committee on the Role and Image of Women." *English Journal* 61 (1972): 710.

Perl, Sondra, ed. *Landmark Essays on Writing Process.* Landmark Essays Series 7. Davis: Hermagoras, 1994.

Phelps, Louise W. "Becoming a Warrior: Lessons of the Feminist Workplace." Phelps and Emig 289–339.

Phelps, Louise W., and Janet Emig, eds. *Feminine Principles and Women's Experience in American Composition and Rhetoric.* Pittsburgh Series in Composition, Literacy, and Culture. Pittsburgh: U of Pittsburgh P, 1995.

Reynolds, Nedra. "Interrupting Our Way to Agency: Feminist Cultural Studies and Composition." Jarratt and Worsham 58–73.

Rich, Adrienne. "When We Dead Awaken: Writing as Re-vision." *College English* 34 (1972): 18–25.

———. "Taking Women Students Seriously." *On Lies, Secrets, and Silence: Selected Prose 1966–1978.* New York: Norton, 1979. 237–245.

Royster, Jacqueline Jones. "When the First Voice You Hear Is Not Your Own." *CCC* 47 (1996): 29–40.

Schell, Eileen. *Gypsy Academics and Mother Teachers: Gender, Contingent Labor, and Writing Instruction.* Portsmouth: Boynton, 1998.

———. "The Costs of Caring: 'Feminism' and Contingent Women Workers in Composition Studies." Jarratt and Worsham 74–93.

Schmidt, Jan Zlotnik, ed. *Women/Writing/Teaching.* Albany: State U of New York P 1998.

Scott, Joan. "Experience." *Feminists Theorize the Political.* Ed. Judith Butler and Joan W. Scott. New York: Routledge, 1992. 22–40

Showalter, Elaine. "Women and the Literary Curriculum." *College English* 32 (1971) 855–62.

Sommers, Nancy. "Between the Drafts." Perl 217–24.

Sullivan, Patricia A. "Feminism and Methodology." Kirsch and Sullivan 37–61.

Taylor, Sheila Oniz. "Women in a Double-Bind: Hazards of the Argumentative Edge." *CCC* 29 (1978): 385–89

"The Students' Right to Their Own Language." *CCC* 25 Special Issue (1974): 1–32.

The Secretary's Report of Executive Committee. "The Student's Right to His Own Language." *CCC* 21 (1970): 319–28.

Villanueva Jr., Victor, ed. *Cross-Talk in Comp Theory.* Urbana: NCTE, 1997.

Welch, Nancy. *Getting Restless: Rethinking Revision in Writing Instruction.* Portsmouth: Boynton, 1997.

Worsham, Lynn. "After Words: A Choice of Words Remains." Jarratt and Worsham 329–356.

3 Class Ethos and the Politics of Inquiry: What the Barroom Can Teach Us about the Classroom

Julie Lindquist

Before I was an English teacher, I was a bartender. When I tell my first-year composition students this as we take turns exchanging getting-to-know-you trivia during the first class session, they laugh—some, I suspect, struck by the improbability of the leap from one profession into the other; others, I know, amused by the irony of ending up with an ex-bartender for a teacher. For these others, sons and daughters of iron workers and auto mechanics and waitresses, my move from barroom to classroom traces the trajectory of their own lives.

When I first began teaching, I thought—or, I have to say I hoped—that the university was the farthest point from the local tavern, and that teaching writing to college students was the furthest thing from opening bottles of Bud for laborers. So I was surprised to find myself, after three years of teaching writing, feeling compelled to return to the bar where I'd worked for several years to do community research into local rhetorical practices. In the ethnographic tale that was to grow out of this research, I wanted to map out connections between class, culture, and rhetoric by investigating how rhetorical genres—and in particular, arguments about politics—participated in the public construction of knowledge in, and ultimately in the production of, working-class culture. I was not, of course, surprised to see my data confirm what I'd already suspected: that this small blue-collar society at the bar differed significantly from the cultures of middle-class academics in orientations to word, work, and world. What did come as something of a

Reprinted from *College Composition and Communication*, December 1999.

surprise, however, were what I have come to recognize as functional parallels between the barroom and the classroom as institutional sites of rhetorical practice. When, as a teacher working in a public university, I question the nature of the service I provide and try to understand the dynamics of the relationship I have with my student "regulars," I am struck by how handily the questions I ask myself about my role in the classroom can be expressed in the same language I might use to reflect on the nature of my job at the bar: What am I selling? Who are my customers, and where do they come from? Why are they here? Do I get to decide what's on tap—and to decide when a customer has had enough? To what extent do I mediate the talk that goes on, and when should I attempt to contain or redirect it? Do I have the right to decide when someone's language is inappropriate and bounce him out? Such questions (suggestive as they are of parallels between the roles of bartender and teacher in their respective institutional contexts) have motivated me to further question how the barroom might compare to the classroom. What does each institution mean to the community it serves? What does each *do* for the populations it serves? And what discourse(s) are sanctioned by each?

I want to suggest that an examination of rhetorical practices at the local bar is instructive for two reasons: (1) the barroom is predictably different from the university writing classroom; and (2) the barroom is surprisingly similar to the university writing classroom. A look at how neighborhood bars are qualitatively different from classrooms can teach us about our working-class students' rhetorical motives, and a recognition of how they are functionally similar can teach us something about our own. As repositories of cultural values, the working-class bar and the university writing classroom are, of course, quite different. As institutional spaces where public knowledge is constructed according to private rules and where conventional discourses are routinely—even ritually—performed, they have much in common. Just as the university writing classroom is an institutional context within which rhetorics—ways of speaking and of knowing—of the middle-class academic community are sanctioned and performed, the neighborhood bar functions as an institution in which rhetorics of working-class communities are routinely transacted. Within each institution is an economy of discourse, and it is within the terms of that economy that rhetoric—the sum of the discourse-knowledge equation—is produced.

No longer do we assume that classrooms are happily homogenous and insular "communities" that are somehow exempt from the market forces of other linguistic economies. Thus in a recent article Virginia Anderson characterizes classrooms as "rhetorical situations, sites of complex interactions between speakers, audiences, subjects, and codes," a situation she trusts that "teachers all along the continuum between activism and neutrality recognize" (198). But I believe that having recognized these complexities, we still have plenty to learn about what kinds of rhetorical situations writing classrooms are—especially insofar as they are constituted by competing (academic and local) discourses. It would help, I think, to conceive of the classroom as a kind of rhetorical marketplace, one that constitutes a complex scene of rhetorical performances, performances that take on value as cultural capital and are symbolically meaningful as currency.[1] As middle-class writing teachers working with students from working-class communities, we need to make it a priority to cultivate an awareness of how our own class capital—*as well as* our institutional power—positions us as rhetors in such a marketplace. Such an awareness would serve us well in moving us closer to a resolution of the ethical problem (of ethics *and* of ethos) that Frank Farmer identifies as the problem of "knowing how to teach in manner that both respects our students' views and, at the same time, questions the complacencies which too often inform these views" (187). Thinking of the writing classroom as a marketplace where discourses operate as symbolic capital can help us to understand how the rhetorical strategies that we use to establish our class(room) identity may delimit our authority to influence belief even as they allow us to enforce belief; and further, to see why it may be unconvincing to sell what functions as capital in the private marketplace of the academy as a transcendent rhetoric of moral integrity or political empowerment.

The problematics of social class and higher education in the United States have received a good deal of attention by Marxist educators and proponents of critical teaching such as Ira Shor, Peter McLaren, Stanley Aronowitz, and Henry Giroux. The autobiographical narratives of working-class academics like Mike Rose and Victor Villanueva have further enriched conversations about confrontations between local working-class and middle-class academic ways of knowing. Researchers such as Tom Fox have conducted ethnographic investigations into the composing strategies of working-class students to understand what it means for these students to grapple with the (social and rhetorical) demands of university writing instruction. Still, inquires into the class-based cultural affiliations of the students who turn up in our writing classrooms have lagged behind inquires into the pedagogical implications of identity and difference based on race, ethnicity, or gender. Since Lynn Z. Bloom complained in the October 1996 issue of *College*

English that her call for papers on "intersections of race, class, and gender in composition studies" for the 1993 meeting of the MLA drew one lone proposal on class in contrast to 12 on race and 94 on gender (657), little has changed. We continue to operate with a thin understanding of the social knowledge—by which I mean epistemological habits rooted in community practice and emerging from material conditions—working-class students bring with them to that space.

What is worse is that when we do recognize this social knowledge, we too often regard it as a bad habit to be broken. Thus Jeff Smith finds in the words of Marshall Alcorn powerful evidence for his complaint that we seriously undervalue students' social obligations, arguing that when Alcorn "speaks of disabusing students of their 'commitments' without seeming to realize, or care, that he is thereby admitting students have commitments (not just wishes, commitments!) different from the ones he would like them to have" (303). Though I have reservations about the kind of instrumental approach to writing instruction Smith appears to recommend, I share his concern that well-intentioned writing teachers—often those most concerned with issues of social justice—seem to give little attention to the material circumstances from which students' local knowledge emerges.

It is perhaps symptomatic of this problem of inattention to the meaning of students' commitments that the approach to writing instruction most concerned with investigating institutional rhetorics to uncover the formative processes of social knowledge seems at times to be so unwilling to consider the specifics of local practice or to acknowledge the ways in which even the most "critical" or "multicultural" classroom works as a site of cultural reproduction. Cultural studies-derived pedagogies aim to have students interrogate the material conditions of their lives, and thus to help them arrive at a fuller understanding of their own (and others') socioeconomic predicaments. While I see this as a worthy goal, I question the means, which seem not to put nearly enough energy into the enterprise of learning what is at stake (and in particular, what is at stake for working-class students) in assenting to such critiques, into figuring out what resistance to cultural-studies projects might mean. For these reasons, it is important that we look beyond the university to see what happens in institutions where working-class identities and values are publicly invented and ritually affirmed.

In what follows, I offer a view of rhetorical practice in one such community institution. I offer examples of the public discourse of the barroom to show that the rhetoric that is valued most highly in today's writing classroom—that is, the rhetoric of conjecture and speculation—not only operates differently as currency in the working-class institution of the barroom, but often becomes, in that rhetorical economy, a powerful class symbol, one that occasions expressions of the problematics of working-class identity. Since speculative rhetoric—the discourse of inquiry—tends to be highly valued as currency in the classroom (and especially in the cultural-studies classroom, where inquiry into social and institutional power structures is the explicit goal), my hope is that teachers of composition will be encouraged not only to examine their assumptions about what this rhetoric is worth and why, but to consider how their authority to teach it is a function of the ethos they create by their own claims of rhetorical capital. Such considerations will, I believe, better equip teachers not only to understand the terms of working-class resistance to their critical teaching agendas, but to understand the nature (and consequences!) of their own resistance to working-class agendas. It is imperative that we learn how to manage (if not transcend) these resistances if we wish to rescue the classroom from its current predicament as the site of a standoff between working-class students' goals of entry into institutions of power and teachers' goals of critique of these same institutions.

"The Problem with You Is That You Ask So Many Questions!"

The Smokehouse Inn,[2] the bar where I both worked as a bartender and conducted ethnographic research into working-class rhetoric, is more than just a place for the locals to get good barbecue and cold beer: it is a neighborhood institution. The barroom of the Smokehouse, though it functions in part to service the adjoining family-style restaurant, serves the local community as a kind of public forum where members of this suburban Chicago community—laborers, machinists, Teamsters—can congregate to meet with friends and fellow workers, to drink, and to participate in conversation and debate with others about how to make sense of current issues and political events.

   Though a relatively small sample of the larger population participates in the social life of the Smokehouse, the bar nonetheless plays an important role in the life of the community. In many working-class neighborhoods, local bars like the Smokehouse have long served as public spaces where private rhetorics are enacted. Historian Roy Rosenweig points out, for example, that barrooms have historically functioned as sanctuaries for expressions of working-class identity, and came to represent an institutional articulation of working-class resistance to middle-class values (145). Despite changes in the industrial landscape, the barroom persists as a site where working-class concerns are given voice. Writes Stanley Aronowitz:

> We live in a postindustrial service society in which the traditional markers of working-class culture survive—especially, the barroom, where waves of male industrial workers have congregated to share their grievances against the boss, their private troubles, their dreams of a collective power and individual escape. (204)

Ethnographic studies of working-class communities have, as well, demonstrated the importance of taverns to the production of knowledge and flow of information in these communities. In E. E. Le Masters' study of lifestyles in a working-class bar in a Midwestern town, for example, the author concludes early on that "the tavern in this small community was the center of social life," to the extent that "the proprietor had an amazing amount of knowledge about the residents of the town" such that "he could predict election results with great accuracy" (17). While neighborhood demographics have changed since the time of Le Masters' study, it remains true that bars continue to function as public forums in many working-class communities. (Though there are many people in such communities who have no direct involvement with bars, local taverns nonetheless act as important sites for the construction of working-class identity.) As such, they are likely to serve as a general point of reference for others in the community, including those who are (legally) considered too young to patronize them. Given the status of bars as neighborhood institutions, young working-class adults—even adolescents—are likely to feel the influence of local bars even if they have never set foot in one. Yet given as well the tendency of working-class adolescents to assume adult roles earlier on, chances are that they will in fact have had direct experience with bars.[3] As a teenager growing up in a blue-collar neighborhood, I experienced bars as an important rite of passage from childhood to adulthood—one that has as a functional parallel, I would venture, the passage undertaken by young middleclass adults first going "away" to college. My experience, while perhaps not universal, is far from unique.

The Smokehouse, where working people come together to publicly invent a private culture, is not in fact situated in what one thinks of as a traditional white-ethnic enclave. However, the community it serves largely comprises working whites who moved from such southside enclaves to flee the southward migrations of urban African-Americans. One could argue, in fact, that the Smokehouse is all the more important as a community institution now that the community itself has been geographically "displaced." Most of the men and women who participate regularly in the social life of the Smokehouse work in traditional blue-collar jobs: The men are skilled laborers (telephone linemen, woodworkers, plumbers, truck drivers, machinists) and the women work in service jobs (as waitresses, bartenders, clerks, child-care providers, and hairdressers).

The voices who have featured most prominently in my story of Smokehouse rhetoric belong to the men and women who were "regulars" at the bar: that is, to those who treated the bar as a kind of home-away-from-home and who enjoyed an established role in the social network there. Many of these "regulars" spent several hours a day, several days a week at the bar. Though at the time I conducted my research most of the regular bar patrons were men, the bar did have its share of women who enjoyed status as regulars, as well.[4] The regular Smokehousers who are at the core of my study are Walter, a retired foreman for a farm equipment manufacturer; Arlen, a 60-year-old cook and bar manager; Joe, a 40-year-old machinist; Maggie, a young mother who has worked at the Smokehouse as waitress, hostess, and bartender; Roberta, waitress and fifteen-year Smokehouse veteran; and Jack, entrepreneur and former steelworker. There have been constellations of others as well, regulars and droppers-in who have moved in and out of the Smokehouse scene, and with whom I have chatted, joked, commiserated, and contended.

Since I had lived in the area for many years and was well-connected in the community, I got the Smokehouse job through a friend of a friend who had been a bartender there. Within a week from the day I first showed up to work the bar at the Smokehouse, I found (or rather, was relegated to) my niche in the small society of the barroom. My prior commitment to the neighborhood meant that I was regarded by the Smokehouse "establishment" as an insider, even as my status (then) as a graduate student clearly marked me as an outsider. This ambiguous identity earned me a distinctive place in the social structure of waitresses, bartenders, and regular customers. I like to describe my role at the Smokehouse as that of friendly antagonist, since my status as insider and place in the network depended on my willingness to provide occasions for argument by challenging conventional values and beliefs. To be an insider, in other words, I had to cultivate a performative persona as outsider. It was in my capacity as bartender that I worked as ethnographer, using my position behind the bar to record the political arguments that took place with such frequency, and such apparent fury.[5]

As bartender/ethnographer—and, as worker/graduate student—I often found myself to be a central actor in these speech events. My own presence at the Smokehouse offered a reference point in terms of which Smokehousers could express themselves as a coherent sociopolitical body by articulating who and what they were not. For this reason, my own conversations and confrontations with others at the Smokehouse were responsible for generating data that is richly suggestive of Smokehouse orientations to truth and language, and of the relationship between rhetorical practice and class identity. Often quite against my will, I "helped" those at the Smokehouse to articulate the conventional wisdoms of the community by taking part in arguments in which oppositions to middle-class rhetorics (and in particular, academic rhetorics) were ritually dramatized.

I expect that the terms of my place among others at the Smokehouse will sound (perhaps painfully) familiar to anyone who has ever found himself or herself struggling to negotiate the space between local working-class and middle-class academic social spheres. Smokehousers publicly spoke about my associations with the university in ways that revealed that I came to represent an orientation to work and knowledge that was vastly different from local norms. Any mention of my "other life" as student and teacher of English, for example, invariably inspired much lively commentary from the regulars at the bar, much of it derisive: Wendell, a union laborer and Smokehouse regular, would often ask me if I was "done with school yet," and would remark on my status as a "professional student." On one occasion, he leaned over the bar to me and demanded to know if I was "*still* in school." When I assured him that I was, Wendell turned his attention to the others at the bar, and addressing them, remarked, "This one here's the only one I know gonna be collecting her social security checks from a goddamn *college*!" Though he does not articulate my transgression against community norms in terms of social class, his quip suggests that as a graduate (and therefore "professional") student, I symbolize an unnatural, or at least unhealthy, identification with the university—and a defection to middle-class values and lifestyle. For Wendell, and presumably for the audience he addresses in his commentary, I clearly represent a departure from local norms which dictate that public identities are built on the fundamental values of work and community. My involvement and identification with the university meant that what I came to signify for others in Smokehouse society was an orientation to all things academic, pedantic, and ultimately without value in the everyday life of the "real world" of work. Once, in a conversation about race relations in the aftermath of the Rodney

King verdict, Walter threw up his hands in exasperation and complained, "The problem with you is that you ask so many questions that sooner a later, a guy runs out of answers!" My rhetorical habit of speculating and raising questions, a strategy that is so richly rewarded within the academic institution, was apparently seen by Walter and others at the Smokehouse as both unproductive and manipulative. However (as I shall argue), the contempt Smokehousers such as Wendell and Walter show for the habit of "asking so many questions" has at least as much to do with (what they perceive to be) my *use* of it as a status claim as it does with their attitudes toward this rhetoric more generally. That is, the Smokehousers' responses to me have less to do with any negative assessment of my personal integrity or with wholesale rejection of a particular rhetorical practice than with their critique of the public self they saw me as trying to invent in my arguments with them.

Social scientists have long struggled to describe the class situation in the United States quantitatively, in terms of material conditions. But the place of political argument in the everyday life of the Smokehouse community indicates the extent to which "working-class" is a cultural category, and hence, a rhetorical construct. Richard Ohmann, taking as an example his own class experience, describes class "membership" as a discursive process: "in all my doing from day to day I and the people I mingle with and am affected by constantly *create* my class position. . . . From this perspective, class is not a permanent fact, but something that continually *happens*" (qtd. in Fox 73–74). Though of course the everyday realities of people in traditional blue-collar jobs are shaped by material conditions, these conditions are always subject to (and the subject of) invention and interpretation; the barroom at the Smokehouse is just one example of a site where working-class identity is under construction. This collective identity is, however, conflicted and problematic: in a sense, contentions about how it should be named are what define the group as a social unit. In the absence of an articulated consensus about how the class to which they belong should experience itself as a sociopolitical body—people at the Smokehouse tend to believe that they can claim neither the established power that accrues to those at the top of the socioeconomic hierarchy, nor the emergent power of historically marginalized "minority" groups—their social identity comes, in large part, from managed dissent.

One important way the Smokehousers express class solidarity is through participation in performances of agonistic discourse. Political argument at the bar functions as a conventional speech genre, knowledge of the conventions of which establishes one's place among others—at the Smokehouse, and in the world. Further, ritual performance of conventional speech genres establishes and authorizes the "official" discourse of the institution. *Topoi* for barroom debates are shaped in relation to that official discourse, which functions as a conservative but negotiable public epistemology, one that maps out the rhetorical territory on which contenders in performed arguments position themselves in staging their disputes. Though individuals may occupy different positions on this discursive terrain, the official discourse serves as the heuristic *in terms of which* class identity is invented. My presence as a dissenter helps to resolve the tension between individuating and consolidating functions of rhetoric—that is, it both opens possibilities for inquiry (thus freeing individuals to claim distinctive positions) and inscribes the parameters of social knowledge (thereby allowing the Smokehousers to articulate what they have in common). In their arguments with me, that is, the Smokehousers could show dissent without showing themselves to be *dissenters.*

One topic that functions as a site for—and implicates me as "teacher" in—the process of invention and identification is that of education. Though most people who work and play at the Smokehouse have not attended college, they urge their children to "stay in school and work hard," seeing higher education as a means to economic opportunity. Many at the bar have been quietly supportive of my academic career, have congratulated me on my efforts to "make something of myself." Yet this valorization of my success in achieving whatever economic mobility my education makes possible— often by the very people who publicly devalue it—bespeaks a deeply ambivalent attitude toward the kind of capital higher education has to offer. Smokehousers privately approve of those who strive to join the middle class, but publicly disapprove of those who embrace the rhetoric of its institutions: Earning a degree is seen as a route to upward mobility even as identification with the university is perceived as a kind of cultural abandonment.

Attitudes about the role of education are connected in complex ways to views regarding the value of work; attitudes about the meaning of work are an essential component of the institutional discourse. In the terms of that discourse, work tends to be defined in opposition to play or leisure, a distinction that reflects a deeper structural opposition in Smokehouse conventional wisdom between doing and thinking, producing and philosophizing. Speaking to me one-to-one in an interview, Walter articulates an investment in practice as the distinctive feature of Smokehouse sociopolitical identity.[6] His response to a question I posed about what is to be learned from institutional versus experiential education suggests that he sees the world of formal education as a world of artifice, one that sets itself in opposition to the "real" world of work. Walter explains that you "learn more" outside of school than in it:

> The first thing they [employers] almost always—everyone'll tell you: First thing you gotta do is, forget what you learned in school! "Cause you're out in the so-called real world-that's where it's at. There's more to be learned outside of college than there is inside of college . . . with the exception, now, of, ah, let's say, uh, engineering, ah, medical professions, uh, some disciplines like chemistry . . . you just can't do without college . . . there's where you learn, you learn the basics. Uh, the real test comes when you get out in the field . . . uh, I, um, here I go again—you're gonna think I'm really hung up on this subject—but I am! Ah, I judge an educated man by his ability to *do*. You understand? That really says it all.

Walt will concede the value of higher education, but only if it doesn't come with indoctrination into middle-class values, values here represented by identification with rhetoric-for-its-own-sake. He speaks for many at the Smokehouse in insisting that the value of formal education lies in its ability to convey immediately applicable, practical knowledge—not in training in speculative rhetoric.

Though the official discourse serves as a heuristic for public debate, the conventional wisdoms it encodes are by no means professed with equal enthusiasm by all. Rather, one's position with respect to the official discourse has everything to do with how one is positioned within the group. Walter, who describes himself as "working class," does in fact identify strongly with the conventional wisdom, and in public arguments, tends to perform views that affirm group solidarity. Walt is the voice of consensus at the Smokehouse, and he is often called upon to give voice to the public view in response to challenges from "outside." In this sense, he occupies a much different role in the Smokehouse network from that of Perry, the owner of the Smokehouse. In private interviews with me, Perry clearly attempted to position himself *against* what he perceived to be working-class cultural habits and Smokehouse conventional wisdoms. He told me that he thought of himself as "lower middle-class," and his commentaries on the uses of higher education are suggestive of his middle-class identification and his approval of upward mobility. Perry spoke to me of the humanistic potential of a college education, and remarked often on its capacity to allow for social mobility. He remembered his own college experience, for example, as a time when he was free to break from local norms:

> I think that the friends I made, the ah, black friends that I had in col-
> lege that were my best friends, had something to do with shaping
> my life . . . so yeah, in some respects you learn a tolerance, that you
> can't pick up if you don't get an education . . . if you don't spend
> time with a variety of people, and around learned people. If you're
> just gonna be—you know, if your life is sitting around a bar, entirely,
> then that's all you're gonna know . . . is those people, it's those *red-
> necks* out there, that you're gonna be doing most of your learning
> from. Unless you really are a person who can rise above it . . .

In looking at the conflicting responses of Walter and Perry, it becomes clear
that Smokehousers' attitudes toward the value of higher education have
much to do with how it is claimed as an identification strategy. To simply
attend college is not enough to set one apart: to inhabit its philosophical
world, however, is.

For Walter—himself a skilled rhetorician—to claim the rhetorical is suspect, because it confuses the practical with the theoretical, mixes work with
play. Walter voices this attitude in valorizing those who "do," while
devaluing those who merely "talk." As an illustration of the preferable former
type, he holds up as an example another Smokehouse regular, Joe:

> You got people around here that—and I don't want to mention any
> names—but, uh, that are very quick, and very responsive, and uh uh
> blah blah blah, they got the floor all the time, but they, uh, when it
> comes to the ability to *do*, earn a living and take care of yourself—
> Joe is head and shoulders above 'em.

Walt's sly reference to my own rhetorical posturing sets me up as a point of
reference against which to contrast Joe as a man of action. For Walt (who
doesn't always agree with Joe, and who frequently tries to bait him into
arguments) Joe's refusal to play rhetorician and to claim rhetorical prowess as
a source of prestige marks him as someone who exemplifies class loyalty
and with whom it is appropriate to identify. Walt's praise of Joe is consistent
with a view, expressed by Smokehousers time and time again, that doing
rhetoric—performing and philosophizing at the same time—is essentially
dishonest, is a play for status motivated by personal vanity, and not
necessarily by concern for truth or for the public good. While Smokehousers
regularly use the barroom as a place to stage elaborate verbal performances
demonstrating individual prowess in agonistic rhetoric, they hold in
suspicion those performers who are obviously adept at the game—the better
one speaks, in other words, the less he or she can be trusted. (Not
surprisingly, Walter himself was often accused of being a "bullshitter" by

other Smokehousers who suspected *him* of enjoying argument as a
rhetorical exercise.)

Though the official discourse of the Smokehouse serves a solidarity
function in setting itself in opposition to the middle-class practice of speculative rhetoric, in arguments individuals stage performances to distinguish
themselves as rhetoricians in the group even as they publicly declaim
skepticism about the usefulness of rhetoric-as-inquiry. In barroom arguments
I was consistently scripted into the role of one who, as teacher (and therefore
as one who asks questions for a living), cannot therefore do (anything *really*
productive). This was the part in which I was cast even though people at the
Smokehouse knew me first in my capacity as worker: My alliance with the
university and its ways of knowing worked to divest me of the authority to
speak the truth on matters of "real life" and to provide meaningful
commentary on the world of work and action. In performed arguments, I
was consistently cast by others at the Smokehouse into the role of
"teacher"—that is, I was called upon to give dramatic voice to what, in terms
of orientation to discourse and knowledge, the academic institution
represented to the Smokehouse community.

An excerpt from one argument in particular illustrates how argument
operates in the domain linking rhetorical practice to class identity. The argument
from which these data are taken took place among several Smokehouse
regulars and workers on a Friday evening as I worked behind the bar, and
features Walter and me as primary players. The exchange began as a discussion
about then-candidate Bill Clinton's qualifications for the office of president
given his history as a "draft dodger," and quickly grew into a more philosophical
debate about the general morality of refusing to serve in the military during
wartime. I held that there were indeed circumstances under which one might
refuse to participate in war; others at the bar, and most notably Walter, argued
that the duty to serve one's country is an absolute moral imperative:

> WALT: [indicating a man seated across at the bar]: I
>   wanna talk about this young man, here. Next
>   year we get involved in a war—and he's ripe. Do
>   you think that he's got the prerogative to say, "I
>   don't *like* this war, so I'm not going!"?
>
> ME: It depends entirely on the circumstances. Now
>   why don't you ask him what *he* thinks?
>
> WALT: There's no *circumstances!* The law says—the law
>   says, we've declared war on . . . ah . . .
>   Mesopotamia . . .

ME: So what if we declared war, and it . . . it did not seem like a just cause?

WALT: *We* didn't declare war on anybody! Well, this is why I say I can't ever discuss anything with you, because here you always say, "What if, what if?" *Bullshit on "What if"*! When our country says we're at war, it's his [points again at the man across the bar] job to go!

A VOICE
FROM
ACROSS
THE BAR: That's what *I* say!

ME: So you should do whatever your country says to do, regardless—

WALT: That's right!

ME: So what if you lived in Germany—

WALT: Same thing! I don't care *where* it is! If your country says you go, *you go*!

ME: But who makes these decisions? Aren't—aren't you, the people—this is a democracy—aren't—

WALT: Ooooh, *fungu* on your goddamn *bullshit! Now* you're changin' the argument—who makes the laws, who done this, who done that . . . I wanna ask you one—

ME: *You* said—

WALT: (pounding on the bar to punctuate each word) I wanna ask you *one* question, and *one question only*! Do you think that each man has an individual right to obey the law or disobey it?

ME: Sure, but I *also* think people—since this is a *democracy*—

WALT: I don't want to hear it! I want a yes or no answer.

ME: [with exasperation] Wal-ter . . . !

ROBERTA: Wait, wait—I gotta ask one question—

ME: You're imposing all these conditions

ROBERTA: Do you think—

ME: —and you won't let me impose my own!

What is most immediately striking about this exchange is how operatic the argument is in its exaggerated rendering of moral opposites, and how much it depends for dramatic effect on the performances of individual actors. While individuals work to display their talents to the audience of others (each player functions by turns as performer and as audience), they also work together to express the thematic structure of a unified dramatic composition. As performance, the argument is in effect cordoned off as ceremonial space where the script of public knowledge is enacted. Within this generic dramatic structure, however, Walter performs a role that gives voice to the deep assumptions that are fundamental to the institutional discourse of the Smokehouse. What is dramatized by Walt in his performance for the larger audience of people at the Smokehouse bar is his (and, by implication, the audience's) contempt for my privileging of theory over practice—that is, for my investment in the hypothetical *what-if* at the expense of the constative *it-is*. Walt's dramatization of the importance of practice over theory, then, enacts the institutional philosophy regarding the place of *what-if* in the cultural marketplace in which the Smokehouse participates.

And *yet*—while it tends to be something of a commonplace among middle-class academics that the working-class is characterized as a group by a kind of stubborn literal-mindedness—it is important to understand that Walt's rejection of my rhetorical strategy *does not mean that Walter and others at the Smokehouse do not practice what-if rhetoric.* Notice how Walter himself proposes a hypothetical scenario immediately prior to his grand dismissal of my own what-if question. (In fact, the barroom—as a place for leisure, a place apart from work—is the official site, the appropriate institutional space for *what-if.*) It means, rather, that in this particular rhetorical economy, I will not be granted the authority to claim the rhetoric of *what-if* as capital. As illocution, Walt's declamation can be understood to mean something like "bullshit on people who use what-if to show they're better than me!" While the bar is seen as a place of *play* and therefore as an appropriate place for what-if games, my status as one who takes part in a marketplace where *what-if* has actual value as *work*—in which theory is practice—undermines my persuasive ethos and makes me an occasion for cultural performance. In other words, at the Smokehouse it is appropriate to practice what-if rhetoric only *if* one neither publicly claims (or proclaims) it as a way to make knowledge nor identifies with institutions where theory *is* practice, where talk *is* action. *What-if* is particularly suspect when it becomes clear that someone outside the community is trying to use it as a way to claim a position of privilege: in the absence of an alternative rhetoric which makes it possible to conceive class in other than crudely economic terms, *what-if* becomes the site of agonistic performance when it is suspected to activate claims of symbolic capital. (Consider, if you will, another example of how *what-if* is linked to persuasive authority: Almost without exception, those at the Smokehouse supported the presidential candidacy of Ross Perot, a anti-politics politician whose persuasive ethos was predicated on his wholesale rejection of all things political. Having demonstrated a commitment to *getting things done*, Perot was free to spin hypothetical scenarios illustrating just what would be different if he were president. In other words, Perot can be forgiven for his material capital—he can still be *real*—as long he doesn't claim rhetorical capital.) To use *what-if*, and to publicly advocate its uses, is predicated on the ethos one can only establish by refusing to use it to claim class privilege. This powerful association of *what-if* with cultural capital has obvious implications for middle-class teachers working in middle-class institutions to teach middle-class rhetorics to working-class students.

Teachers, Students, and the Politics of Inquiry

Of course, Walter doesn't speak for all working-class students, or even for most. How students will receive the critical agenda of the writing classroom has to do with how they perceive rhetoric to work as currency in marketplaces in which they currently trade, on the one hand, and aspire to claim membership, on the other. The population of a writing class is not a mere random sample of the larger population, as Jeff Smith points out. "For," he says, stating the obvious but often overlooked truth, "students have *already* passed through gates en route to our classrooms." He goes on to remind us that as different as our students may be from us and from each other, what they have in common is that they have chosen to come to college (102). Clearly, the writing students who show up in our classrooms have—unlike Walter—demonstrated a commitment to the middle-class enterprise of higher education. But though the very presence of a working-class student at the university would seem to indicate his or her belief in the virtue of upward mobility (or at least, if such a desire is not fully realized, an ambivalence toward identification with the working class), such a student may not be equipped to trade in the kind of rhetorical currency we're offering. The place of *what-if* in the rhetorical economy of the

Smokehouse suggests that it is not learning the habits and conventions of inquiry that is troublesome for working-class students—since, as we have seen, what-if rhetoric *does* happen in working-class institutions—but rather, that the politics of identification in the use of this rhetoric is what these students find truly problematic.

Quite obviously, the barroom differs from the classroom in the social values it sanctions. As institutional sites, barroom and classroom embody different sets of cultural prerogatives. In "Freshman Composition as a Middle-Class Enterprise," Lynn Z. Bloom argues that whatever else we may think we're doing in the writing classroom, we are promoting—through teaching style, writing assignments, evaluation, everything—a set of clearly identifiable middle-class virtues. She goes on to list some of the values university writing instruction promotes: respectability, decorum and propriety, moderation and temperance, thrift, efficiency, order, cleanliness, punctuality, delayed gratification; and, finally, critical thinking. It is easy to see how working-class bars represent the violation, indeed the antithesis, of this middle-class value structure: the typical corner bar appears to be a place of fierce solidarity, vice, aggression, drunkenness, profligacy, leisure, chaos, sloth, and excess. But it is the final item in Bloom's list, the one that does not participate quite so neatly in the above list of oppositions, that we as writing teachers use most often, and most insistently, to define ourselves and our classroom discourses against local institutions and local rhetorics: the virtue of critical thinking.

Though we still haven't reached a consensus about the means and ends of freshman writing instruction, I think it's fair to say that most teachers—and particularly those who see themselves as working to advance the aims of a "critical pedagogy"—are committed to teaching the transformative power of rhetoric both for self-discovery and social change. This would include any writing teacher who participates in current conversations in composition studies, from process-approach specialists to proponents of Freireian liberatory pedagogy to those who take a cultural-studies approach to the teaching of writing. In other words, it implicates anyone who believes that an important goal of first-year writing instruction should be to educate students in ways to approach discourse "critically"; that is, to both interpret and invent strategic uses of text. Marilyn Cooper articulates this common philosophical ground in noting that most compositionists "believe in the value of critical thinking, cognitive dissonance, and adopting different perspectives—all of which are based on the central value of coming to know through reading and writing" (55).

What is productive as an educational goal, however, is likely to be counterproductive when claimed as a moral virtue. I would go so far as to argue that the rhetorical habits Cooper describes are habits in which we as compositionists not only believe, but identify—that is, we claim their practice as a moral virtue which we then use to locate ourselves in relation to our students and the institutional rhetorics they represent. While addressing the needs of working-class students demands that we become aware of the ways in which the classroom is different from the barroom in the rhetorical gestures it rewards, it would also serve us well to note that as a rhetorical marketplace, the classroom has much in common with the barroom. Like the barroom, the classroom is a place where (though different market values may obtain) insiders trade in cultural currencies and claim their places in the institution through generic cultural performances.

While it's important that we remain aware that we speak from a position of institutional power and therefore have a moral obligation to speak responsibly to students in our classrooms, the difficulty as I see it has as much to do with how to be persuasive *at all* as with how to decide what kind of influence to have. As politically sensitive instructors, we worry endlessly about the ideological messages we convey to our students, but my work and field experiences at the bar have given me to suspect that we're giving ourselves rather too much credit.[7] In her recent work exploring the meaning of authority in the postmodern composition classroom (1996), Xin Liu Gale argues that teachers working within institutions of higher education have always had coercive power, a power that derives from their associations with the institutions themselves, but she gives rather less attention to the question of what kind of coercion this power implies, and to how it actually affects students' ways of thinking about their lives. I do think it is safe to assume that, just as persuasive authority is unevenly distributed among rhetoricians at the Smokehouse, the academic institution does not wholly, unequivocally, or unproblematically determine the authority of individuals working within it. If working-class students have had limited participation in marketplaces in which intellectual capital holds currency, then what is to say that they will regard writing teachers—who are often rich in symbolic capital but do not display signs of material capital—to have the kind of *ethos* that effectively persuades them of the value of *what-if* as a resource?

It seems doubtful that we will be able to make the necessary ethical appeals to convince students to engage in the kind of writing-as-inquiry we value when we claim what-if as capital at the same time we fail to demonstrate social and economic power.[8] In their discussion of the nature of authority in the writing classroom, Mortensen and Kirsch call into question the idea that authority as it functions in the classroom "community" is a linear process or static condition that works independently of particular discursive contexts, observing that "relations in communities are in part defined by differences in knowledge, experiences, and status—differences in power that endlessly shift with and across social contexts (557–58). To identify different kinds of authority in the social dynamic of the classroom, Mortensen and Kirsch suggest that a functional distinction be made between the power to enforce belief and the power to influence belief, calling the former "authority of office" and the latter "authority of expertise"(559). In one sense, what we lack when we fail to persuade of the value of *what-if* is the authority of expertise—i.e., we have somehow failed to demonstrate the profitable uses of our knowledge-as-capital, even as the authority we enjoy by virtue of our office within the institution gives us the power to dictate classroom policies and procedures. From another perspective, the crisis of persuasive authority can be located in the relation between the authorities of office and expertise, insofar as our failure to persuade of the value of *what-if* originates in our failure to make apparent to our students the specificity of the relationship between the authorities of office and of expertise. In other words, what we have failed to demonstrate is that the kind of expertise we are selling—the capacity to engage speculative rhetoric—does in fact have something to do with the authority of offices outside the academy. When we display a kind of capital that appears to be without value in the larger social economy, we have not succeeded in persuading students from working-class communities that expertise in *what-if* confers power in socioeconomic institutions that exist in (as such a student might put it) "the real world."

Writing about problems feminist teachers face in attempting to persuade students to ally themselves with feminist concerns, Virginia Anderson calls upon the Burkean idea of identification to explain that such attempts fail because they misapprehend the rhetorical situation in which they operate, and misunderstand the role of ethos in the process of identification. In her critique of Dale Bauer's tactics for persuading students to realign themselves with her feminist agenda, Anderson argues that it is Bauer's own ethos that is largely responsible for her failure to persuade. Explains Anderson: "[Bauer] presents herself as an embodiment of her political agenda, and hence as a site, intrinsically valid and appealing in itself, where students will one day decide they want to end up . . . [But] sites are seldom intrinsically persuasive; identification is created. We induce it through the tactical choices we make—our own moves in the rhetorical alignment and the types of arguments we construct" (200). She speculates that feminist teachers go wrong in that "they align themselves with those students hope never to become, and they depict themselves as enemies of what many students are" (203). I am suggesting that a similar dynamic is at work in the attempts of middle-class teachers to persuade working-class students to identify with the practice of *what-if*—that teachers who claim *what-if* as capital while encouraging critique of other symbols of middle-class capital do not themselves embody persuasive sites. In making conventional symbols of middle-class capital the subject of our critical performances, we not only set ourselves in opposition to the discourse of working-class institutions but also demonstrate class privilege by aligning ourselves with an economic predicament working-class students are trying desperately to transcend. In a recent issue of *CCC*, Frank Farmer confesses that his students, upon being asked for their responses to essays critical of popular culture forms for an advanced composition course, were more interested in figuring out what the critics stood to gain in their rhetorical performances than they were in evaluating the validity of the critiques themselves. Far from accepting the claims of the pop-culture critics uncritically, Farmer's students suspected that the critics were motivated by an urge to assert class distinction at the expense of the average, unenlightened reader (190–92).

What I have come to understand since Walter pounded his fist on the bar at the Smokehouse and declared "bullshit on 'what if'!" is that he was right in suspecting me of trying to win the game by claiming *what-if* as capital. I was, admittedly, more concerned with characterizing myself as something other than the ill-informed, literal-minded working stiff I imagined (and constructed) him to be—was more concerned, that is, with showing myself to be middle-class—than I was with trying to move the conversation into a place where we could engage in mutual inquiry into the truth of the matter. I knew immediately that Walter was using me as a foil against which to construct a public persona, but it took me longer to see that I was just as eagerly doing the same.

I worry that what we are doing is convincing students who have strong local ties that the only use of *what-if* is as a strategy for identification with something they don't necessarily want to be. While some students (those who, like Perry, are driven by a desire to set themselves apart from "those rednecks out there") might be persuaded to identify with us and with the institutional rhetorics for which we speak, this hardly encourages critique of dominant institutions, nor does it produce humane, informed citizens. It merely teaches working-class students a trick of achieving class distinction, a trick that entails seeing those in their home communities—and worse, those parts of themselves that remain at home—as dupes. I worry that when we construct *what-if* as class capital and ourselves as examples of successful investors in such capital, students who wish to buy into *what-if* must necessarily identify *against* the "rednecks."

What, then, can we do to create an *ethos* that is persuasive to students who may be inclined, like Walter, to say, "bullshit on 'what if'"? We need to make the uses and powers of *what-if* the very subject of deep inquiry in the writing classroom—to focus, for example, on the relationships between the practice of *what-if* and socioeconomic power, and to pose such questions as, Who has the "right" to engage in *what-if*, and under what circumstances? What is the relationship between the ability to perform speculative rhetoric and capacity to achieve one's social, economic, and political goals? At the same time that we work to understand students' reasons for their resistance to us and to what we stand for, we should also interrogate the terms of our resistance to what *they* stand for. We need to communicate our efforts in both respects. We can begin, for one, by responding not with contempt or derision for such students' vulgar instrumentalism, but by demonstrating a willingness to open a space in the classroom for inquires into the relationship between academic writing and *what-if*, to interrogate the different instrumentalities *what-if* might have. It is important, I think, that we as teachers remain open to what sometimes may strike us as the (distressingly) utilitarian motives of first-year students, and to work to open a dialogue between writing-as-critical-inquiry and writing-as-instrument; between means and ends. When students invested in acquiring practical knowledge want to know what learning to write in the ways we sanction will do for them, we should take the question seriously.

The way to persuade working-class students of the value of *what-if*, then, is to openly acknowledge functional parallels between the rhetoric of the barroom and that of the classroom. This means that we would make the nature of institutional discourse the focus of our pedagogy, and would encourage students to think about how speculative rhetoric can be of value to them as capital, how it can be useful as currency in the marketplaces in which they wish to participate. Examining how *what-if* can be useful as an instrument in the academic marketplace might then invite inquiries into how much philosophical and instrumental rhetorics are differences in kind, and to what degree they suggest differences in context. The language of *action* and *use* may help to invest us with the authority to persuade students that writing has important uses even when it isn't being *useful.*[9] I am not arguing that we should be concerned only with teaching students how to fill out job applications; I believe that we should encourage them to write in ways that are critical and exploratory. But I *am* suggesting that we need to make it a priority to raise questions about how each text performs, in which domain, and to what ends. This seems essential if we are to demonstrate to students that we are aware of what we are up to in our performances.

Every so often I hear one or another of my colleagues invoke the white-male-in-a-baseball-cap-who-wants-just-the-facts as a symbolic focus for his or her resentment toward student resistance to *what-if* (and to critical pedagogy more generally). Just as Walter publicly identifies me as a symbol of the kind of middle-class intellectual one must not claim to be, teachers construct such students as symbols that are ritually invoked for political ends. Such rhetorical strategies bring to mind the profoundly troubling what-if question Virginia Anderson poses: "What if the real solidarity that appeals to activist teachers is not that solidarity we might achieve with our students, but rather the unity and satisfaction we find in our radical stance?" (212). It is certainly true that working-class students' obvious lack of (middle-class) cultural capital, combined with their apparent political conservatism, may tend to frustrate and alienate teachers whose political views and teaching philosophies work together as valuable symbolic resources within the institution. But while white working-class students may seem to offer a safe opportunity to express such resentments, surely these students are not themselves unaware of their status as the focus of such teacherly frustrations. In setting ourselves in opposition to such students we may succeed in expressing our own class distinction, but we succeed neither in showing solidarity with their needs, nor in constructing an *ethos* that might help us to persuade them of the value of *what-if* in their writing and in their lives.

While it is certainly true that learning about rhetorical practices in working-class institutions helps us to understand the nature of working-class students' (social and rhetorical) commitments, it may also be true that an awareness of the politics of inquiry in our own institutional context better equips us to persuade our more traditional students of the value of inquiry, as well. That *what-if* is so problematically linked to class identification does, of course, mean that working-class students have more to gain, and more to lose, in buying stock in the rhetorical capital of the academic institution. But I am convinced that knowing our own rituals and performances is a way of becoming intimately familiar with who we are as rhetors, with our powers and limitations, with our motives and agendas. If we are truly concerned with teaching the transformative power of writing for political empowerment and social change, then we must understand that our first and most critical task is to assess, and commit ourselves to working within, the rhetorical economy of the writing classroom itself—even when this entails taking an honest look at the terms of our own investments in *what-if*.

Notes

1. Joseph Harris complained years ago of the tendency of compositionists to accept the notion of *discourse community* uncritically, and cautioned that "theories have tended to invoke the idea of community in ways at once sweeping and vague: positing discursive utopias that direct and determine the writings of their members, yet failing to state the operating rules or boundaries of these communities" (12). Harris' caveat has encouraged me to see that the complex socio-cultural dynamics of the classroom "community" might better be understood in Bourdieu's terms, whereby specific social scenes operate as marketplaces within a larger social economy in which products of culture function as currency and take on value as capital (1991).

2. A pseudonym. Since the bar services a barbecue restaurant and is usually filled with a dense haze of cigarette smoke, "the Smokehouse" seemed like the obvious choice of name.

3. In her study of social categories in a suburban Detroit high school, sociolinguist Penelope Eckert demonstrates how working-class students tend to assume adult roles much earlier than their middle-class counterparts, for whom adolescence is preparation for an adult life characterized by stages of upward mobility. Eckert explains that because working-class adolescents tend to look to local networks for social and economic resources, they are not necessarily set off categorically from the social world of adults. "Continuity between high school and early adulthood," writes Eckert, "resides in different spheres [for middle- and working-class adolescents]"(139).

4. It has been noted by linguists and anthropologists who have studied barroom cultures (Le Masters, Spradley and Mann, Bell) that bars have traditionally functioned as spaces where rituals of masculinity are given ceremonial treatment. At the Smokehouse, women are active participants in the social life at the bar—though they earn the right to claim membership by taking part in male-solidarity rituals (such as buying rounds of drinks and participating in performances of agonistic discourse), they nonetheless are an important part of the Smokehouse scene. This participation extends beyond the domain of work, since women who are employed as waitresses and bartenders often spend much of their leisure time at the bar. As a bartender—that is, as one in a central position in Smokehouse social routines—I enjoyed a position of high visibility and status in Smokehouse society.

5. Because of the bar's status as private-space-within-a-public-space, the mechanics of data collection presented particular challenges. My general method

for gathering data was to switch on a small, hand-held tape recorder I kept behind the bar as episodes of conversation happened. Though I did not remind people of the presence of the tape recorder as I recorded each episode of talk, I did discuss my plan to record conversations with the owner of the Smokehouse as well as with those regulars who are featured most prominently in the study. In other words, regulars knew I was working on a research project about "how people talked about politics in the real world," and that I was likely to tape conversations (even if I did not announce my intent to record particular stretches of discourse). Generally speaking (though many at the bar said that they were glad I was going to write something about the way things *really* were among people who worked), my *research* project was regarded as an eccentricity, as further evidence of the peculiar habits of academics.

6. It is, of course, important to bear in mind that even though I conducted interviews with individuals at a remove from the arena of public performance, interviews are themselves performances to an audience—me—perceived to be skeptical of the truth of working-class values.

7. In his research on first-year writing students' responses to critical pedagogy, David Seitz observed that working-class students in a cultural-studies research writing class at the University of Illinois at Chicago learned how to render convincing performances of the kinds of critical discourses sanctioned by teacher and institution. In conducting a series of follow-up interviews with these students, however, Seitz found that the students remained unpersuaded of the truth (or usefulness) of these discourses, and that the architecture of their local knowledge had managed to remain more or less intact (65–73).

8. That teachers operate as signs in the assemblage of texts that is the discursive world of the writing classroom is no great revelation, but it is nonetheless a crucial point in considering what kind of persuasive authority we have with students. No matter what else we may be doing in the classroom at a given moment, we are busily signifying our social allegiances. I am made uncomfortably aware how much I work as signifier beyond (and perhaps in spite of) the more explicit messages I wish to convey each time a student informs me that I don't "*look* like an English teacher." That students perceive my physical self to signify something other than what they've come to expect an English teacher to represent tells me that the signified "English teacher" is associated with a particular and conventional set of signifiers. Clearly, what for middle-class academics functions as valuable currency in their cultural economy—the capital of tastes, manners, language, and style that signals to insiders the power to *reject* the very kinds of material capital to which working-class students aspire—may have no cultural meaning for students "outside," or worse, may be read as signs of failure to achieve socioeconomic success.

9. In William Covino's rhetoric for writing students, *Forms of Wondering,* reader-writers are drawn into a conversation about the means and ends of writing. The book opens with an assignment entitled "What's the Use of Writing?" a dialogue designed to get the writer to create a dialectic between the philosophical and utilitarian functions of writing. While some of the writing tasks in Covino's book may be too generically esoteric to be persuasive to students seeking to learn

forms of writing that perform conventional functions in nonacademic market-places, *Forms'* ongoing dialogue about the goals and uses of writing is an excellent model for teachers wishing to structure classroom activities around such a discussion.

Works Cited

Anderson, Virginia. "Confrontational Teaching and Rhetorical Practice." *CCC* 48 (1997): 197–214.

Aronowitz, Stanley. "Working-Class Identity and Celluloid Fantasies in the Electronic Age." *Popular Culture: Schooling and Everyday Life.* Eds. Henry Giroux and Roger Simon. New York: Bergin, 1989.

Bell, Michael J. *The World from Brown's Lounge: An Ethnography of Black Middle-Class Play.* Urbana: U of Illinois P, 1983.

Bloom, Lynn Z. "Freshman Composition as a Middle-Class Enterprise." *College English* 58 (1996): 654–75.

Bourdieu, Pierre. *Distinction: A Social Critique of the Judgment of Taste.* Trans. R. Nice. Cambridge: Harvard UP, 1984.

Cooper, Marilyn. "Unhappy Consciousness in First-Year English: How to Figure Things Out for Yourself." *Writing as Social Action.* Marilyn Cooper and Michael Holzman. Portsmouth: Boynton, 1989. 28–60.

Covino, William. *Forms of Wondering.* Portsmouth: Boynton, 1991.

Eckert, Penelope. *Jocks and Burnouts: Social Categories and Identity in the High School.* New York: Teachers College P,1989.

Farmer, Frank. "Dialogue and Critique: Bakhtin and the Cultural Studies Writing Classroom." *CCC* 49 (1998): 186–207.

Fox, Tom. *The Social Uses of Writing.* Norwood: Ablex, 1990.

Gale, Xin Liu. *Teachers, Discourses, and Authority in the Postmodern Composition Classroom.* New York: State U of New York P, 1996.

Harris, Joseph. "The Idea of Community in the Study of Writing." *CCC* 40 (1989): 11–22.

Le Masters, E. E. *Blue-Collar Aristocrats: Lifestyles at a Working-Class Tavern.* Madison: U of Wisconsin P, 1975.

Lindquist, Julie. "'Bullshit on "What If'!" An Ethnographic Rhetoric of Political Argument in a Working-Class Bar." Diss. University of Illinois at Chicago, 1995.

Mortensen, R, and Gesa Kirsch. "On Authority in the Study of Writing." *CCC* 44 (1993): 556–72.

Ohmann, Richard. "Reflections on Class and Language." *College English* 44 (1982): 1–17.

Rosenweig, Ray. "The Rise of the Saloon." *Rethinking Popular Culture: Contemporary Perspectives in Cultural Studies.* Eds. Mukerji and Schudson. Berkeley: U of California P, 1991: 121–56.

Seitz, David. "Keeping Honest: Working-Class Students, Difference, and Rethinking the Critical Agenda in Composition." *Under Construction: Working at the Intersections of Composition Theory, Research, and Practice.* Ed. Christine Farris and Chris Anson. Logan: Utah State P, 1998.

Smith, Jeff. "Students' Goals, Gatekeeping, and Some Questions of Ethics." *College English* 59 (1997): 299–320.

Spradley, James, and Brenda Mann. *The Cocktail Waitress: Women's Work in a Man's World.* New York: Knopf, 1975.

4 History in the Spaces Left: African American Presence and Narratives of Composition Studies

Jacqueline Jones Royster and Jean C. Williams

This essay begins with a statement that is fast becoming, if it is not already so, an aphorism: History is important, not just in terms of who writes it and what gets included or excluded, but also because history, by the very nature of its inscription as history, has social, political, and cultural *consequences.*

A Short Review of Histories of Composition

In the last twelve years several scholars have produced historical accounts of composition studies, seeking to define a field which is still, in many ways, in its infancy. Both James Berlin's *Rhetoric and Reality: Writing Instruction in American Colleges, 1900–1985* and Stephen North's *The Making of Knowledge in Composition: Portrait of an Emerging Field* were published in 1987, just one year short of 25 years from the 1963 date they propose as the birth of composition as a discipline. In 1990 Albert Kitzhaber's often copied 1953 dissertation, *Rhetoric in American Colleges, 1850–1900*, was published in book form. In 1991, Susan Miller joined the discussion with *Textual Carnivals: The Politics of Composition*, and since then several other accounts, such as John Brereton's *The Origins of Composition Studies in the American College, 1875–1925* (1995) and Sheryl Fontaine and Susan Hunter's edited volume, *Writing Ourselves into the Story: Unheard Voices*

Reprinted from *College Composition and Communication*, June 1999.

from Composition Studies (1993), have continued to enrich our views and participate in establishing national parameters for the field.

Each of these texts has a different focus and contributes positively, along with others not cited here, to knowledge and understanding. They offer perspectives on the emergence of rhetoric and composition as an academic field; discuss ways in which knowledge has been and continues to be made, applied, disseminated, and interpreted in the field; and address some of the broader trends and issues pertinent to the historical and ideological trajectories of the field. None, however, can be described as comprehensive, definitive, or all inclusive. Each sustains a point of view and occupies an ideological and/or cultural location. In fact, setting aside Kitzhaber for the moment as a scholar who in 1953 was a precursor of the field, neither Berlin nor North as two of the earliest historical accounts make claims to universality. Quite the contrary, Berlin actually warns us that "there are no definitive histories" and that "each history endorses an ideology, a conception of economic, social, political, and cultural arrangements that is privileged in its interpretation" ("Octalog" 8).

The challenge suggested by this comment is twofold. On one hand, researchers who produce discipline narratives are called upon to contextualize historical work so that gaps and limitations in the purview of their work are clearer and so that their interpretive claims do not exceed their reach and thereby serve to disregard, exclude, or misrepresent other viewpoints. On the other hand, and perhaps more importantly, those of us who use he narratives would better serve the discipline if we were required by common practice to re-articulate those gaps and limitations in our own uses of the narratives, rather than drifting in our valorization of them toward the assigning of primacy and the assumption of universality, even by default. The latter challenge is for all of us to have a critical perspective of the extent to which images and valorized viewpoints shape interpretive visions and thereby create consequences, given the interpretive frameworks that grow out of these visions, in terms of knowledge making, policymaking, and day to day operations.

Examples that demonstrate the need for caution are evident in each of the studies cited above. Kitzhaber, the earliest written narrative and, again, a precursor in the field, has certainly achieved a status of high regard. His effort was to look at the nineteenth century from 1850 to 1900 as the backdrop for establishing a shift in English studies and the teaching of rhetoric that made modern composition studies possible. One event, for example, that Kitzhaber identifies as important is the rise of land grant institutions. He says:

> These new state institutions, founded squarely on the notion that it
> was the responsibility of American colleges to offer a wider selec-
> tion of courses than had been commonly available before, were very
> influential in breaking up the older pattern and in supplying a new
> one for the next century. (12)

Nowhere in his analysis, however, does Kitzhaber consider what this statement suggests regarding the seventeen historically African American colleges and universities that constitute what is popularly known in African American academic circles as the "1890 institutions," a label referring to the second round of land grants that permitted federal monies to be used in establishing separate land grant institutions for African Americans in states (primarily in the South) where they could not attend the white land grant institutions established thirty years earlier.

The point to be emphasized for this analysis is that neither Kitzhaber nor the numbers of researchers who have since used his work as a building block have been pushed to specify, not just the groundbreaking strengths of this seminal work, but also the limitations of it in terms of the ideological location of the scholar who has produced it: where he sets the gaze, the particular historical experiences on which he draws, and the intersecting experiences of others whom he does not notice but who could, nevertheless, be written into the story.

Further, while both Berlin and North acknowledge that they do not intend their narratives to be definitive, in a manner similar to Kitzhaber, they also do not permit their own group identity or the politics of location to have visibility or consequence inside their narratives. In essence, though, they do not violate common practice in the field. Historically, the viewpoint of these narratives has not had to be articulated. These scholars operate within the dominant field of vision. In centralizing their historical viewpoints within mainstream experiences, without having to specify their locations as researchers in a more diversified landscape, their narratives become naturalized within this very mainstream, as other such narratives are habitually naturalized, as universal and thereby as transparent. Neither Berlin nor North was compelled at the time of publication by good practice in the field to make clearer the extent to which their narratives represent the dominant perspective. In effect, they may have acknowledged that other viewpoints are possible, but in this type of dynamic the other viewpoints are inevitably positioned in non-universal space and peripheralized, and the exclusion of suppressed groups, whether they intend it or not, is silently, systemically reaffirmed.

By 1991 with the publication of *Textual Carnivals: The Politics of Composition*, Susan Miller holds this dynamic up for interrogation. She says:

> Without "good" stories to rely on, no minority or marginalized major-
> ity has a chance to change its status, or, more importantly, to iden-
> tify and question the "bad" tales that create it. In this case, the
> required new narrative portrays teachers and students of writing in
> American higher education, who have for some time been the sub-
> jects of a marginalizing and negative—but nonetheless widely
> believed—myth. I hope to substitute a new narrative for that degen-
> erating tale by rereading this myth. (1)

She makes a case for seeing the legitimacy of composition and for taking into account the engendering of composition teaching and the implications of other power relationships. She casts a different narrative light, but her story is not all inclusive either and can not be expected to be given how wide the range of marginalized participants can be. Miller acknowledges the existence of other viewpoints, but does not craft a space, for example, for the voices of people of color.

The same holds true in a different way in John Brereton's *The Origins of Composition Studies in the American College, 1875–1925*. In his preface, Brereton does indeed identify rather specific intersections between his work and other narrative viewpoints. Focusing on major trends in composition studies occurring in major institutions, he notes that his research is limited to the public record, a record that he acknowledges does not present the whole story. He states that "the most widely circulated professional documents of the time ignore important trends in writing instruction by women. . . . And a great deal of what we would now regard as postsecondary writing was done by immigrants in settlement houses, by men and women in Bible colleges and normal schools, and at historically black institutions" (xv–xvi).

Brereton also mentions the absence of the voices of African American educators in the general discourse about writing instruction in the fifty years that he covers, but posits that "most black colleges seem to have taught writing in strict accord with the standards of white America" (21). In addition, he creates space for historically African American institutions (HBCUs) and those associated with them by inference, e.g., when he mentions that "very traditional approaches [old-fashioned rhetoric with text books by Blair, Campbell, or Whately] survived at colleges, not universities, in the East and South" (14) into the twentieth century. Since most HBCUs are located in the South, we can infer that the pedagogical practices of HBCUs are included, referentially, in this statement. Further, as a note to the abilities of black students at the time, Brereton also adds that W. E. B. Du Bois, a graduate of Fisk University, elected to take Barrett Wendell's writing course while pursuing graduate studies at Harvard (21). In other words, Brereton does indeed create a space for others, including African Americans, but he does not actually fill the space, or substantially credit African American viewpoints of it, or permit it to enrich, refine, or redefine what he is suggesting is the "larger," publicly documentable story.

Sheryl Fontaine and Susan Hunter, editors of *Writing Ourselves into the Story: Unheard Voices from Composition Studies*, also endeavored to be more inclusive than preceding composition narratives. The purpose of their collection, as the title indicates, was to add voices to the story that are not normally heard. Their intent was to define or extend the parameters of the disciplinary discussion. The contributors include a number of part-time, untenured instructors, primarily women, who carry not only their voices into the text but also the varied voices of their students. As Fontaine and Hunter review the contributors who responded to their call, however, they note their regret that submissions from ethnic minorities were "conspicuously absent" (11) despite their attempts to have the call for submissions broadly advertised and circulated.

In discussing their concerns about the absence of minorities, Fontaine and Hunter state:

> Still, since there are many voices we expected to hear that we did not, we find ourselves wondering why more two-year college faculty did not respond, why ethnic voices are so conspicuously absent. One potential contributor, an ethnic minority, told us that she didn't have much to say about basic writers; instead, she wanted to get back to more empowering concerns about African American writers and multicultural curricula. (11)

Fontaine and Hunter go on to dismiss a reviewer's comment that suggested a lack of professional interest or "savvy" on the part of ethnic minorities in participating in scholarly publication and to put forth their suspicion that "the powerlessness that comes with continually being unheard and uninvited has left them [meaning ethnic minorities] untrusting of our invitation or of their own voices" (12).

While either of these readings of the potential contributor's response may indeed have merit, we wonder whether Fontaine and Hunter were able to see any connection between the place where they were inviting the potential contributor to stand and her refusal, not to participate perhaps, but to speak to the particular issue that they had identified for her? Is it possible that they were conflating ethnicity in higher education with powerlessness and basic writing and assuming that her viewpoint, her place for writing herself into the story as an ethnic minority would be the same as the one that they imagined for her? Did they credit her response that her work, and perhaps her students, did not conform to their images for the collection? Perhaps neither she nor her students, despite the inescapable existence of systemic suppression, saw themselves either historically or currently in these terms. Did Fontaine and Hunter hear that perhaps she did not see her work as marginalized in the same way that they were seeing it, saying it, and drawing the lines of possibility for it? Was, perhaps, her reluctance to "trust" the invitation a resistance to circumscription, even in a project that otherwise sought to celebrate "multivocality, heteroglossia, and nonhierarchical relationships" (9)?

The concerns of Fontaine and Hunter about the participation of ethnic minorities in scholarly projects raise questions about the metaphors and interpretive frames that editors use to solicit contributors from suppressed groups, about what a choice to remain silent portends from various points of view, and about the extent to which editors themselves, given their authority to set the parameters of submission, should assume some responsibility for the ways in which their choices passively and aggressively exclude and circumscribe participation.

What seems consistently clear across these narratives is the point with which we began this section. Those of us who write composition narratives and those of us who use them need to be critically disposed to see the negative effects of primacy, the simultaneous existence of multiple viewpoints, and the need to articulate those viewpoints and to merge them in the interest of the larger project of knowledge making in the discipline.

Representations of Students

As indicated by the preceding section, many of the narratives in composition studies are not directly student centered. The focus is more on conceptions of the field and on pedagogical practices and processes. Recent texts, however, such as Marguerite Helmers' *Writing Students: Composition Testimonials and Representations of Students,* and Harriet Malinowitz's *Textual Orientations: Lesbian and Gay Students and the Making of Discourse Communities,* and Valerie Balester's *Cultural Divide: A Study of African American College-Level Writers* have turned to look at students and how they are depicted or represented in our field. In *Writing Students,* Helmers draws on the lore of the field using the *CCC's* "Staffroom Exchange" column and discusses the stock figure of *"the student, . . .* a character whose inability to perform well in school is the defining feature" (4). She reports that students, as a whole, "have been the subject of despair, ridicule, rhetorical distancing, and fear for centuries" (5). Helmers' description affirms that the good or successful students are not often mentioned in our lore, our practice, or our scholarship. However, we know they are there because they represent the standard by which those *other* students are judged. For Helmers, *the student is* also a generalized term "absent of a specific ethnic or gendered referent" (11). While this seemingly neutral approach could be thought of as placing all students on an equal level, the neutrality often erases the presence of students of color with the resultant assumption that, in not being marked as present, they in fact were not there.

Students who are not generic and also not recognized as present in the field literature become the focus for Malinowitz's study of lesbian and gay student writers. Focusing on student writing, Malinowitz directly confronts prejudice and bias as she questions how "homophobia in society, and as it is reproduced in the writing class, constitute[s] a basic form of interference in lesbian and gay students'. . . writing processes and performances" (xvii). Her issues become not only how teachers construct lesbian and gay students but how the students, in their writing, work toward constructing themselves. Malinowitz's study takes place in an urban multiracial college, and students of color were present in her classrooms. While her text does not contain extended discussions focusing on students of color, her work is noticeably cognizant of issues involving sex, gender, race, and class.

Balester, to her credit, reports that although work has been done on underprepared African American college level students, "we have paid scant attention to the average or superior college student. . . . [and] we can learn a great deal by attending to the texts of *successful* African-American college-level writers" (2). Her actual focus, however, is on Black English Vernacular (BEV), and she describes her students (despite one student's objection to the description) as speakers of BEV who are "attempting to construct a scholarly identity which, as novices, they had not yet fully assumed, and to address audiences of whom they as yet had little knowledge" (2–3). Even though Balester acknowledges the success of these students, she still positions them as non-universal outsiders, as aliens to the traditions to which other students lay claim, and essentially as "basic writers." This narrative furthers this inscription in the Foreword written by M. Jimmie Killingsworth whose opening line reads:

> One of the strongest threads of research and criticism in composi-
> tion studies reveals the inherent consistency, the rhetorical integrity,
> even the brilliant folkways that emerge among students whom we
> have labeled "basic writers" (often as a way of predicting their fail-
> ure). (vii)

Only toward the end of the page, do we learn that Balester's work has an
"interesting twist" because she has decided to study African American
students who have "made it" across "the cultural divide between life in a
second-dialect minority and the life in the educated classes represented by
the American university" (vii–viii). This Foreword assigns monolithically
"second-dialect" status to all of the students in the study, without recognizing
class stratification in the African American community and the class
distinctions, therefore, of this particular group of African American students.
The Foreword also assigns this group a place outside of "the educated
classes represented by the American [our emphasis] university," ignoring the
long-standing presence of African Americans in arenas of higher education
and the possibility that successful students who are African American could
be insiders in American universities, whether these particular students were
insiders or not.

Throughout the text itself, Balester works to fit the African American
students into her framework and to identify them with BEV, even when they
resist that categorization. She describes her students in the same way most
basic writers are described, i.e., as students seeking a way into an academic
culture to which they presumably have no traditional moorings. Balester's
study illustrates that the connections that we have made in the field in
conflating ethnicity, otherness, and basic writing are strong and remain
compelling, despite the extent to which these connections are not
automatic.

The Conflation of Race and Basic Writing

Among the touchstones of student-centered research, Mina Shaughnessy's
Errors and Expectations: A Guide for the Teacher of Basic Writing occupies a
well-respected space, and many scholars have turned to this text for a
description of the basic writer. Despite the popular perception, however, that
Shaughnessy's text contributes to the conflation of students of color and
basic writing, the basic writers in *Errors and Expectations* are actually
broadly constructed. Shaughnessy indicates that because of the protests
taking place in the late 1960s, many four-year colleges began admitting

students who may not have been considered ready for college. While subsequent researchers tend to focus on the 60s as a "decade of protest" in terms primarily of the civil rights protests staged by African Americans, there were also protests against the Vietnam War and the treatment of veterans, for women's rights, for workers' rights, and for the overthrow of what was seen as an elitist, capitalistic system in order to create a more egalitarian system providing for the basic needs of all people. Looking, therefore, at this broader conception of who actually came into the university during this era of protest, Shaughnessy focuses more on economic characteristics than she does on racial ones. She states that the students admitted were:

> academic winners and losers from the best and worst high schools in the country, the children of the lettered and the illiterate, the blue-collared, the white collared, and the unemployed, some who could barely afford the subway fare to school and a few who came in the new cars their parents had given them as a reward for staying in New York to go to college; in short, the sons and daughters of New Yorkers, reflecting that city's intense, troubled version of America. (2)

Shaughnessy does not negate the presence of race in the students admitted. She makes clear that most of the students were from "one of New York's ethnic or racial enclaves . . . had spoken other languages or dialects at home and never reconciled the worlds of home and school" (3). Race, however, never becomes a focal point for her analysis. Even her discussions of BEV are used as points of comparison and example for other racial and ethnic groups as she points out that the syntactic structures of BEV are present in nonblack American-born students such as Jewish students who are influenced by Yiddish, Irish Americans, and Chinese Americans (91). Speaking a language or variety of English other than standard English appears to be much more a contributing factor to Shaughnessy's characterization of basic writers than does race. Where Shaughnessy emphasizes race, though, is in pointing out that the absorption of negative views of language makes learning formal uses of English a more contentious process, and she does say that the "black student has probably felt the bite of this prejudice more persistently and deeply" (158).

Shaughnessy's connection between the politics of racial location and the perception of writing performance is insightful, but this insight suggests more about the impact of persistent oppression than the centrality of a direct association between race and poor writing performance as a predictable consequence. Nevertheless, since the publication of this study, there has been a deepening sense that African Americans entered the university during the 60s era and that, as students of color, they entered quite predictably as basic writers and only as basic writers. The conflation of basic writers with students of color has become deeply embedded in the literature, despite lengthy histories that demonstrate other realities.

Setting aside African American experiences, however, remedial writing programs existed for "traditional" students in historically white colleges and universities well before 1960s protests movements and the establishing of open admissions policies and well before Shaughnessy popularized the term "basic writing" and set in motion processes by which this area became a legitimate area for scholarly study. When we take this alternate point of view and look in the shadows of composition history for a different space for underprepared students, we find that *CCC* is a good resource. Basic writing was actually one of the primary topics addressed during CCCC conferences and in *CCC* articles during the 1950s, the first decade of the organization. Surveys taken during the period and reported in *CCC* relate that the percentage of underprepared freshman students enrolled in what at that point were labeled remedial composition classes often reached ten to twenty percent and sometimes more than thirty percent of the entering.class. What we take note of in these reports is that these articles were not talking about African American students (or even people of color more generally) since, indeed, this group did not command ten to twenty percent of the general college population in the United States in the 1950s.

A number of colleges and universities also reported that they had offered remedial composition courses since the 1920s—the era of progressive education which focused on the democratization of education and which clearly had consequence, as continues to be the case, in composition teaching as a critical point of acculturation for the university itself. In looking from these viewpoints, the point to be emphasized is that controversies about underprepared students did not start in the 1960s and were not historically connected with people of color. Historically, we could look for narratives of underpreparedness at several places other than the 1960s: in the late nineteenth century when Harvard instituted its written entrance examination; at the rise during the progressive era of standardized testing; at the moment in 1956 when the University of Illinois decided to drop its remedial classes. In this latter case, while many institutions followed suit, many others remained committed to having classes that would serve a wider range of students, including those who were inexperienced in college environments and in writing. All of these moments are before the 1960s and the perception that people of color, and particularly African Americans, came into colleges and universities and created "the basic writer."

A Historical View of African Americans in Higher Education

If, then, African American students as active participants in higher education, are not substantially yoked to the open admissions processes of the 1960s and to basic writing programs, where can we set the gaze to get a fuller understanding of their historical presence in academic arenas, and thereby in composition studies? We find that looking at the 19th century rather than the 20th century is a good place to begin.

According to Carter G. Woodson (1919; 1991), the first organized efforts in the United States to offer higher education to African Americans began in 1817 when advocates of the American Colonization Movement, i.e., the movement to send people of African descent, especially free ones, back to Africa, opened a school in Parsippany, New Jersey. In political contrast with this effort, many African Americans and white abolitionists who disagreed with this movement were determined to establish colleges that supported the making of a life at "home," i.e., in the United States. This latter strategy led to the incorporation of Avery College in Allegheny City, Pennsylvania, in 1849. Moreover, an ongoing strategy was also to open the doors of white institutions to African Americans, an effort that resulted in:

- John B. Russwurm (who would become the editor of the first African American newspaper in the United States, *Freedom's Journal*) becoming the first college graduate when he completed studies at Bowdoin in 1828.

- Oberlin College opening its doors to African Americans (and to women and other racial minorities) in 1833.

- A small but steady stream of African American men and women during the nineteenth century who enrolled, successfully matriculated, and consistently graduated from *American* colleges and universities.

In addition, there were two other historical moments that add light to the participation of African Americans in higher education. The earlier of these moments came before the Civil War in 1856 when Wilberforce University in Ohio and Lincoln University in Pennsylvania were established as institutions focused specifically on the education of African Americans. After the Civil War, with support from the African American community, the Freedmen's Bureau, the American Missionary Society, and other philanthropic groups, these two institutions were joined in the endeavor to educate African Americans by a collective of other private institutions, mostly in the South, who one hundred years later constitute the thirty-nine colleges and universities associated with the United Negro College Fund.

The dominant educational philosophy of these institutions is captured by a statement made by Mary McLeod Bethune, President of Bethune-Cookman College (an HBCU in Daytona Beach, Florida), in 1932 at the celebration of the twenty-fifth anniversary of Henry Lawrence McCrorey as President of Johnson C. Smith University (an HBCU in Charlotte, North Carolina). Bethune was one of several prestigious speakers who gathered during the anniversary celebration for critical dialogue on higher education among African Americans, past, present, and future. Bethune spoke for the future in an address entitled, "What Should Be the Program for the Higher Education of Negroes for the Next Twenty-five Years?" She said:

> This age increasingly demands that the Negro youth, along with the youth of every other race, know the truth about the world in which he lives. While facing facts, he must prepare himself to function successfully in that world as a happy individual. He must develop power of independent thought and effective expression. Within large areas he will discover that he must make compromises and adjustments to the religion, ethics, and economic principles of the dominant group that surround him. To make these adjustments adequately, he must be capable of formulating for himself a philosophy that will sustain his courage and his self-respect. The future college for the higher education of Negroes must bear the tremendous responsibility of guiding this youth in his search for truth, of developing his innate capacities, and of unfolding to him a philosophy of life that will encourage him ever to keep his face toward the sun. (Mckinney 59)

As implied by the attention to effective expression and the development of critical thought in Bethune's address, this network of institutions was indeed committed, not only to a strong liberal arts focus, but to the specific development of literate abilities, including writing abilities. Moreover, the student populations in these institutions varied widely in terms of students who were well prepared for college experience and students who were variously underprepared, such that the popular sentiment among these institutions was that their tradition was to take students from wherever they were in terms of knowledge and performance and to educate them, a view that demonstrates a general commitment to a student-centered approach and to educational progress.

The second historical moment occurred on July 2, 1962, when Representative Justin S. Morrill of Vermont succeeded in getting the Morrill Act inscribed in law. This Act authorized the establishment of one land grant institution per state, providing federal funding through the sale of public lands for education in practical professions, such as agriculture, mechanical arts, and home economics. As indicated earlier in this article, thirty years later with the Second Morrill Act in 1890, seventeen historically African American institutions were incorporated into this system, creating a core group for what we now recognize as the network of historically African American publicly supported colleges and universities.

To be noted in rendering a narrative about African American presence in higher education is Howard University. This institution, established in 1867 in Washington D.C., stands separately from both sets of the institutions cited above as a university intended primarily, but not exclusively, for African Americans. While private donations were also its primary source of funding, what marks one distinction for this university is that for many decades, it was semi-supported by appropriations from Congress, semi-monitored by the United States Office of Education, more stable in its base of funding than most of the other colleges in the private network, but not tied to the practical professions as other publicly funded African American institutions of this era.

To be highlighted, then, is that Howard University shared in the dominant educational philosophy of historically African American institutions generally, and it also held its own secure place as a premier institution in the liberal arts tradition. Among the collective of historically African American institutions, Howard helped to set the pace, along with Atlanta University, Fisk University, Talledega College, Tougaloo College, Hampton University, Tuskegee University and others throughout the network, in scholarly production and in the creation of academic spaces for intellectual development and leadership in the African American community. Historically African American colleges and universities served as beacons of light for academic excellence and for the nurturing of talents and abilities across a full range of academic experience and potential.

The Recovery of Contributions

The recovery of contributions to composition history by African American teachers and scholars is a complex enterprise also. Given the historical place of African Americans as a suppressed group in the United States, the work of these professionals has not been historically celebrated in arenas of the dominant academic culture, and it has not typically been visible in prime documentary sources of the dominant community. Evidence of this work does exist, however, and the rendering of it within the context of other stories of the profession creates a provocative view of what we have come to know historically as the study and teaching of rhetoric and composition. If we take just three cases in point, we can see how these exemplars contributed to the field distinctively in terms of the general ways in which we value excellence in theory, practice, and professional activity, and we can also see how they do so in ways that are distinguishable from each other. In other words, neither they nor their contributions are one dimensional. They cover a spectrum of the types of achievements that we *normally* honor in the field. We have chosen to highlight:

- *Alain Locke*, for his work as a cultural theorist, literary and arts critic, and educational philosopher.
- *Hallie Quinn Brown*, for her expertise in developing literate abilities through her pedagogy and textbook production, and also for her own expertise as an orator.
- *Hugh M. Gloster*, for his role as a literary critic, as the editor of an anthology of African American writers, and also for his pioneering leadership in the development of English professional organizations.

Alain Locke

Alain Locke was the son of educated parents who had professional careers in teaching and government. He received a BA degree with honors (Phi Beta Kappa, magna cum laude, winner of the Bowdoin Prize for an essay in English) from Harvard University in 1907. He was the first African American to be awarded the prestigious Rhodes Scholarship, attending Hertford College of Oxford University (after being denied admissions by five other Oxford colleges) where he studied philosophy, Greek, and literature from 1907 to 1910. From 1910 to 1911, he attended the University of Berlin, and in 1918, he received the Ph.D. from Harvard.

While at Oxford, Locke was a founder and the secretary of the African Union Society, a group established with other men of African descent to nurture leaders, to encourage broad interests in matters of race as a global concept, and to establish a global network among leaders. Returning to the United States in 1912, Locke was appointed to the faculty of the Teachers College at Howard University as assistant professor of English, where he remained throughout his career, with various periods in between devoted to an incredible range of intellectual and sociopolitical activities, from participating in 1924 in the re-opening of the tomb of Tutankamen in Luxor, to a stint with the League of Nations to study the development of African education since World War II, to a well-funded project to evaluate adult education programs in Atlanta and Harlem which led to the establishing in 1935 of the Associates in Negro Folk Education.

In light of this wide array of experiences and achievements, Locke is nationally recognized as a pioneer in comparative ethnic studies who made contributions in several areas, including education, literary and arts criticism, philosophy, and cultural studies. He published extensively, but is perhaps best known for his edited collection, *The New Negro* (1925), a demonstration of the cultural and social progress of African Americans in creative writing and literary scholarship. What may be more critical for this analysis is that Locke, in collaboration with other intellectual leaders at Howard University (including the President, Mordecai Johnson, and his fellow faculty members: Sterling A. Brown, Kelly Miller, Margaret Just Butcher and several others) conceptualized a culturally rich liberal arts curriculum that included the teaching of writing and the development of what we now call critical literacies.

Hallie Quinn Brown

Hallie Quinn Brown, the daughter of freed slaves, was born c. 1845. She received a bachelor's degree from Wilberforce University in 1873, began her teaching career in the public schools of Mississippi, South Carolina, and Ohio, and took the opportunity while teaching in Dayton, Ohio, for further training in the art of speech and oratory by attending in the summers the Boston School of Oratory. From 1885 to 1887, Brown administered a night school for adults in South Carolina and served as Dean at Allen University (an HBCU in Columbia). From 1892 to 1893, she served as Dean of Women at Tuskegee Institute (an HBCU in Alabama), and in 1893, she accepted an appointment as professor of elocution at Wilberforce University, where she remained until her death in 1949.

During these years, Brown was simultaneously building a sterling record as a charismatic speaker who was actively involved as a member of the Black Clubwomen's Movement, various women's temperance associations, and the Woman's Missionary Society of the African Methodist Episcopal Church. She lectured nationally and internationally in the interest of a variety of social concerns; she founded the Neighborhood Club in Wilberforce; she was active in the formation of the National Association of Colored Women, of which she was president from 1920 to 1924; she was president of the Ohio Federation of Colored Women's Clubs; she was vice president of the Ohio Council of Republican Women and in 1924, she spoke at the Republican National Convention in Cleveland (Hine). Her appointment as professor of elocution at Wilberforce, therefore, is not, in hindsight, a surprise.

For the purposes of this article, what stands out most distinctively about her professional activities in light of composition history is that as professor of elocution at Wilberforce University from 1893 to 1923, Brown produced pedagogical materials, as documented most recently by Susan Kates, that innovatively enriched the learning experiences of her students. As Kates says:

> She raised questions about the relationship between schooling and social responsibility, using and transforming mainstream elocution theory in order to address these issues. The goal of Brown's pedagogy was an "embodied rhetoric," that is to say, a rhetoric located within, and generated for, the African American community. (59)

In essence, Hallie Quinn Brown embraced a student-centered approach to the development of literate abilities, centralized, as we do today, the notion that there should be some relationship established by curriculum and pedagogy between home knowledge and academic knowledge, and fashioned both a theoretical perspective as well as practical classroom activities that permitted her students to do as Bethune suggested, to lift their faces toward the sun with courage and self-respect and to enhance their expressive abilities.

Hugh M. Gloster

Hugh M. Gloster received a bachelor's degree from Morehouse College (an HBCU in Atlanta) in 1931, a master's degree from Atlanta University, and the Ph.D. in English from New York University in 1943. Gloster taught in English departments, directed communication programs, and served in administrative positions in colleges and universities in the United States, Africa, Asia, Europe, and the Caribbean. He authored *Negro Voices in American Fiction* (1965) and co-edited with Nathaniel P. Tillman, *My Life, My Country, My World: College Readings for Modern Living* (1952). In 1967, he was appointed President of Morehouse College and retired from this position in 1988 (see Jones 1967).

Given the focus of this current analysis, what is most informing about Gloster's work is that in 1937, as a professor of English at Lemoyne College (an HBCU in Memphis, Tennessee), he sent out a call to teachers of English in historically African American colleges to gather in dialogue, and on April 23, 1937, the participants became charter members of the Association of Teachers of English in Negro Colleges (ATENC). In his letter of invitation, Gloster had stated:

> Believing that the main burden of the educational task rests on cor-
> rect language usage and that a college should at least require a
> knowledge of the language skills, many institutions of higher edu-
> cation have undertaken a critical evaluation of current curricular
> practices for the purpose of raising standards of proficiency in the
> use of the English language. As a result of this investigation, many
> constructive changes have been made. The fact still remains never-
> theless, that there is need for further improvement in oral and writ-
> ten expression, and that a valuable and mutually beneficial program
> might be developed by those who are in daily contact with the prob-
> lem. (Fowler 3)

This concern was a central one for ATENC, but as a professional organization in English Studies, this group had other concerns as well, including the teaching of literature, the ongoing production of creative works, and research and scholarship on African American culture. They sustained an agenda to encourage publishers to include African American writers in anthologies, and they recognized the need to have a space in which African American scholars could flourish, despite the chilly reception that they received in other professional organizations, such as the Modern Language Association (MLA). To be noted, as suggested by this latter concern, is that members of ATENC were certainly active in ATENC, but they were also members of other national organizations and active in them to the extent that the particular organizations permitted.

In 1949 at the ATENC in New Orleans, the Committee on Resolutions recommended and the members approved a change in the name of the ATENC. It became the College Language Association (CLA), an organization that remains viable and active among contemporary professional organizations in English Studies. One further connection also emerged in 1949 with the founding of the Conference on College Composition and Communication (CCCC) of the National Council of Teachers of English (NCTE). As an organization interested in the development of oral and written language abilities, CCCC also drew members from CLA as they had previously been drawn to NCTE and MLA. In fact, the formation of the Black Caucus of NCTE/CCCC in 1970 was very much informed by the multiple alliances of many of the African American members who were also members of CLA, as demonstrated by the CLA documents that were shared with the new group and thereby helped to shape their ideology.

Over the years, CLA has sustained its own vitality as an organization dedicated to excellence in scholarship, teaching, and professional development; to the preservation of African American culture; and to ongoing cultural production. Beyond this mission, however, CLA has also carried these interests into other organizations, influencing these groups variously, as CLA members through their multiple alliances have been actively involved in MLA, NCTE, CCCC, and other professional organizations. This process was originally enabled by the vision and collaboration of Hugh M. Gloster with colleagues across the network of African American scholars in English studies, such that from one point of view, without attempting to be totalizing in scope, one might say that the ripple effects of the vision of Hugh Gloster and the other charter members of ATENC have been considerable.

Implications

This essay has focused on history in the spaces left and has sought to bring light to the effects (i.e., the social, political, and cultural consequences) of officialized narratives. Our specific goal has been to adjust the historical lens by shifting the gaze to the experiences of African Americans. Our intent has been to counter mythologies about African American presence in composition studies in two ways: 1) by acknowledging that in officialized narratives, the viewpoints of African Americans are typically invisible, or misrepresented, or dealt with either prescriptively, referentially, or by other techniques that in effect circumscribe their participation and achievements; and 2) by identifying more instructive ways of looking at African American experiences that support a different view of presence, in terms of:

- an historical view of African Americans in higher education that begins in the nineteenth century, not the twentieth century.
- representations of students that are not keyed by the metaphor, "basic writer."
- a recovery of specific contributions that suggest a history of scholarship and a tradition of professional engagement.

In choosing the title of the essay, we have based the central image "history in the spaces left" on an image used by William Cook in his 1992 CCCC Chair's address, "Writing in the Spaces Left." In that address, Cook asserted that historically our "official" national narratives have excluded from metaphors of universality groups that have been systemically suppressed by sociopolitical constructions of power. Inside these narratives, such groups are typically unacknowledged and rendered invisible, or positioned as non-universal or "other," or inscribed in ways that circumscribe and often misrepresent them. Cook asserted, however, that the members of these groups have persistently resisted this treatment and taken the authority to write themselves in more animated ways onto the narrative landscape, as we have ventured to do in this essay.

Cook cites Olaudah Equiano, Frederick Douglass, Richard Wright, Ralph Ellison, Ann Petry, Toni Morrison, and Maya Angelou as writers who, by their insistent narrative presence, have reconfigured the story. He demonstrates that even though their perspectives and experiences have not been authenticated historically by "official" narratives, these writers and others have, nevertheless, tampered with "the word," inserting themselves boldly into the spaces left, and they have literally changed the page—that is, the historical narrative that might be rendered instead. In like manner, we have claimed an insistent presence for African Americans that, if acknowledged, could also reconfigure the story of composition.

The problem, as Cook suggested and as mirrored in this essay, is not simply that, given our national history of sociopolitical suppression, opportunities for remarkable exclusions exist and need correction. The problem is that these official narratives have social, political, and cultural consequences, a situation that is exacerbated by the ways in which the officializing process itself grants the privilege of primacy to texts. The privilege of primacy—that is, the status of being the official viewpoint—sets in motion a struggle between these "prime" narratives and other narrative views (that for whatever reasons the official narratives exclude) for agency and authenticity and, most of all, for the rights of interpretive authority. "Official" narratives set the agenda for how and whether other narratives can operate with consequence, and they also set the measures of universality— that is, the terms by which we assign generality, validity, reliability, credibility, significance, authority, and so forth.

As illustrated by this analysis, such a struggle shows itself vibrantly in composition studies as we examine *our* own national narratives and the metaphors that we use to talk about or not talk about members of historically suppressed groups. As in other officializing processes, as existing histories of composition acquire an "official" status, they participate in the making of metaphors and the symbolic systems of reality by which we draw the lines of the discipline and authenticate what is "real" and not, significant enough to notice and not, or valuable and not. These constructions set the default boundaries, and, in effect, determine the range of what can be rendered in composition history in "mainstream" or "traditional" terms, and what is consistently rendered in the terms of exception or "other."

In wanting field narratives to be more inclusive of historically suppressed groups, our view is that we need to take a critical stance in composition studies against the negative effects of primacy. The imperative is to emphasize the need for historicizing practices that both contextualize the historical view, as composition narratives typically do, but that also go beyond contextualizing to treat that view as ideologically determined and articulated. This imperative indicates that, while we recognize that narratives of composition have been successful in increasing our understanding of long-range views of the field, we recognize also that these same narratives have simultaneously directed our analytical gaze selectively, casting, therefore, both light and shadow across the historical terrain. In acknowledging areas of both light and shadow, we suggest that there is a clear and present need to pay more attention to the shadows and to how unnoticed dimensions of composition history might interact with officialized narratives to tell a reconfigured, more fully textured story than we now understand.

When we render stories of composition from points of view other than dominant academic perspectives, we have the opportunity to see the historical page in ways that subvert the negative effects of primacy. Instead of always measuring progress and achievement by the tape of mainstream experiences (Du Bois 1903), and discounting viewpoints that do not match them, we have the opportunity to set the terms of historical engagement with a more critical view, to shift locations, and to raise questions, previously unasked, that might more fully animate knowledge and understanding.

The basic commitment in such shifting is to ground both our assumptions and our experiences with the intent of clarifying the purview of our gaze. In this way, claims and assertions do not seek so easily or immediately for universal status. We can ask, instead, basic questions, such as: For whom is this claim true? For whom is it not true? What else is happening? What are the operational conditions? In the interest of the larger enterprises of knowledge making and public policy making, we are encouraged by such strategies to resist primacy and to operate in a more generative and less offensive manner.

As suggested by the preceding pages, this type of paradigmatic shift is consistently demonstrated by the case of African Americans as one historically suppressed group. Consider, for example, the data reported in *Souls of Black Folk* by William E. B. Du Bois who noted that by the turn of the century, 35 years after the end of chattel slavery, approximately 2000 African Americans had received college degrees from 34 historically African

American colleges. He noted also an additional 400 African Americans who received bachelor's degrees from historically white northern colleges and universities such as Harvard, Yale, and Oberlin. These data were for the turn of the century—that is, sixty plus years before the era of open admissions and the emergence of people of color as substantive entities in mainstream composition narratives. Even without the preceding interrogation of composition histories, we might well imagine, if we were inclined to do so, the tradition of academic achievement generated by this cadre of graduates and others since them. These data alone suggest that the prevailing view of the participation of African Americans in composition histories is, at the very least, a specific case of an inadequate representation. Composition histories show that when we consistently ignore, peripheralize, or reference rather than address non-officialized experiences, inadequate images continue to prevail and actually become increasingly resilient in supporting the mythologies and negative consequences for African American students and faculty, and also for their culturally defined scholarly interests, which in their own turn must inevitably push also against prime narratives.

Ultimately, then, our goal in presenting this viewpoint is to raise a call for both a clearer understanding of the past and better practices in the present and future. In composition studies, we suggest:

A systematic commitment to resist the primacy of "officialized " narratives.

We might begin this process with a basic framework for resistance: The writers of composition histories can obligate themselves to contextualize the historical view and to specify their own ideological position. The users of composition histories can remind themselves to systematically re-articulate the limitations of that viewpoint and the accompanying ideological position. In other words, the imperative is for both historians and users of history to acknowledge both areas of light and areas of shadow.

A search for better interpretive frames that are capable of accounting more richly for the participation and achievements of the many rather than just the few.

In other words, when we resist primacy, traditional paradigms for seeing and valuing participation, even in composition studies, are inadequate. They obviously miss the experiences and achievements of many, and they privilege by this process the viewpoints and the interpretations of the officialized few, whether they are acknowledged as prime or not. The challenge then is to broaden the research base, the inquiry base, the knowledge base from which interpretive frameworks can be drawn, not simply to say that we know that we don't know but to do the work of finding out. We need methodologies for seeing the gaps in our knowledge and for generating the research that can help us to fill those gaps.

A renewed interest in using the knowledge and understanding acquired through suggestions one and two in order to help a broader range of students to perform at higher levels of achievement.

In other words, what has constituted progress and achievement in the past and what might be meaningfully used to nurture progress and achievement in the present and future seems better tied to knowledge-making processes that are recursive, ones that allow us to re-see and re-think.

This list of suggestions indicates that at the fiftieth anniversary of *CCC*, we can benefit greatly from an interrogation of the relationships of "suppressed" experiences in the field to our considerably anointed ones. Our sense of the landscape is that a more positive and productive future in composition studies actually depends, and rightly so, on finding less exclusive ways to envision our horizons, whether we are setting the gaze in the past, the present, or the future. The cautionary tale, then, is the statement with which we started. History is important, not just in terms of who writes it and what gets included or excluded, but also because history, by the very nature of its inscription as history, has consequences—social, political, cultural. As instruments of ideological processes, histories of composition, like our other national narratives, have participated in the generating of a record of misdeeds—exclusions, misrepresentations, negative stereotyping, and non-hearings. Our view is that we would be well advised to acknowledge this record and its systemic modes of operation in our research, scholarship, and pedagogy, but that we would be even better advised, especially at this moment of critical reflection, to build into our work systematic practices of both acknowledgement and resistance.

Works Cited

Balester, Valerie M. *Cultural Divide: A Study of African-American College Level Writers.* Portsmouth: Boynton, 1993.

Berlin, James A. *Rhetoric and Reality: Writing Instruction in American Colleges, 1900–1985.* Carbondale: Southern Illinois UP, 19S7.

Brereton, John, ed. *The Origins of Composition Studies in the American College, 1875–1925.* Pittsburgh: U of Pittsburgh P, 1995.

Charmaine, Sylvia. "Land-Grant Colleges and Universities: 100 Years of Excellence." *About . . . Time* (Nov. 1990): 12–15.

Cook, William. "Writing in the Spaces Left." *CCC* 44 (1993): 9–25.

Du Bois, W. E. B. *The Souls of Black Folk.* (1903) Greenwich: Fawcett, 1961.

Fontaine, Sheryl, and Susan Hunter, eds. *Writing Ourselves into the Story: Unheard Voices from Composition Studies.* Carbondale: Southern Illinois UP, 1993.

Fowler, Carolyn. *The College Language Association: A Social History.* Ann Arbor: UMI, 1988.

Gloster, Hugh M. *Negro Voices in American Fiction.* New York: Russell, 1965.

Gloster, Hugh M., and Nathaniel R. Tillman, eds. *My Life, My Country, My World: College Readings for Modern Living.* New York: Prentice, 1952.

Helmers, Marguerite H. *Writing Students: Composition Testimonials and Representations of Students.* Albany: State U of New York P, 1994.

Hine, Darlene Clark, ed. *Black Women in America: An Historical Encyclopedia.* Brooklyn: Carlson, 1993.

Jones, Edward A. *A Candle in the Dark: A History of Morehouse College.* Valley Forge: Judson, 1967.

Kates, Susan. "The Embodied Rhetoric of Hallie Quinn Brown." *College English* 59 (1997): 59–71.

Kitzhaber, Alben R. *Rhetoric in American College 1850–1900.* Dallas: Southern Methodist UP, 1990.

LaPati, Americo D. *Education and the Federal Government: A Historical Record.* New York: Mason/Charter, 1975.

Locke, Alain, ed. *The New Negro: An Interpretation.* New York: Boni, 1925.

Logan, Rayford W., and Michael R. Winston, eds. *Dictionary of American Negro Biography.* New York: Norton, 1982.

Malinowitz, Harriet. *Textual Orientations: Lesbian and Gay Students and the Making of Discourse.* Portsmouth: Boynton, 1995.

McKinney, Theophilus Elisha, ed. *Higher Education among Negroes.* Charlotte: Johnson C. Smith U, 1932.

Miller, Susan. *Textual Carnivals: The Politics of Composition.* Carbondale: Southern Illinois UP, 1991.

North, Stephen M. *The Making of Knowledge in Composition: Portrait of an Emerging Field.* Upper Montclair: Boynton, 1987.

"Octalog: The Politics of Historiography." *Rhetoric Review* 7 (1988): 5–49.

Shaughnessy, Mina P. *Errors and Expectations: A Guide for the Teacher of Basic Writing.* New York: Oxford UP, 1977.

Woodson, Carter G. *The Education of the Negro Prior to 1861.* 1919. Salem: Ayer, 1991.

II Assessment

As Kathleen Blake Yancey notes, "writing assessment has always been at the center of work in writing" (p. 99). The year 1999 was no exception and the focus was on portfolio assessment. The articles highlighted here deal with the theory of assessment and how portfolios are now the assessment tool of choice. Indicating the centeredness of the portfolio, however, are the critical arguments about portfolios. Not only do we have the practical processes of making portfolios work, but we are also now developing the critical stance to fully explore their validity.

In "Looking Back as We Look Forward: Historicizing Writing Assessment," Yancey reminds us that the nature of communicating invites assessment, and that CCCC's history includes a rich discussion of how we assess, what that assessment means, and what we need to pay attention to as we continue our assessment. She traces assessment through the history of CCCC, arriving at the maturity of portfolio assessment.

Alexis Nelson provides a thoughtful piece on student reaction and development through portfolio assessment in "Views from the Underside: Proficiency Portfolios in First-Year Composition." She studies portfolio use at a university and reflects on its values at a community college, helping us to see the value and worth of portfolios in multiple settings.

Sue Ruskin-Mayher's "Whose Portfolio Is It Anyway? Dilemmas of Professional Portfolio Building" explores the issue of making portfolios meaningful through student ownership. Too often the portfolio is developed to fulfill a requirement rather than to develop and display the intellectual growth of the student. Ruskin-Mayer's article provides insight on how to make the portfolio a reflection of the student's growth.

What about the student's perspective on portfolios? While assessors have embraced the portfolio as the best current method of understanding the full learning of the student, the student often has a different take on the process. It might be important to remember that for most students, school in any form is an experience to survive; education sometimes accompanies survival. In "Inside the Portfolio Experience: The Student's Perspective," C. Beth Burch provides the results of her study of student attitudes and activities.

5 Looking Back as We Look Forward: Historicizing Writing Assessment

Kathleen Blake Yancey

Even if by another name, writing assessment has always been at the center of work in writing: and it surely was there in 1950 when CCCC began. It wasn't called assessment then, of course; that language came later. During the first of what I'll identify as three waves in writing assessment, it was called *testing*, and it permeated the entire institution of composition—the contexts surrounding writing classes as well as the classes themselves, from the admission tests students completed to determine who would enroll in "sub-freshman English" and who in the "regular" course, to the grades that were awarded within the classroom, to the exit and proficiency tests that marked the single way out of many a composition program. Ironically, assessment in composition studies in those early days wasn't just routine: it was ubiquitous—and invisible.

Like composition studies itself, however, writing assessment has changed during the past half century. One way to historicize those changes is to think of them as occurring in overlapping waves, with one wave feeding into another but without completely displacing waves that came before. The trends marked by these waves, then, are just that: trends that constitute a general forward movement, at least chronologically, but a movement that is composed of both kinds of waves, those that move forward, those that don't. The metaphor of waves is useful conceptually, precisely because it allows us to mark past non-discrete patterns whose outlines and effects become

Reprinted from *College Composition and Communication*, February 1999.

clearer over time and upon reflection—and whose observation allows us in turn to think in an informed way about issues that might contribute to future waves.

An Overview

During the first wave (1950–1970), writing assessment took the form of objective tests; during the second (1970–1986), it took the form of the holistically scored essay; and during the current wave, the third (1986–present), it has taken the form of portfolio assessment and of programmatic assessment. This is the common history of writing assessment: the one located in method. But as Kenneth Burke suggests, other lenses permit other views; particularly when brought together, they allow us to understand differently and more fully. We could also historicize writing assessment, for instance, by thinking of it in terms of the twin defining concepts: validity and reliability. Seen through this conceptual lens, as Brian Huot suggests, writing assessment's recent history is the story of back-and-forth shifts between these concepts, with first one dominating the field, then another, now both. A related approach constructs the history of writing assessment as the struggle between and among scholars and testing practitioners and faculty, those who speak the terms validity and reliability quite differently: the old *expert*; the new *non-expert*. From this perspective, the last 50 years of writing assessment can be narrativized as the teacher-layperson (often successfully) challenging the (psychometric) expert, developing and then applying both expertise and theory located not in psychometrics, but in rhetoric, in reading and hermeneutics, and, increasingly, in writing practice.

Still another way to trace the history of writing assessment is through its movement into the classroom; multiple choice tests standing outside of and apart from the classroom have become the portfolios composed within. And finally, writing assessment can be historicized through the lens of the self. Which self does any writing assessment permit? As important, given that "tests create that which they purport to measure" (Hanson 294), which self does an assessment construct? Portfolio assessment, with its multiple discourses and its reflective text, has highlighted this second question, certainly, but it's a question to be put to any writing assessment seeking to serve education.

Significantly, these lenses don't just frame the past; they point to the future, specifically to three issues. First, the role that the self should play in any assessment is a central concern for educators. It is the self that we want to teach, that we hope will learn, but that we are often loath to evaluate. What is the role of the person/al in any writing assessment? A second future concern has to do with programmatic assessment: how can we use this kind of assessment—which is quite different than the individual assessment that has focused most of our attention for 50 years—to help students? A third concern focuses on what assessment activities can teach us: it's only recently that assessment was seen as a knowledge-making endeavor. Which raises a good question: what (else) might we learn from writing assessment? And how would we learn? Underlying these concerns is a particular construct of writing assessment itself: as rhetorical act that is both humane and ethical.

In itself, that understanding of writing assessment is perhaps the most significant change in the last 50 years.

A Context for a History of Writing Assessment: Spheres of Influence

During the first wave of writing assessment, dating from around 1950 to 1970, writing assessment was young, complex, conflicted. It was a critical time in that most of the issues that currently define the field were identified. Consequently, in our practices today, in the questions that continue to tease out some of our best thinking, we can trace the outlines of yesterday's concerns.

Much of the lore about the early days in writing assessment is accurate. It's true that "objective" tests, particularly multiple choice tests of usage, vocabulary and grammar, dominated practice. It's true that most testing concerns focused on sites ancillary to the classroom: typically, on the placement exercise used to "place" students into "appropriate" writing courses. And, in general, it's true that in the early days of CCCC, classrooms were defined, at least in part, by what we could call a technology of testing—not only by means of the tests that moved students in and out of classrooms, but also by way of contemporaneous efforts to bring "our work" ie., the reading and grading of student work—into line with testing theory. The early issues of *CCC* speak to these practices and aspirations convincingly: in summaries of CCCC workshops where the usefulness of objective tests is explained to the lay teacher, for instance, and in endorsements of *national* grading standards.

What's at least as interesting is a specific account of why these issues gained attention, why testing didn't include writing samples more often, why people who knew well how to read and value texts would turn to test theory when it came time to read and evaluate student texts. One contextual factor was demographic: the numbers and kinds of students that were beginning to attend school in the early 50's, students that seemed more and different than students we'd seen before. Consequently, there were genuine questions as to what to do with these students: where to put them, how and what to teach them, and how to be sure that they learned what they needed.[1] In theory, those three tasks—(1) where to put students and (2) how and what to teach them and (3) how to be sure that they learned what they needed—belonged to all educators. In practice, the tasks initially divided themselves into two clearly demarcated spheres of influence that characterize the first wave of writing assessment: the process of *deciding what to teach* the students belonged to educators, those who would become new compositionists; the process of *moving students about*, to testing specialists.

During the second two waves of writing assessment in composition studies—those of holistically scored essay tests, and next portfolios and program assessments—the two spheres merge and overlap, with administrators and then faculty taking on institutional and epistemological responsibilities for testing previously claimed by testing experts, and in the process developing a new expertise and a new discipline: *writing assessment.*

This history is also that story.

Methods and Sampling: Two Sides of the Same (Assessment) Coin

From the perspective of method, changes in writing assessment appear straightforward and familiar: from first-wave "objective" measures like multiple choice tests, largely of grammar and usage, to second-wave holistically scored essay tests to third-wave portfolios. Put another way, first wave evaluation relied on an "indirect" measure—a test of something assumed to be related to the behavior, but not the behavior itself (e.g., items like comma usage questions and pronoun reference corrections). Within twenty years, during the second wave, we began employing a "direct" measure—a sample of the behavior that we seek to examine, in this case a text that the student composes. Once the direct measure becomes accepted and even routinized as the measure of choice, the "one essay" model is soon replaced by a set of texts, so that: a single draft becomes two drafts; two drafts become two drafts accompanied by some authorial commentary; two drafts plus commentary become an undetermined number of multiple final drafts accompanied by "reflection," and the set of texts becomes the new: *portfolio assessment*. As important as the method of assessing writing in this account is the *sampling* technique. The question "How shall we evaluate writing?" concerns itself not only with methodology, but also with behavior: which behavior should we examine? Sampling was critical, in part because sampling was (and is) the stuff of everyday classroom life: day in and day out, faculty assign, read, and evaluate student texts. In this sense, *teaching writing is itself an exercise in direct measure*. Accordingly, (1) teachers saw the difference between what they taught in their classes—writing—and what was evaluated—*selection of homonyms* and *sentence completion exercises*; (2) they thought that difference mattered; and (3) they continued to address this disjunction rhetorically, *as though the testing enterprise could be altered*—first on their own campuses; also at composition studies conferences like CCCC, later and concurrently at testing-focused conferences like the National Testing Network in Writing and the NCTE conferences on portfolio assessment; and concurrently in articles and books.

Still, it took over 20 years for this critique to make an impact, over 20 years for the second wave to occur. It's fair to ask, then: if compositionists saw this disjunction between classroom practice and testing practice early on, why did it take over two decades to shift from one sampling technique to another, from one methodology to another? And the waves are overlapping, not discreet: why is it that even today, 50 years later, multiple choice tests continue to be routinely used in many assessment exercises (Murphy)?[2] The responses to these questions, phrased themselves as four general questions, are inter-related, each of them located in or deriving from the methods and sampling issues:

- What roles have validity and reliability played in writing assessment?

- Who is authorized and who has the appropriate expertise to make the best judgment about writing assessment issues?

- Who is best suited to orchestrate these questions, design an assessment based on the answers, and implement that design? In other words, who will wield this power?

- What, after all, is the overall purpose of writing assessment in an educational situation?

Each one of these questions points to one understanding of writing assessment; each one identifies a dimension of writing assessment still in contest.

Validity and Reliability: The Pendulum Swinging

Writing assessment is commonly understood as an exercise in balancing the twin concepts validity and reliability. Validity means that you are measuring what you intend to measure, reliability that you can measure it consistently. While both features are desirable in any writing evaluation, advocates of each tend to play them off against each other. Accordingly, which one should dominate, assuming only one could be favored, has generated considerable discussion—and change.

During the first wave, reliability prevailed; we see this, first, in the kinds of assessments that were commonly employed, and second, by the rationale for using them. That such tests were common is confirmed by various survey data. One survey in 1952, for example, included over 100 responding institutions and provided an all-common portrait: 90% of the responding institutions administered placement tests to entering freshmen, 84% of those tests were standardized, and most of those tests were created by external experts (Sasser 13). Similarly, the same survey reported that nearly half of the reporting institutions (44%) also included a test at the conclusion of the course, a "follow up re-test," with half of the schools folding that test score into the course grade. From placement to exit, then, objective testing defined the borders of many first-year composition courses, and in doing so, it also influenced what went on inside.

Such testing was theorized persuasively. Perhaps the most articulate theorist for this perspective was Paul Diederich, the ETS researcher whose *Measuring Growth in English* was the first monograph to address the specifics of postsecondary writing assessment. As unofficial representative of the testing community, Diederich—at nearly every CCCC during the 1950s's and within the pages of *CCC*—repeatedly explained the value of the reliable measure, taking as his primary exemplar the prototypic placement test:

> The best test to use at the college entrance level to pick out good, average, and poor writers is not a writing test at all but a long, unspeeded reading test. That will usually yield a correlation of about .65 with good teachers' estimates of the writing ability of their own students in excellent private schools, in which a great deal of writing is required. Next best is a good objective test of writing ability; it will usually yield a correlation of about .60 with such judgments. A long way down from that is a single two-hour essay, even when it is graded twice independently by expert College Board readers. It will usually correlate .45 to .50 with such estimates. Furthermore, if you

> test the same students twice—in the junior and again in the senior year—the two reading tests will correlate about.85 with one another, while the two essays will correlate only about .45 with each other. Thus the reading test will not only pick out good and poor writers each year better than the essay but it will also pick out the same one both years, while the essay tends to pick out different ones. (qtd. in Valentine 90)

The logic here, admittedly, is compelling in its own way. If you want to predict how students will perform and if you want to do this in a fair, consistent, and efficient way, you go the route of objective testing—because even to generate the most favorable conditions with an essay, which of course are considerably less than those of the standardized test, you have to use *expert College Board readers* (an impossibility for the average campus), and even then the texts don't *correlate* well *with one another.* Teachers' *estimates* are just that: they cannot compete with *correlations.* Properly understood, then, the placement exercise is an exercise in numbers, not words.

Not that Diederich and other testing specialists didn't consider the essay test (which, in fact, Diederich's monograph both touts and complicates). It's just that from both psychometric and administrative perspectives, the testing task as they construct it is almost insurmountably difficult because error-prone, inefficient, and expensive. You'd need, they say, "*Six two-hour papers, each written in a separate testing session,*" read by "*Four well-selected and trained readers, who will read and grade each paper independently,*" a process that costs "$100 per student" (qtd. in Valentine 91). What it all comes down to is twofold: (prohibitive) cost, of course, but also "the inevitable margin of testing error," a *margin* that is a given in a testing context, but that can be minimized. According to this view of placement (and testing more generally), what we need to do is to rely on "reliability of measurement"; "it is only when we use highly reliable tests that we come close to coming up with scores for an individual that are just measures of his ability—that don't seriously over-value him or under-value him" (Valentine 91).

The first wave of writing assessment is dominated by a single question: not the question we might expect— "What is the best or most valid measure of writing?"—but a question tied to testing theory, to institutional need, to cost, and ultimately to efficiency (Williamson)—"Which measure can do the best and fairest job of prediction with the least amount of work and the lowest cost?"

The answer: the reliable test.

The Discourse of a *Writing* Assessment: Tables Turned

But what about validity? This question, raised often enough by faculty, dominated the second wave of writing assessment. Faculty teaching in new open admissions schools and elsewhere saw new and other kinds of students; and an obvious discrepancy between what they did with their students in class and what students were then asked to do on tests (White *Teaching and Assessing Writing*). Their concern with validity was also motivated by the fact that by the 1970s, faculty had begun to identify themselves as compositionists. They *knew more* about writing: about writing process, about teaching writing process, about writing courses and what they might look like, about what composition studies might be. Given what we were learning, it made increasingly less sense to use tests whose chief virtues were reliability and efficiency. The shift to what did seem obvious— the essay test—had to be orchestrated, however, and it was, by two rhetorical moves, both of which worked inside psychometric concepts to alter assessment practice: first, to make validity (and not reliability) the testing feature of choice; and second, to undermine the concept of correlation as a criterion for evaluating tests.

   Edward White took the first approach. As a faculty member who became an administrator—the first director of the California State University (CSU) Freshman English Equivalency Examination Program—he understood the three variables that had to be accounted for in order to make essay testing feasible:

> While some . . . chancellors, regents and the like are impervious to argument, most are not; many of those who employ multiple-choice tests as the only measure of writing ability are properly defensive of their stance but will include actual writing samples if they can be shown that writing tests can be *properly constructed, reliably scored, and economically handled*. (*Teaching* xiv, my italics)

Which is exactly what White and others—Richard Lloyd Jones, Karen Greenberg, Lee Odell and Charles Cooper, to name but a few—set out to do: devise a writing test that could meet the standard stipulated by the testing experts. To do that, they had to solve the reliability dilemma: they had to assure that essay tests would perform the same task as the objective tests. Administrators like White thus borrowed from the Advanced Placement Program at ETS their now-familiar "testing technology." Called holistic writing assessment, the AP assessment, unlike the ETS-driven placement tests, was a classroom-implemented curriculum culminating in a final essay test that met adequate psychometric reliability standards through several quite explicit procedures: (1) using writing "prompts" that directed students; (2) selecting "anchor" papers and scoring guides that directed teacher-readers who rated; and (3) devising methods of calculating "acceptable" agreement.[3] By importing these procedures, test-makers like White could determine both what acceptable reliability for an essay test should be and, perhaps more important, how to get it.[4] The AP testing technology, then, marks the second wave of writing assessment by making a more valid, classroom-like writing assessment possible.

At the same time that administrators and faculty were showing how a more valid measure could also meet an acceptable standard of reliability—and therefore how testing could be more congruent with classroom practice—other administrators and faculty were demonstrating in the language of testing why the reliable-only test was particularly *incongruent*. In 1978, for instance, Rexford Brown made this case not only by appealing to the *context* of assessment, but also by connecting that test to the context of the larger world:

> *Of course* these [objective] tests correlate with writing ability and predict acadenric success; but the number of cars or television sets or bathrooms in one's family also correlate with this writing ability, and parental education is one of the best predictors there is. All existing objective tests of "writing" are very similar to I.Q. tests; even the very best of them test only reading, proofreading, editing, logic and guessing skills. They cannot distinguish between proofreading errors and process errors, reading problems and scribal stutter, failure to consider audience or lack of interest in materials manufactured by someone else. (3)[5]

The *correlations* here correlate with more than predictive ability: they are themselves a measure of affluence, of *the number of cars or television sets or bathrooms in one's family,* and of another variable, *parental education.* Are these, Brown implicitly queries, the items we seek to test? Moreover, given the discrepancy between the items on the test and what we in our classrooms teach, what could such *scores* based on such items really *mean,* anyway? Meaning is, after all, located in more and other than correlations: it is intellectual and rhetorical substance.

By working both within and against the psychometric paradigm, then, faculty and administrators moved us during the second wave of writing assessment closer to classroom practice.

The Third Wave: New Assessment as Politics of Location

During the second wave of writing assessment, not all faculty, and not all institutions, were carried along: many of both continued the objective measures of the first wave, particularly when they engaged in placement assessments, and many continue these practices today. The first wave, in other words, hasn't disappeared. And yet, at the same time, waves feed into other waves: just as the first wave fed into the second wave, the second wave itself began to make room for the third, again because classroom assumptions and practices could be translated into an assessment scheme. Put simply: if one text increases the validity of a test, how much more so two or three texts? In responding to this question, Gordon Brossell forecast the preferred technology of the third wave, the portfolio:

> we know that for a valid test of writing performance, multiple writing samples written on different occasions and in various rhetorical modes are preferable to single samples drawn from an isolated writing instance. But given the sizable and growing populations of test takers and the increasing costs associated with administering tests to them, the problems of collecting and scoring multiple writing samples are formidable. Until we find ways to reduce testing costs and to improve the validity of the assessments, the whole enterprise is not likely to serve any purposes higher than routine sorting and certifying. (179)

As Writing Program Administrators, Peter Elbow and Pat Belanoff in the mid-1980s found a purpose *higher than routine sorting* when they directed a first-year composition program that—like the programs of the 1950s—required an exit exam. Dissatisfied with its form (it was a second-wave essay test), Elbow and Belanoff used classroom materials to create a writing assessment embodying Brossell's description: *multiple writing samples written on different occasions and in various rhetorical modes.* Or, a portfolio.

This model of writing assessment, with its different genres and multiple texts and classroom writing environment, seemed more valid still. But built into the model was another new feature, a reliability based not on statistics, but on reading and interpretation and negotiation. Rather than use an elaborated holistic scale (with a 1–6 scoring range, for instance), theirs required a simple dichotomous (if still holistic) decision: pass or fail. The "raters" were the classroom teachers themselves. They were not *trained* to agree, as in the holistic scoring model, but rather released to read, to negotiate among themselves, "hammering out an agreeable compromise"

(Elbow, *Portfolios* xxi). Elbow called this a "communal assessment," and argued that it was both more realistic and productive:

> the more we grade with others, the more attuned we become to community standards and the more likely we are to award grades fairly to all. Even though we know, for example, that we are passing a paper because of the quality of its language, we can become aware that the rest of the group would fail it for faulty thinking, and we can then recognize that all of us need to rethink and perhaps adjust our standards. And the greatest benefit of all comes when we return to our classrooms enriched by new ways of commenting on student texts which have come to us during discussions with our colleagues. (xxi)

In the late 1980s and into the 1990s, other portfolio systems developed, notably the portfolio-based basic writing program at Purdue University, the exemption program at Miami University, the placement program at the University of Michigan, and the rising junior portfolio at Washington State University. Simultaneously, individual faculty began using writing portfolios, sometimes as a means of formal assessment, sometimes as a way of learning. All of these portfolio assessments expressed a direct connection to classroom practice.

The Elbow-Belanoff model, however, was the first to raise several interesting, still-unresolved questions challenging both theory and practice in writing assessment. First, this model quite deliberately conflated two different processes—*grading*, typically a non-systematic classroom evaluative procedure, and the more psychometrically oriented operation called *scoring* (which involves the technology of scoring described above). Consequently, psychometric reliability isn't entirely ignored, nor is its historical concern for fairness—Elbow and Belanoff stipulate that *award[ing] grades fairly to all* is a prime objective. But the mechanisms of classic reliability are supplanted by different understandings and larger concerns: (1) about how raters can be led to agree (through "negotiation" rather than training); and (2) about the value of such agreement (desirable, but not required nor expected). Second, faculty are readers, not raters. As readers, they are guided rather than directed by anchor papers and scoring guides; and they are asked to read portfolios with the understanding that readers necessarily will value texts and textual features differently, that they will disagree, that they should negotiate. In sum, we see in this model a shift from a desire for the uniform replication of scoring practice to an assumed negotiation and acceptance of different readings. It's only through the articulation of difference and negotiation, Elbow and Belanoff say, that *community standards* are developed, and through these standards that fairer grades can be derived. Moreover, they claim, this process enables us to refine responding skills that can be taken back to the classroom. This model of assessment, then, functions three ways: (1) as a sorting mechanism (pass-fail); (2) as a check on practice; (3) as a means of faculty development.[6]

It's worth noting that this model of assessment—one that emphasizes validity at the same time it re-contextualizes reliability—emerged from a different context than the one primarily responsible for shaping earlier assessments. During the first and second waves of writing assessment, the common reference point against and from which reform occurred was the placement exercise, which is conducted as an extra-curricular exercise, one prior to college matriculation. By contrast, *in early iterations of programmatic portfolio assessment, the initial reference point is curriculum-based*, occurring (like the AP exams) at the *end of a course*—where it's difficult to ignore the program you've just delivered, to bifurcate that program from a high-stakes assessment marking the students you've just taught in that program.[7] Or: like other disciplines, writing assessment functions out of a politics of location.

Faculty experience with portfolios has raised three other, also-unresolved theoretical issues related to portfolios and to assessment more generally: (1) the nature of reading processes and their relationship to assessment; (2) the role of scoring procedures in an assessment; and (3) what writing assessments can teach us when they are located in practice.

Precisely because portfolios are "messy"— that is, they are composed of multiple kinds of texts, and different students compose quite different portfolios, even in the same setting and for the same purposes, which in turn can make evaluating them difficult—they invite several questions. Certainly, portfolios should be read: but how? Initially, it was assumed that faculty would read portfolios similarly (Hamp-Lyons and Condon), but this given has been contradicted experientially. More specifically, several recorded communal "readings" have suggested at least two quite different portfolio reading processes—one, a linear process; and a second, "hypertextual"— and these different processes have called into question *how any text is read* in an assessment context unconstrained by the technology of holistic scoring (Allen et al., "Outside"). A second issue focuses on the propriety of portfolio scoring; like Elbow and Belanoff, others have questioned whether or not portfolios should be scored at all. A perhaps more interesting and related question has to do with whether a single holistic score is appropriate given the complexity of the materials being evaluated (e.g., Broad). A third issue inquires into the nature of collaborative scoring—a later version of communal scoring—and the value of including a mix of perspectives from various "stakeholders," for instance, a set of outsider and insider readers, or a set of administrative, faculty, and external reviewers (Allen et al., "Outside," *Situating*; Broad). A fourth issue focuses on what can be learned about our own practices from portfolios; exemplifying this aspect is Richard Larson's review of curriculum as it is evidenced in a set of working folders.

Together, these concerns illustrate a new function identified for writing assessment during the third wave: creating knowledge about assessment, of course, but also about our own practices. When writing assessment is located within practice, its validity is enhanced, to be sure. But equally important, it reflects back to us that practice, the assumptions undergirding it, the discrepancy between what it is that we say we value and what we enact. It helps us understand, critique and enhance our own practice, in other words, because of its location—in practice—and because it makes that practice visible and thus accessible to change.

Experts and Amateurs

Another way of understanding writing assessment in the last 50 years is to observe that expertise in writing assessment has been redefined and created anew. During the first wave, testing specialists dominated the field, articulating in a testing jargon why (testing) things are. To create the second wave, a new, hybrid expertise developed: one influenced by testing concepts like validity and reliability, but one also influenced by pedagogical knowledge, composing process research, and rhetorical study. Simply put, we had a clearer sense of what we were doing in class, we began to administer programs, and so we began looking for ways to accommodate the assessment needs of our institutions to our own classroom practices. To do that, we, like Sylvia Holladay, began to develop our own expertise, an expertise located in two disciplines—*writing* and *assessment*. Likewise, we began to develop the disciplinary machinery that would support and disseminate such expertise: organizations like the National Testing Network in Writing; and books like Charles Cooper's and Lee Odell's NCTE edited collection *Evaluating Writing*, the Faigley et al., *Assessing Writers' Knowledge and Processes of Composing*, and the Williamson and Huot edited volume *Validating Holistic Scoring for Writing Assessment*.

In the third wave, another shift regarding expertise is underway; this one appears to be bimodal. On the one hand, as indicated in documents like the

CCCC Bibliography, the CCCC Position Statement on Writing Assessment, and the CCCC program proposal forms, composition studies recognizes writing assessment as a field; we have a journal devoted exclusively to the discipline, *Assessing Writing*; and graduates of programs in rhetoric and composition contribute to their own programs as well as to the composition studies literature (books like *New Directions in Portfolio Assessment* and *Assessing Writing across the Curriculum*; articles in WPA: *Writing Program Administration* and the *Journal of Teaching Writing* as well as in *CCC*).

On the other hand, there still continues reluctance at best, and aversion at worst, to writing assessment. Sometimes it appears in resistance to grading practices (see Tchudi); sometimes it's identified as the villain when a major educational disenfranchising event occurs (as with the current eradication of many basic writing programs); often it's evidenced in a generalized faculty reluctance to take on the tasks entailed in any assessment. And sometimes, discomfort at least is articulated quite clearly when faculty practicing assessment presume to something quite different, a *deliberately non-expert status*, as Elbow and Belanoff suggest:

> First, we note that we are not assessment specialists. We have not mastered the technical dimensions of psychometrics. That doesn't mean we don't respect the field; we agree with Ed White that one of the greatest needs is for practitioners and theorists like us to talk to psychometricians. But we don't feel comfortable doing that so long as they continue to worship numbers as the bottom line. We think teaching is more important than assessment. (21)

Still associated with number-crunching and reductionism, assessment expertise is, at least sometimes, foiled against a teaching grounded in humanism. Ironically, it's expertise rooted twice, in teaching knowledge and in assessment non-expertise; they seem to work together. At the same time, other new experts—theorists like Huot and theorist-practitioners like Michael Allen and Jeff Sommers and Gail Stygall—understand writing assessment itself as the grounds for that same humanism. They argue that the humanistic endeavor requires a student-informed and -informing assessment and the expertise that can create it.

Faculty experience with portfolios as an assessment technology has focused our attention from yet another perspective: that of practice. The effect of this practice has been to suggest new understandings about the kinds of expertise that might inform our assessment practices, with the specific effects of democratizing, localizing, and grounding expertise of three kinds: student expertise, reader expertise, and theorist expertise.

- First, *student expertise.* Through the reflective texts in portfolios,[8] students are asked to demonstrate a kind of expertise about their own work; their "secondary" reflective texts are used as confirming evidence of student achievement as documented in a primary text (Yancey, "Reflection"). Writing well is thus coming to mean twofold: writing well and being an expert on one's writing.

- Second, *reader expertise.* Assessment specialists are looking more carefully at what they are calling "expert" readers, based on a second-wave holistic model that Bill Smith used at Pittsburgh and was later adapted for portfolio assessment by Washington State (Haswell and Wyche-Smith). In this model, readers are expert in a local sense—authoritative about the relationship between a student and a specific course, one that the teacher-reader has very recently taught. Conceived of this way, reliability is not a function of agreement, directed or otherwise, among raters so much as it is a function of rater experience with particular curricula.

- Third, *theoretical expertise* that grows out of and is integrated with practice. The practical work in assessment undertaken during the third wave has created a body of rich data permitting theories of writing assessment to emerge. The theories are developing in two ways: as elaborations and new applications of assessment theory generally (Huot); and as readings of practice suggest (Broad; Allen; Allen et al., "Outside").

Orchestrating Assessment: Politics of Location, Plural

Closely related to the issue of expertise is that of power. During the first wave of writing assessment, faculty seemed content to allow testing specialists to direct the tests while they directed classroom activities: a kind of specialization of effort mimicked what appeared as a co-distribution of power. During the second wave of writing assessment, faculty began to see writing assessment as something that wasn't tangential to the classroom, but important in its own right, as Daniel Fader suggests: ". . . writing assessment is to be taken seriously because its first purpose is to determine quality of thought rather than precision of form. As our students, our readers, and our network of cooperating teachers have told us, it matters because it tries to test something that matters so much" (83). Assessment within the classroom thus took on increased emphasis and importance. Two examples—one focused on the role of error and another on response to student texts—

illustrate how assessment concerns begin to move inside the classroom, become transformed in that context, and generate new questions for assessment specialists and compositionists alike.

During the first wave of writing assessment, error (by means of test items) outside the classroom determines which classroom a student enters: error has an ontological status of its own. During the second wave, error comes inside the classroom: taken together, errors weave a pattern amenable to teacher observation and intervention (Shaughnessy). Still understood as mistakes, they become clues allowing a teacher to plot where to start and what to do. During the third wave, pattern of error is its own discourse: errors work together to create unconventional readings that evidence their own uncommon logic (Hull and Rose). Originally an external marker of deficit, error thus moves into the classroom and becomes its own legitimate text, a means of knowing for both student and teacher.

A similar kind of movement occurs with response to student writing. During the first wave of writing assessment, considerable comment is provided on how important response is in helping students: the early pages of *CCC* speak to this near-universal concern eloquently. But assessment as a discipline, located outside the classroom, includes no provision for response: it's a null set. During the second wave, we see the first formal study of response, conducted by Nancy Sommers in 1981. Located not outside the classroom but inside, Sommers' study is based in and oriented toward recommending good classroom practice. During the third wave of writing assessment, modes of response and their functions—when to praise, how to help students move toward reflective writing, and how students interpret our comments to them—have become a central concern (Daiker; Anson; Chandler). A current debate: should preferred response always be non-directive (Straub and Lunsford), or should it be situated (Smagorinisky)? As significant, response is theorized newly, not as an evaluative end, but rather as an inventive moment in composing. It's a text in its own right, another place to continue what Joseph Harris calls the opportunity for writers to "change not only their phrasings but their minds when given a chance to talk about their work with other people" (68). Moving inward now—into the classroom and then into and within composing itself—writing assessment becomes social act.

As social act, writing assessment exerts enormous influence, both explicitly and implicitly, often in ways we, both faculty and students, do not fully appreciate. Certainly, writing assessment has been used historically to exclude entire groups of people: White makes the point that a primary motivation for holistic scoring was explicitly political, to enlarge and diversify the student body. Portfolios, for many, developed from similar impulses, as Catharine Lucas notes: portfolios provide for what she calls "'reflective-evaluation,' a kind of formative feedback the *learners give themselves*" (2). Through this technology, then, "students' own evaluative acuity is allowed to develop" (10). That is the hope. As others make clear, the hope is not yet realized. Two of the early portfolio models no longer exist: the Elbow Belanoff model is now defunct, a victim of politics; the University of Michigan portfolio program is rumored to be in demise along with its Composition Board; many other models oppress more than make possible, as Sandra Murphy and Barbara Grant detail. Beyond portfolio as technology, scholars continue to look, with depressingly frugal effect, for assessments more congruent with other epistemologies, like that of feminism (Holdstein); with other rhetorics, like that of African Americans (Ball); with other composing technologies, like that of hypertext (Yancey, "Portfolio").

How these issues play out—and how we compositionists alleviate or exacerbate them—is a central and largely unexamined question for assessment, as Pamela Moss explains, one ideally suited to program assessment. This kind of assessment provides another lens through which to understand our practices and their effects, so that we might, ultimately and in a reflective way, take on the central question that doesn't seem to surface often enough: whose needs does this writing assessment serve? (Johnston) In detailing such a program assessment, Moss focuses on the power of naming and of forming that assessment wields: how, she asks, do students and others come to *understand themselves* as a result of our interpretations, our representations, our assessments? How does such an interpretation impact students' "access to material resources and [how does it] locate them within social relations of power" (119). Moss argues that in taking up these questions, it is insufficient merely to interview and survey students. "Rather, it is important to study the actual discourse that occurs around the products and practices of testing—to see how those whose lives a testing program impacts are using the representations (interpretations) it produces" (119). Writing assessment here, then, is rhetorical: positioned as shaper of students and as means of understanding the effects of such shaping.

Writing Assessment and the Self: A Reflecting Lens

As Lester Faigley and James Berlin have suggested, education ultimately and always is about identity formation, and this is no less true for writing assessment than for any other discipline. What we are about, in a phrase, is formation of the *self* and writing assessment, because it wields so much power, plays a crucial role in what self, or selves, will be permitted—in our classrooms; in our tests; ultimately, in our culture. The self also provides a lens through which we can look backward and forward at once, to inquire as to how it was constructed during the three waves of writing assessment as well as how it may be constructed in the fourth.

During the first wave of writing assessment, the *tested self* of course took very narrow forms. In multiple choice tests, the self is a passive, forced-choice response to an external expert's understanding of language conventions. Agency is neither desired nor allowed. During the second wave, the self becomes a producer—of a holistically scored essay—and thus an agent who creates text. Still, there is less agency there than it appears. The text that is created is conventionally and substantively determined—some might say overdetermined—by an expert who constrains what is possible, by creating the prompt, designing the scoring guide used to evaluate the text, training the readers who do the scoring. Given these constraints, the authorship of such a text is likely to be a static, single-voiced self who can only anticipate and fulfill the expert's expectations, indeed whose task is to do just that (Sullivan). At best, agency is limited; a self-writing is permitted, but it is a very limited self, with very circumscribed agency. The text does not admit alternative discourses conceptually or pragmatically: it's text as correct answer.

During the third wave of writing assessment, the self emerges, and it's often multiple, created both through diverse texts and through the reflective text that accompanies those texts. And yet many are uncomfortable with this model of assessment, as Charles Schuster argues. He takes issue particularly with the reflective text since it invites portfolio readers to "fictionalize" authors:

> In effect, fictionalizing student authors moves readers away from normed criteria, replacing careful evaluation with reader response. . . . Presumptions concerning personality, intention, behavior and the like skew readings or turn assessment into novel reading. . . . Such fictionalizing serves a useful purpose within a classroom. . . . Writing assessment, however, demands that we exclusively evaluate what the student has produced on the page in the portfolio. Fictionalizing in this context can only obscure judgment. (319)

Others, however, aren't so sure, some pointing out that such fictionalizing occurs even within singular texts (Faigley; Sullivan), and others that such "narrativizing tendencies" are inevitable (Schultz, Durst, Roemer):

> This narrativizing tendency constitutes one of our primary ways of understanding, one of our primary ways of making sense of the world, and is an essential strategy in comprehension. As far as portfolio evaluation is concerned, rather than say that narrativizing is right or wrong, perhaps we should start by admitting its inevitability, and by advising teachers to be aware of this tendency and not overvalue the stories we create. (130)

The questions raised within this portfolio assessment, then, take us back to reliability and link it to the personal: how *do* we read, particularly this kind of text; what do we *reward* when we read; and what (different) role(s) should the answers to these questions play in both classroom and external assessment? Or: where and when does the self belong, and why?

A final point: the self is constructed quite explicitly through reflection, it's true. But the self is constructed as well through multiple school discourses—academic writing, writing connected to service learning, writing within disciplines, writing for the workplace, writing for the public. Each of these rhetorical tasks assumes a somewhat different self: how are these selves represented—or even evoked—in writing assessment? Or: how *could* they be represented in writing assessment, particularly one that is linked to democracy?

The Role of CCCC: Writing Assessment within Composition Studies

Through its conferences and within the pages of its journal, as the many citations here attest, the Conference on College Composition and Communication has provided the place where postsecondary writing assessment has developed as a discipline. Reading through 50 years of volumes impresses one with the sophistication of the issues raised, the commitment of compositionists to their students, the frustration that easier answers were not to be had. In addition to numerous articles of various kinds—theoretical, pedagogical and research—the pages of *CCC* include writing assessment's disciplinary consolidation, as we see in ever-longer, ever-more-complete and rhetorically informed bibliographies—in 1952, in 1979, and in 1992. It was likewise within the pages of *CCC* where the first comprehensive statement about writing assessment was published, The Position Statement on Writing Assessment, which moves from what we know to include *what that means*: what we can and must do because of what we know. Because literacy is social, this statement claims, assessment must be specific, purposeful, contextual, ethical. And because it is social, we—students, faculty, administrators, legislators—all have rights and responsibilities.

Which is not to say that the story of writing assessment is a narrative of uninterrupted progress; it's rather a narrative of incomplete and uncompleted waves: the early wave, governed by the objective measure; the second wave, which saw the move to the more valid holistically scored essay; the third wave, where portfolios contextualized our students' work and invited us to consider how we read, how we interpret, how we evaluate. At the same time, energies are currently accumulating as though to gather a fourth wave. Perhaps this next wave will focus on program assessment as epistemelogical and ideological work; perhaps it will focus more on individual assessment as interpretive act; perhaps it will take on the challenges posed by non-canonical texts (e-mail, hypertext, multi-generic writings); perhaps it will address the kinds of expertise and ways that they can construct and be represented in writing assessment; perhaps it will include topics that are only now forming.

What is certain is that writing assessment is now construed as a rhetorical act: as its own agent with responsibilities to all its participants. What's also certain is that practice has located assessment, even during the first wave, and that practice has motivated successive waves of development, permitting a kind of theorizing that is congruent with a composition studies that is art and practice. Grounded in such practice, then, writing assessment is becoming more reflective about that practice and the practices to which it connects, uncovering assumptions we bring to texts and that we create as we read texts, understanding our work in the light of what others do, apprehending that what we do is social and thus entails both ideological and ethical dimensions that themselves are increasingly very much a part of both theory and practice.

Acknowledgments

Thanks to Russell Durst, to Cynthia Lewiecki-Wilson, and to a third anonymous reviewer for their clarifying and productive remarks on this essay.

Notes

1. Of course, how and what to teach them—that is, what the content of the English course should be—was also a frequent topic in the early days.

2. Even as I write this, there is a call on the listserv WPA-L inquiring into how multiple choice tests can assist in placement.

3. As I suggest later in this paper, the fact that this is a classroom based program is significant.

4. And White demonstrates: "the actual reliability of the essay test therefore lies between the lower limit of .68 and the upper limit of .89; in practice, this means that any two readers of the test, working independently on a six-point scale, agreed (or differed by no more than one point) approximately 95 percent of the time" (*Teaching* 27).

5. Ironically, what Brown recommends seems considerably less progressive: "Use computers. Have people mark off T-units in the essays so you can gather information about number of words per T-unit, number of clauses per T-unit, number of words per clause, number of adjective clauses, number of noun clauses, and so on—information about embedding, in short, which ties you directly to indices of syntactic maturity" (5).

6. Assessment—or the specter thereof—has sparked many a faculty development program. See, for instance, Toby Fulwiler and Art Young's account of the way the WAC program at Michigan Tech began, in their introduction to *Assessing Writing across the Curriculum*.

7. The first books on writing portfolios all concern themselves with portfolio practice as it occurs in classrooms or just after. See Belanoff and Dickson, and Yancey, *Portfolios*.

8. Reflection is increasingly a part of nonportfolio placement exercises: at Coe College, for instance, at Morehead State, and at Grand Valley State College. And these practices show how waves overlap in still other ways, here in a second-wave essay format enriched by a third-wave reflective text. For more on self-assessment in placement, see Royer and Gilles' "Directed Self-Placement."

Works Cited

Allen, Michael. "Valuing Differences: Portnet's First Year." *Assessing Writing* 2 (1995): 67–91.

Allen, Michael, William Condon, Marcia Dickson, Cheryl Forbes, George Meece, and KaWeen Yancey. "Portfolios, WAC, Email and Assessment: An Inquiry on Portnet." *Situating Portfolios: Four Perspectives.* Ed. Kathleen Blake Yancey and Irwin Weiser. Logan: Utah State UP, 1997. 370–84.

Allen, Michael, Jane Frick, Jeff Sommers, and Kathleen Yancey. "Outside Review of Writing Portfolios: An On-Line Evaluation." *WPA* 20.3 (1997): 64–88.

Anson, Chris. "Response Styles and Ways of Knowing." *Writing* and *Response: Theory, Practice, Research.* Ed. Chris Anson. Urbana: NCTE, 1989. 332–367.

Ball, Arnetha. "Expanding the Dialogue on Culture as a Critical Component When Assessing Writing." *Assessing Writing* 4 (1997): 169–203.

Belanoff, Pat, and Marcia Dickson, eds. *Portfolios: Process and Product.* Portsmouth: Boynton, 1991.

Berlin, James. *Writing Instruction in Nineteenth-Century American Colleges.* Carbondale: Southern Illinois UP, 1984.

Broad, Robert. "Reciprocal Authority in Communal Writing Assessment: Constructing Textual Value in a New Politics of Inquiry." *Assessing Writing* 4 (1997): 133–169.

Brossell, Gordon. "Current Research and Unanswered Questions in Writing Assessment." Greenberg et al. 168–83.

Brown, R. "What We Know Now and How We Could Know More about Writing Ability in America." *Journal of Basic Writing* I.4 (1978): 1–6.

CCCC Committee on Assessment. "Writing Assessment: A Position Statement." *CCC* 46 (1994): 430–437.

Chandler, Jean. "Positive Control." *CCC* 48 (1997): 273–274.

Cooper, Charles and Lee Odell, eds. *Evaluating Writing: Describing, Judging, Measuring.* Urbana: NCTE, 1989.

Daiker, Donald. "Learning to Praise." *Writing and Response: Theory, Practice, and Research.* Ed. Chris Anson. Urbana: NCTE, 1989. 103–114.

Elbow, Peter. Introduction. Belanoff and Dickson ix-xxiv.

Elbow, Peter and Pat Belanoff. "Reflections on an Explosion: Portfolios in the 90's and Beyond." *Situating Portfolios: Four Perspectives.* Ed. Kathleen Yancey and Irwin Weiser. Logan: Utah State UP, 1997. 21–34.

Fader, Daniel. "Writing Samples and Virtues." Greenberg et al. 79–92.

Faigley, Lester. "Judging Writing, Judging Selves." *CCC* 40 (1989): 395–412.

Faigley, Lester, Roger Cherry, David Jolliffe, and Anna Skinner. *Assessing Writers' Knowledge and Processes of Composing.* Norwood: Ablex, 1985.

Fulwiler, Toby and Art Young. "Preface—The WAC Archives Revisited." *Assessing Writing Across the Curriculum: Diverse Approaches and Practices.* Eds. Kathleen Blake Yancey and Brian Huot. Greenwich: Ablex, 1997. 1–7.

Greenberg, Karen, Harvey Wener, and Richard Donovan, eds. *Writing Assessment: Issues and Strategies.* New York, Longman, 1993.

Hamp-Lyons, Liz and William Condon. "Questioning Assumptions about Portfolio-Based Assessment." *CCC* 44 (1993): 176–190.

Hanson, E A. *Testing Testing: Sodal Consequences of the Examined Life.* Berkeley: U of California P, 1993.

Harris, Joseph. A *Teaching Subject: Composition Since 1966.* Upper Saddle River: Prentice, 1997.

Haswell, Richard and Susan Wyche-Smith. "Adventuring Into Writing Assessment." *CCC* 45 (1994): 220–36.

Holdstein, Deborah. "Gender, Feminism, and Institution-Wide Assessment Programs." *Assessment of Writing: Politics, Policies, Practices.* Eds. Edward White, William Lutz and Sandra Kamusikiri. New York: MLA, 1996. 204–26.

Holladay, Sylvia, guest ed. *Teaching English in the Two-Year College* 20.4 (1993). Special Issue on Writing Assessment.

Hull, Glynda, and Mike Rose. "This Wooden Shack Place: The Logic of an Unconventional Reading." *CCC* 41 (1990): 287–98.

Huot, Brian. "Toward a New Theory of Writing Assessment." *CCC* 47 (1996): 549–567.

Johnston, Peter. "Theoretical Consistencies in Reading, Writing, Literature, and Teaching." NCTE, Baltimore, 1989.

Larson, Richard. "Using Portfolios in the Assessment of Writing in the Academic Disciplines." Belanoff and Dickson 137–51.

Lucas, Catharine. "Introduction: Writing Portfolios—Changes and Challenges." *Portfolios in the Writing Classroom: An Introduction.* Ed. Kathleen Yancey. Urbana: NCTE, 1992. 1–12

Moss, Pamela. "Response: Testing the Test of the Test." *Assessing Writing* 5 (1998): 111–23.

Murphy, Sandra, and the CCCC Committee on Writing Assessment. "Survey of Postsecondary Placement Practices." Unpublished ms, 1994.

Murphy, Sandra and Barbara Grant. "Portfolio Approaches to Assessment: Breakthrough or More of the Same?" *Assessment of Writing: Politics, Policies, Practices.* Eds. Edward White, William Lutz, and Sandra Kamusikiri. New York: MLA, 1996. 284–301.

Royer, Daniel J., and Roger Gilles. "Directed Self-Placement: An Attitude of Orientation." *CCC* 50 (1998): 54–70.

Sasser, E. "Some Aspects of Freshman English." *CCC* 3.3 (1952): 12–14.

Schultz, Lucy, Russel Durst, and Marjorie Roemer. "Stories of Reading: Inside and Outside the Texts of Portfolios." *Assessing Writing* 4 (1997): 121–33.

Schuster. Charles. "Climbing the Slippery Slope of Writing Assessment: The Programmatic Use of Writing Portfolios." *New Directions in Portfolio Assessment: Reflective Practice, Critical Theory, and Large-Scale Scoring.* Eds. Laurel Black, Donald Daiker, Jeffrey Sommers, and Gail Stygall. Portsmouth: Boynton, 1994. 314–25.

Shaughnessy, Mina. *Errors and Expectations.* New York: Oxford UP, 1977.

Smagorinsky, Peter. "Response to Writers, Not Writing: A Review of Twelve Readers Reading." *Assessing Writing* 3: 211–21.

Sommers, Nancy. "Revision Strategies of Student Writers and Adult Experienced Writers. *CCC* 31 (1981): 378–88.

Straub, Richard, and Ronald Lunsford. *Twelve Readers Reading.* Creskill: Hampton, 1995.

Sullivan, Francis. "Calling Writers' Bluffs: The Social Production of Writing Ability in University Placement Testing." *Assessing Writing* 4 (1997): 53–81.

Tchudi, Stephen, ed. *Alternatives to Grading Student Writing.* Urbana: NCTE, 1997.

Valentine, John. "The College Entrance Examination Board." *CCC* 12 (1961): 88–92.

White, Edward. "Pitfalls in the Testing of Writing." Greenberg et al. 53–79.

———. "Holistic Scoring: Past Triumphs, Future Challenges." *Validating Holistic Scoring for Writing Assessment.* Ed. Michael Williamson and Brian Huot. Creskill: Hampton, 1993. 79–108.

———. *Teaching and Assessing Writing.* San Francisco: Jossey-Bass, 1985.

Williamson, Michael, and Brian Huot, eds. *Validating Holistic Scoring.* Norwood: Ablex, 1992.

Williamson, Michael. "The Worship of Efficiency: Untangling Practical and Theoretical Considerations in Writing Assessment." *Assessing Writing* 1 (1994): 147–174.

Yancey, Kathleen Blake. *Portfolios in the Writing Classroom: An Introduction.* Urbana: NCTE, 1992.

———. *Reflection in the* Writing *Classroom.* Logan: Utah State UP. 1998.

———. "Portfolio, Electronic, and the Links Between." *Computers and Composition* 13 (1996): 129–35,

Yancey, Kathleen Blake, and Brian Huot, eds. *WAC Program Assessment.* Norwood: Ablex, 1997.

6 Views from the Underside: Proficiency Portfolios in First-Year Composition

Alexis Nelson

> Portfolios make you do a good job or else. Instead of just "You have to do it for the teacher," now you have to do it for the school or the department. I think it's good. [Readers] don't even know who you are. I think that's a lot better because they're not discriminatory. They're not gonna hold it against you because you're somebody they know or anything like that. And you're not gonna get any free handouts.
>
> —Sally

Introduction

It would be difficult to imagine a conversation about writing assessment in which no one mentioned portfolios. Entire state K-12 systems compell their use (Kentucky and Vermont); Peter Elbow's, Pat Belanoff's, and Kathleen Yancey's presentations and essays tout them; and assessment specialist Ed White supports their use. Like other journals, *TETYC* has published an array of articles about portfolios. Some writers describe department-mandated competency portfolios at the end of the first-year composition course (Christian; Baumflek, et al.); others describe them as an evaluation device used by individual teachers (Metzger and Bryant; Lewicki-Wilson); and still

Reprinted from *Teaching English in the Two-Year College*, March 1999.

others describe their uses in literature courses (Sommers; Tomkins). The literacy activities and assessment practices covered by the umbrella term "portfolio assessment" seem quite broad.

If more has been written about portfolio assessment in the last five years than about all writing assessment in the last twenty, then good reason exists to consider what it reveals about the profession. One might well ask whether it is only a bigger, more popular fad or here to stay. One thing seems clear. Portfolio assessment has been successful because it appeals to teachers at many levels:

- as evidence that the curriculum reflects a process approach to writing,
- as an activity that invites students' judgment about their reading and writing,
- as a way for teachers to maximize students' attention to writing and to minimize the tyranny of grading,
- as a repository of the changes learners undergo in rereading literary texts and their responses to those texts,
- as a means of creating dialogue among colleagues about writing and evaluation, and
- as evidence of the socially constructed nature of all learning.

Portfolios would seem to satisfy teachers' needs for pedagogy, for assessment, and for theory.

The evident satisfaction with portfolio assessment had struck me as one-sided, revealing the predilections of those who create curricula and assessments. Students abide all assessments, but I wondered whether their experience would sustain claims about portfolios' merit. Having read about portfolios, instituted a competency portfolio for first-year composition at my community college, and heard the call for empirical investigation of portfolios, I undertook an ethnographic study of the ways students understand portfolios.

In 1992, I left the two-year college where I teach to study composition classes at another institution, a large state university, the goal being to see English and competency portfolios from the students' angle.[1] I wanted to learn how students understood portfolios within the context of their particular composition course and to discover the sense they made of a device that bore little resemblance to their other experiences of writing assessment. I attended the classes of two teachers, both TA's; did the work required of all students in the course; made field notes; interviewed at length eight students from those classes three times during the semester; transcribed, sorted, and analyzed the interview data.[2]

I listened with a critical ear to students' interpretations of portfolios. The account that follows, then, is not a grand argument in support of portfolios nor an attack on them. Rather, I hope it provides what Lucas called for early on: "ethnographiic research that 'looks into' the portfolios rather than attempts to prove them worthwhile" (7). In doing that, the essay reveals some of the fault lines surrounding portfolio assessment and the successes accruing to it in an effort to provide teachers with a practical sense of the issues involved in implementing such assessment.

The Portfolio Assessment Program

The portfolio assessment program at Seneca State University (a pseudonym) was designed to assure students and faculty that those completing first-year composition were competent academic writers. SSU's portfolio assessment was a close facimille of that employed at SUNY-Stony Brook (Elbow and Belanoff). At midterm, students submitted a single essay which was marked "satisfactory progress," "revision needed," or "unsatisfactory progress." In the final portfolio, students submitted one impromptu and two revised essays, one of which involved research and exceeded four pages. That portfolio either passed or failed, and if it failed after further revision, the student had to repeat the course. Both portfolios included preliminary and polished drafts and a letter of introduction describing the portfolio's contents and the writer's process. Readers of both the midterm and fictional portfolios could rate the writing in fourteen categories such as focus, clarity, truth, syntax, documentation, and mechanics.

The first interviews of students took place after they had received the official department description of portfolio assessment in their composition classes and well before they had any personal experience with it. For the most part, they understood portfolios to be about the university's practice of sorting, bewildering, or threatening its newest members. Two students articulated this confusion quite clearly. Madeline was enthusiastic about her writing course but baffled by portfolios and remained so for most of the semester. She first said of them, "I don't get it. I don't understand. Just because you do all the work, you may not pass English if the people think your work is not adequate? And I'm like, 'Geez, that's pretty deep.'" Jeremy was less baffled than angry. He growled:

> They don't affect the final grade . . . [but] they can either say pass
> or fail, and there goes the course for you. Which is a lot of wasted
> time for the freshman . . . who thinks he might be doing good. There's
> just that chance of somebody doing well in class and then failing. I
> don't think our chance is that big. I just think it's outrageous that it
> could actually happen.

These initial responses suggest the foreignness of writing portfolios to first-year students, who did not know what to make of them. Even though both teachers distributed the department handout describing portfolios and talked about them in class, most students had difficulty understanding this university practice, the motive for which was either "deep" or sinister.

In my second round of interviews, after the midterm portfolios, the students understood the assessment device to have almost nothing to do with their final grades in English. Because grades are the familiar assessment and one's portfolio did not affect the grade if it passed, then portfolios had to be about something other than writing assessment. Students worked hard to construct a meaning for such a quirky evaluation practice, and the meaning that more than half ascribed to portfolios was this: portfolio assessment has to do with teacher supervision. John, a "kicked-back" computer engineering major, said, "Somebody's looking over the TA's shoulders." Isabella, a lively double major in art and business, said, "Maybe they'd look at [the portfolio] as how she's been teaching us? It's all well and good to get input and say, 'Oh, you passed,' but I think it's more; they're trying to get a reflection on what she's been doing for us." Another engineering major, Charles said, "My guess is that it's to keep the TA's so they know what they're doing and also to let us know how well we write." And Jeremy, ever irritated by the process, said with genuine sympathy, "I'm sure that undermines a teacher's confidence a little bit. Teachers like feeling students believe in them. So I don't think that [the portfolio process] helps the teaching process a lot specially 'cause she's a TA, and basically like a little child here."

Students obviously ascribe to the English Department very different motives for assessment than "official" sources would suggest. What caught my attention in all their description was location: with one exception, the students who identified teacher supervision as the reason behind portfolio assessment had the same teacher, Emily. In order to allay her students' fears about their portfolios and to emphasize her own rigorous standards, Emily had told her class that portfolios were more an assessment of her teaching than their writing. They took her at her word. Her students constructed a meaning for portfolios that deflected their attention from their writing and stood in opposition to the stated goal of the portfolio program. In other words, the students could conclude that helping them become academic writers was of less institutional value than overseeing the teachers for whom they wrote.

In the third interviews, after the final portfolios were evaluated, I heard quite different stories, ones revealing genuine disappointment when the writers received less feedback on the final portfolio than they had on their midterm ones. Both the midterm and final verdict sheets provided space for the reader to comment on the writing as well as to evaluate it, but on the final round, readers commented only when a portfolio failed. If the portfolio passed, the writer was congratulated, period. The change in form is critical. Several students used what they had learned on their midterm portfolios to revise their work. Isabella, for example, radically overhauled an essay because of her reader's assessment. To revise her essay, a review of David Lynch's film *Twin Peaks: Fire Walk with Me*, Isabella watched the film again twice on video. She said:

> I've seen this movie three times now, and each time I've understood it a little bit more. And I realize how confusing the movie actually is, so when I revise it again . . . I'll just incorporate that as a flaw in the film, saying [Lynch] is not reaching everyone he could. It's a confusing film, but it's also confusing, I think, to read any of the reviews if you haven't ever seen the [TV] show.

The response of an additional reader at midterm, then, caused Isabella to engage in several writerly activities. She saw the film again, reconsidering its impact on its audience and acknowledging that what was a given for her—Lynch's originality as a director—could confuse naive viewers. She identified herself with a community of writers, that is, film critics who had treated both the TV and film versions of *Twin Peaks*. She refined her thesis into a more narrowly focused piece of advice for her audience. The contrast between the consequences of the first and second rounds of assessment is striking. Isabella said, "I don't think I got any [feedback]. You know, just checks. There aren't any comments or anything. It didn't mean anything, so I felt like it was pointless to even try. Getting them back, you get so irritated 'cause there's nothing." Like every informant who completed the final portfolio, Isabella bristled at the lack of response. Finding many typos and spelling mistakes in her final portfolio that her reader had not noted, Isabella grew skeptical of her reader's thoroughness. More important, the final round of assessment shifted her attention away from writing to typing concerns.

Isabella was not alone in her distaste; in fact, all the students whose portfolios passed complained despite their having passed. Having received formative feedback from their midterm assessors, they were disappointed not to receive it from their final assessors. They had typified the process in one way—as offering them information from a reader responding to them as writers. When the final portfolios lacked a reader's response, that is, when they were evaluated rather than engaged as writers, their previous understanding was destroyed and the assessment enterprise laid open to question. The once-foreign, then-familiar practice of portfolio assessment had been made strange again, and the students bristled. Such distress is telling: though teachers occupy the same classrooms as students, they do not necessarily understand the same activity similarly. To seasoned evaluators, the change in the form makes sense: the time for formative evaluation had passed and the time for summative evaluation had arrived. To students, the change could only seem capricious or worse.

Portfolio partisans may not be pleased by these students' construction of portfolios as teacher-assessment, nor can they be happy to see the way the final portfolio reading ruptured students' belief that the assessment had something to do with treating them as writers to whom readers respond. Nevertheless, advocates can delight in the way portfolios sharpen less sophisticated writers' ideas about audience and revision. It is a commonplace that many students write for themselves or for their teachers and consequently have trouble seeing revision as anything more than tidying the mechanics.

The baffled Madeline was stuck for a good part of the semester trying to determine her audience and acting as though it were she herself. In our second interview, she said of her teacher, "I want her to read it how *I* read it, but she won't *ever.* . . . She's *soooo* nit-picky." Wanting to follow directions and please, Madeline had trouble revising because she considered only her teacher's marginal notes: "Like in revision, I have not made any more changes than what she says, and I don't know if I should or what. Does she want me to change more than she's marked? I guess she does. But what if it's not right? Then I'll be in even deeper hot water." Like several others, she went through much of the semester with a very mechanical notion of revision; however, it was clear when she spoke of her final portfolio that she had made a breakthrough to another view of education and another understanding of writing. She too was disappointed with the puny response to her final portfolio, saying:

> I wish they would have said something. I mean, OK, it passed, but
> something that I could possibly learn from. If they don't want to cor-
> rect spelling, they don't have to. But if they just want to say, "This is

a little confusing here." They're not suggestions, but I could have thought it through.

How important such change is. First, Madeline recognizes that concern about spelling is of less value than learning where her prose confuses a reader. Second, she understands herself to benefit rather than to smart from suggestions about how she might revise. By the end of the course, she has caught on to the explicitly rhetorical dimension of writing, and she says:

> [The portfolio] was a hassle, but it's really just to prove you can write [when] you're a future employee . . . when you graduate. It kinda makes sense too. I mean, you have proof that you can do it. And that people from a college think you can too.

Portfolio assessment, then, gave Madeline a collection of her work upon which the university had passed a favorable judgment. Similarly, portfolios pulled the balky Jeremy toward increased awareness of his audience. The sting of his middling evaluation at midterm pushed him to examine his assumptions about writing. He recalled that essay:

> I guess I didn't really have a lot of emphasisis on why *Road Warrior* was such an original movie. Sometimes I get so caught up and think it's so great in my mind that it sometimes loses it on the paper. Sometimes you can look at [a piece of writing] and [say] "This is my writing. Anything wrong with it?" And then you do have to be critical of yourself: You see: "What the hell was I doing? Where was I going?" It clearly expresses my opinions to me, but it's not clear to everybody else *and that's my main problem because it's more than writing for me* (emphasis added).

Not only has Jeremy revised an essay, he has revised his understanding of writing, seeing finally that his essays must be reader-centered rather than writer-centered. When he assembled his final portfolio, he redoubled his efforts, including in it the essay he had written arguing against the English department's policy of portfolio assessment. He said:

> [I selected that paper] so they would think. It's the most well written paper, the most opinionated paper, and I think I hit the point and I hit the point hard. I had reasons for every point I made. But I'm worried about getting another paper as strong as this. I don't want to give just a strong [paper] and one that's kinda mediocre.

What writing teacher or program administrator would not celebrate these writerly developments in Jeremy: the self-criticism, the desire to affect his audience, the willingness to revise in order to make his writing consistently strong?

The benefit of portfolio production is not limited to those whose portfolios pass. John, whose midterm and final portfolios failed, incorporated his readers' suggestions into his revisions until he finally passed. For him alone, the final portfolio provided feedback, which he appreciated:

> I'm sure it helped with the grade I got after I turned it back in to her because I worked on a lot of the stuff that this person had mentioned. And then when I got this back, Barbara [his teacher] had a copy of the paper and when she handed it back, it said a lot of the stuff [my reader] did. So I already had the revisions ready to turn in, and so it was kinda easier in that way.

Because of portfolio assessment, John gained an opportunity denied the more successful writers; he used the suggestions of his reader to revise his research essay, thereby improving his grade. Although John did not like his reader's tone, he, nevertheless, used the response to advantage.

Using Student Stories to Construct Academic Practice

This essay is not the place to rehearse the arguments made on behalf of portfolio assessment, for they have been articulated (Elbow and Belanoff; Belanoff and Dickson) and refined elsewhere (Black, et al.; Yancey; Gill; Yancey and Weiser). Instead, I use the stories of students' experiences to suggest several concerns relevant to implementing department-wide competency portfolios. Foremost among these is the importance of any given teacher's understanding of this methodology. Students will understand portfolio assessment in the way their teacher represents it to them. If she sees the assessment as the students' opportunity to get feedback additional to her own, then they regard it as an occasion for further response and an aid to their learning. On the other hand, if she says the process is meant to evaluate her teaching more than their writing, then students will not disagree. Should their attention be shifted from their writing and toward instruction, they are robbed of a helpful evaluation tool and simultaneously armed with a weapon against the instructor.

The SSU episode exemplifies Kathleen Yancey's concept of the two curricula: "the delivered (the teachers', the institutions') and the experienced (the students' version of that delivered curriculum), and when courses work well, they provide a point of intersection between the two" ("Teacher" 250–51). In one class I observed, the delivered and the experienced curricula intersected around portfolio assessment; in the other class they did not. The story seems less about one SSU teacher's subverting the department's assessment goals and more about the different ways any two teachers construct academic practice with their classes. Clearly, what teachers do and say about institutional practice matters. Students get the curricula of their institutions through the agency of particular teachers, some of whom are enthusiastic, some muddled, some indifferent, and some skeptical purveyors of any given feature of that curriculum. Certainly the dissatisfaction of one teacher I studied was evident (and her concerns were shared by other TA's not included in this study). That dissatisfaction suggests teachers should share not only the theoretical framework but also the experiential framework that makes a particular practice sensible, whether that practice be portfolios, peer feedback, revision, or others.

An ancillary concern related to individual teacher practice is that of grading. Advocates of portfolio assessment appreciate that it allows the teacher to defer grading, yet many teachers grade individual essays. Certainly both TA's in whose classes I participated graded every draft and revision, as do many teachers in my department. Several reasons account for this readiness to grade: students understand grades instantly, teachers feel obliged to tell students where they stand, and grades provide all parties with evidence of teacher authority. Grades are the most familiar evaluation practice, and teachers often rely on the familiar. But individually graded essays can make portfolio assessment a bumpy ride. A student will be frustrated when a disinterested evaluator says her *B* essay needs substantial revision in order to be termed proficient, and she is likely to vent her spleen on the teacher. At the very least, teachers who wish to grade everything would be wise to postpone the practice until the midterm portfolio has been read.

The larger issue, consistently applied local standards, is a piquant one, revealing that the Platonic form of the *B* essay (or the *C* essay) is not shared by all members of the department. Establishing consistent grading standards among a range of teachers is no simple chore, but it is a task that portfolio assessment begins to address as teachers talk about how they judge writing, the relative value they place on originality, argument, organization, mechanical correctness, and verbal dexterity. Any decision about undertaking portfolio assessment, then, should be accompanied by discussion of grading: how writing traits are evaluated and how grading itself works to promote or inhibit revision. The possibility of extensive revision, after all, makes this assessment device appealing.

The last caveat I would draw from the students' stories is one centering on the rituals of assessment. These students typified the assessment process differently after the final reading than after the midterm reading; they regarded the final round skeptically because the frame around portfolios had shifted. Evaluators stopped being coaches and became judges. Of course, professionals in the assessment community would call the preliminary round formative and the final round summative evaluation and see a different purpose for each. Students, however, are not assessment professionals. Teachers should, therefore, talk about the different purposes for each round of assessment and about differences in official documents conveying the evaluation. An additional element of the assessment ritual relates to time. These students grew skeptical because the final portfolios required less time to read than their midterm ones.[3] Only the most naive student thought the fuller portfolio had gotten as careful a reading as the earlier one. Because predictability is so important to students' constructing their academic lives, because these writers had learned from their readers' midterm responses, and because they knew there was more and better prose for their readers in their final portfolios, institutional effort should be directed toward consistency in the two portfolio readings.

Doing Portfolios: A Community College Faculty Story

It would be a mistake to allow the complexity of portfolio assessment to blind us to its benefits. Community colleges seem at least as well—if not better—situated than large universities to reap the benefits of portfolio evaluation. First, faculty rather than graduate students teach the composition courses. Whether full-time or adjunct, those teachers usually have a bigger stake in assessment practices than have people who teach the curriculum they are told to teach and move though the system in 2-6 year cycles. Having tied their professional fortunes to the college, two-year faculty members have authoritative voices and influence over policy. While skeptical about assessment schemes decreed from the top, teachers can effect curricular and assessment change from within the ranks. University graduate students will assess as they're told, juggling that demand as one responsibility among many. Community college faculties, on the other hand, are well served when assessment is an integrated part of instruction rather than an additional demand. Portfolio assessment is but one site on a continuous loop in composition, giving feedback about the curriculum to students and to the teachers who develop and sustain it with their classroom practices. And community college teachers will talk, tinker, and revise curriculum until it satisfies their instructional needs. Only if portfolio assessment serves faculty—in clarifying shared expectations, in maintaining standards, in supporting difficult judgments—can it succeed.

Second, portfolio assessment provides a stage on which teachers do publicly together what they routinely do privately in solitude: evaluate writing. Norming and reading sessions become a sort of miniature contact zone where teachers of the same course "meet, clash, and grapple with each other" (Pratt 34). My department's experience might illustrate this contact zone. At the middle and end of each quarter, we meet for a day of norming and reading. We do not squeeze portfolio readings into the cracks of already overcrowded weeks; instead, the dates are scheduled at the start of the term and composition classes suspended so that undistracted reading can occur. When teachers put these dates into their syllabi, they notify the students that the faculty works together and values the assessment. We begin by reading 2-3 sample portfolios drawn from the current quarter and identified by the teacher as borderline portfolios; that is, the teacher has trouble deciding whether the writer's work is competent (we've defined competency as worth a C rather than C-).

After everyone has read a portfolio and marked a response sheet stating the criteria we expect the writing to meet, we tally the sheets and talk about our differences, which usually are several. Some teachers are willing to let slim detail pass because a student struggled with an ambitious topic, maintained clear organization, and demonstrated control of mechanics. Others are less willing. We try to discuss every reader's concerns and to reach consensus, but we do not expect consensus in every case. Often reading the second or third portfolio, with quite different strengths and problems, makes us think self-critically about the ways we impose these criteria. Having done this work for twenty-seven quarters, we know the established "softies" and "hard-liners"; their comments identify the issues and occasionally surprise us. We rethink our judgments when a softie fails a portfolio or when a hard-liner sees virtues in a mediocre one that our particular concerns had obscured. In short, we regularly become a professional community that practices evaluation together.

Baumflek et al. have identified the ways portfolio assessment can be perceived as threatening to part-time faculty, indeed to anyone without tenure. The negotiations about standards can be heated, particularly when tied to the writing of one's students and thus to one's teaching. If the portfolio reading groups are ill-constituted or if the department atmosphere is one that permits some faculty to use student performance as the occasion for rude remarks to others, then portfolios will provide an endless source of internecine conflict. On the other hand, if department members enjoy the experience of disagreement in the norming negotiations, if they can argue civilly and even relish diversity among colleagues as well as among literary texts, then portfolios serve an ongoing department need for collegial engagement. That collegiality is tied to instruction rather than to social exchange in the lunch room. Durst, Roemer, and Schultz acknowledge the danger of exposing our judgment to our colleagues' scrutiny, and they argue that "the trauma of this experience seems largely unavoidable, and better faced head-on as a group than left to private terrors and individual nightmares" (290). Portfolio assessment allows the faculty to identify the fault lines and negotiate them together instead of in isolation.

Third, norming discussions provide faculty acculturation and ongoing development. Quiet and attentive, our new teachers see portfolio norming as their best cue about the local expectations of students' writing; moreover, they begin to feel confident that they assign and evaluate work in a way that is consistent with others in the department. Conversely, senior faculty have realized that our new hires often construct better prompts and make audience consideration a part of each writing task. These twice-quarterly days have become occasions for all of us to learn from one another. We see one anothers' assignments and the results of those assignments in the essays students compose. Portfolio readings make it easy to find the teachers with the effective, provocative writing prompts and to begin conversations that result in the exchange of ideas. We share the howlers our students produce, and we occasionally read portfolios of astonishing quality. Portfolios allow each of us to read and commend good writing from other classes. We can give no better encouragement to a novice writer than a fresh reader's comment, nor to ourselves than the pleasure of reading a splendid portfolio and congratulating the teacher who elicited it.

The current adage is that portfolios do not compel us to agree but rather help our disagreements to bear fruit. Portfolios foster discussion and collaboration. To argue effectively about student texts, a teacher must convince colleagues of the strength of her position; she must support her claim about its quality with evidence from that text, not from knowledge of the student writer. It is ambiguous, demanding work—work that lies at the very core of rhetoric and of the academy itself. Argument and judgment in the presence of ambiguity characterize the discourse community of higher education, the very world we invite our students to join through their writing. Wiggins suggests that "an authentic test not only reveals student achievement to the examiner but also reveals to the test-taker the actual challenges and standards of the field" (704). Portfolios reveal teachers values to students and thereby make the tacit curriculum more explicit; they promote students' enfranchisement in the academic world; and they afford students insights into the worlds of their readers that impinge upon them as writers. In these multiple ways, they benefit both the students and teachers who produce them.

Notes

1. I explored portfolios at a university rather than my own college for two reasons. First, it seemed more methodologically rigorous to investigate where I was unknown and had no authority that might influence the data I gathered; second, portfolios had been in place at the university for five years and were not considered experimental. Because the course in which portfolios were used was the ubiquitous first-year composition, these findings seem relevant to teachers of that course on almost any campus.

2. This study is informed by Berger and Luckmann's theory that reality is socially constructed; consequently, I attended to the ways natives talked about the artifacts and activities of their daily lives. This frame seemed useful because first-year students are natives to schooling but novices to higher education.

All the informants' names are pseudonyms, as is that of the university. I followed these textual conventions: ellipsis to indicate pauses in an informant's speech rather than omission, italics to indicate the speaker's emphasis unless otherwise stated, and brackets to indicate where my words supplement the speaker's.

3. At midterm, teachers collected portfolios of a single essay to exchange within their reading groups and returned them one week later. The final portfolios, with three essays, were collected on Wednesday and returned in the next class, Friday.

Works Cited

Baumflek, Sylviane, et al. "Part-Timers, Full-Timers, and Portfolio Assessment." *Teaching English in the Two-Year College* 24 (1997): 308–16.

Belanoff, Pat, and Marcia Dickson, eds. *Portfolios: Product and Process.* Portsmouth: Boynton, 1991.

Berger, Peter L., and Thomas Luckmann. *The Social Construction of Reality: A Treatise in the Sociology of Knowledge.* Garden City: Doubleday, 1966.

Black, Laurel, Donald A. Daiker, Jeffrey Sommers, and Gail Stygall, eds. *New Directions in Portfolio Assessment: Reflective Practice, Critical Theory, and Large-Scale Scoring.* Portsmouth: Boynton, 1994.

Christian, Barbara. "Freshman Composition Portfolios in a Small College." *Teaching English in the Two-Year College* 20 (1993): 289–97.

Durst, Russel K., Marjorie Roemer, and Lucille M. Schultz. "Portfolio Negotiations: Acts in Speech." Black, et al. 286–300.

Elbow, Peter, and Pat Belanoff. "Portfolios as a Substitute for Proficiency Examinations. *College Composition and Communication* 37 (1986): 336–41.

———. "State University at Stony Brook: Portfolio-Based Evaluation Program." *New Methods in College Writing Programs: Theories in Practice.* Ed. Paul Connelly and Theresa Vilardi. New York: MLA, 1986. 95–105.

Gill, Kent, ed. *Process and Portfolios in Writing Instruction.* Urbana: NCTE, 1993.

Lewiecki-Wilson, Cynthia. "Teaching in the 'Contact Zone' of the Two-Year College Classroom: Multiple Literacies/'Deep Portfolio.'" *Teaching English in the Two-Year College* 21 (1994): 267–76.

Lucas, Catharine. "Introduction: Writing Portfolios—Changes and Challenges." Yancey. 1–11.

Metzger, Elizabeth, and Lizbeth Bryant. "Portfolio Assessment: Pedagogy, Power, and the Student." *Teaching English in the Two-Year College* 20 (1993): 279–88.

Pratt, Mary Louise. "Arts of the Contact Zone." *Profession* 91. New York: MLA, 1991. 33–40.

Sommers, Jeffrey. "Portfolios in Literature Courses: A Case Study." *Teaching English in the Two-Year College* 24 (1997): 220–34.

Tomkins, Sandra Lee. "How Does a Reader Make a Poem Meaningful? Reader Response Theory and the Poetry Portfolio." *Teaching English in the Two-Year College* 24 (1997): 317–24.

White, Edward M. "Portfolios as an Assessment Concept." Black 25–39.

Wiggins, Grant. "A True Test: Toward More Authentic and Equitable Assessment." *Phi Delta Kappan* 70 (1989): 703–13.

Yancey, Kathleen Blake, ed. *Portfolios in the Writing Classroom: An Introduction.* Urbana: NCTE, 1992.

———. "Teacher Portfolios: Lessons in Resistance, Readiness, and Reflection." Yancey and Weiser 244–62.

Yancey, Kathleen Blake, and Irwin Weiser, eds. *Situating Portfolios: Four Perspectives.* Logan: Utah State UP, 1997.

7 Whose Portfolio Is It Anyway? Dilemmas of Professional Portfolio Building

Sue Ruskin-Mayher

As the field of English Education continues its ongoing self transformation, the need for assessment tools which reflect the authentic forms of work which we now require of students has grown. Striving towards the kind of authenticity of performance which Wiggins (1989) recommends, many of us have begun to use portfolios as our major assessment tool. We find the portfolio to be particularly suited to the kinds of ongoing reflection which we now require of our students. We have come to recognize that tests and essays function as snapshots which tell us something about a student's learning at a particular moment in time. In the larger picture of a student's learning, they tend to be reductive, providing a picture of only a fragment of what has really been learned. They do not represent the complexity of the knowledge attained, or of the learning process itself. They do not make connections between bits of knowledge, and they do not tell us or our students anything about how knowledge changes as students construe and reconstrue meaning. Portfolios, on the other hand, rather than presenting unrelated, individual snapshots, provide more of a collage, a collection of individual bits of knowledge which students must use their meta-cognitive skills to piece together. Portfolios give students the opportunity to find their own unique themes, so that the reader will come to the same understandings that the portfolio builder has about what has been learned.

Reprinted from *English Education*, October 1999.

Gordon (1995) compares the process of portfolio construction to that of making a quilt. The job of the portfolio constructor is similar to that of the quilter in that they both must create relationships between separate items in order to achieve a sense of harmony and balance in the final product.

In the traditional model of assessment, the student as "self" tries to reiterate what has been learned either from the teacher, or from the text, in a manner which will be acceptable to the teacher whose role as assessor demands that he/she be cast as powerful "other." The two become totally separate entities, in harmony only when "self" magically reproduces what is in "other's" mind. Paradoxically, the duality of these positions serve to inhibit creation of self, as, in this structure, it is only when "self" and other function with one mind that the student can achieve academic success.

Portfolios, at their best, allow us to break out of these roles and form a learning partnership in which student and teacher can become collaborators, co-creating meaning in an ongoing dialogic process. Though many of us see the potential for true classroom change through portfolio development, there is little in our own educational backgrounds to support us in transforming our assessment practices. Transformation of practice does not take place in isolation. It is an outgrowth of a change which has taken place within the teacher him/herself. As a teacher educator, I am particularly concerned with creating experiences for my students which will result in a transformation of thinking and of practice. The route to such change lies in our own reflections on our classrooms, on our practice, on our lives. The professional portfolio proves to be an excellent vehicle for this kind of reflection.

I first became acquainted with the concept of the professional portfolio at an Association of Teacher Educators conference in the 1980's. The professional portfolios which were exhibited there were being used as exit criteria from schools of education, as well as for certification. I liked the idea of the portfolio, but was dissatisfied with the formulaic approach which the teacher education programs were taking to the portfolio itself. Surely, as collections of student work, they represented the world of the student for the duration of the teacher education program, both in courses and in the field. Yet the finished products seemed constrained by the assessment rubrics which accompanied them. I felt that there were two essential ingredients missing. The first was any real sense of connection to the portfolio builder's sense of him/or herself as a teacher/learner, and the second was any sense of connection to a larger tradition. "Whose portfolios were these anyway?", I asked myself as I viewed Xeroxed versions which had been passed around for workshop participants to examine. The heart and soul of portfolio building was missing. That intimate conversation with self and others which Sunstein (1996) refers to as reflective and reflexive encounters were certainly not what these portfolios communicated to me as I struggled to understand the teacher/learner in the text, or to differentiate one writer from another. Nor was there any sense of the educational tradition from which these writers had come, or the stands they were taking as they were poised on the verge of passing this tradition on to others. It was difficult to distinguish between these portfolios and the more traditional test with regard to standardization of product. What was the point of creating a "new " hoop for pre-teachers to jump through, rather than fully exploring the potential of portfolio development for reflection and growth.

What seemed most lacking in these portfolios was any tangible evidence of concentrated reflection or meaning making. I visualized a student who had been handed a list of criteria which she obediently fulfilled. The portfolios seemed to have been created in a vacuum. The portfolio creators had not located the "self" in the portfolio. As a result, these portfolios had no distinguishable voice. The voice which says this portfolio is mine, and tells my story, and I want to share it with you so you will understand it and therefore me. This is the voice which can only be achieved through intense self reflection.

Reflection does not come naturally to teachers. It is our tendency in structuring learning situations to create a framework in which students can move sequentially from step to step, building skills and comprehension as if linearity were the sole dimension of understanding which students possess and can apply. Learning is, however, more like a wave which builds in intensity until it reaches a crest of understanding. Once crested, it then recedes to gather more information until, full with new meaning, it crests again, repeating this recursive pattern while meaning is built, modified, changed. This recursive property of learning is, then, best nurtured through ongoing reflection which supports the making of connections between new learning and old. Reflection alone, however, can not communicate one's understandings of practice to others, which is the ultimate goal of any professional portfolio.

Sunstein (1996) identifies three types of encounters which underlie the portfolio experience. She calls these the reflective encounter, the reflexive encounter, and the dialectical encounter. In a reflective encounter, a portfolio builder "resees" herself, peering into a mirror of her own creation. In a reflexive encounter the expectations of the "other" become considered, as the portfolio builder strives to demonstrate the ways in which the portfolio fulfills the expectations of the institution or the learning community. In the dialectical encounter, a teacher acts as mediator between the portfolio builder and others, easing the communicative process. Together these form a trinity of meaning making which allow a portfolio builder to understand and communicate her unique understandings of her practice. Through the completion of these encounters, the portfolio builder invites the "other" into her conceptual universe creating the voice in her portfolio.

As a teacher educator functioning as the mediator between the portfolio builder and the "other," it is my job to facilitate the reflection and reflexion processes. How to best support these became my challenge. In writing about these reflective encounters, Sunstein cites Rob, a college student who writes:

> I didn't really see the interactions in my portfolio until recently. I knew I had a collection of things which demonstrated my various literacies. . . . but I didn't see the duet being performed: for nearly every piece of writing or performing there is a complementary piece of reading or decoding. My lyrics and the record of CD purchases. My record of a baseball game serves as a reading made writing. Music to be interpreted and changed by me and music written by me to be read by another interpreter. (p.17)

As Rob found his portfolio "voice," he was making intraportfolio connections. Further, he was making connections between his work and the work of others. He was beginning to connect to other parts of his life, and to other people within his personal tradition. How different from the workshop portfolios which I had viewed. These were the connections which I hoped to encourage my students to make. I began to see each portfolio as having an individual voice, and the process of portfolio construction as a journey on which I could launch and guide students, while they captained their own ships. It was clear to me that if their "encounters" were truly going to achieve the level of reflectivity for which I was striving, that it would have to be their own work, and that the kinds of assessment rubrics which I had seen would be limiting rather than broadening and deepening. Primarily, I wanted to help students use reflection as a vehicle for growth and change. I was searching for a process which would rely on my students' own understandings to frame the portfolio building process.

Donald Schön (1987) discusses the need for professionals to do a form of reflection in action. He describes a process of learning their craft, performing their craft, and reflecting on their craft as a way of transforming their approach to their work. This synthesis of activity takes place in a reflective practicum with the teacher functioning as coach. While I could not be in the field with my students, the idea of a class which would meet regularly and would provide a basis for reflecting on experience began to make sense to me. I entered into a negotiation with my last semester graduate students to develop a course which would follow their action research course. In this new course, they would create portfolios which would begin with reflection upon who they were as teachers and learners, and weave the threads of their personal and professional experience into a complex tapestry of self exploration. At the beginning of February 1996 we began.

How to inspire teachers to reflect on their practice in ways that would be meaningful to them, and then be able to communicate that meaning to others was more complex than I had initially imagined. Available texts on professional portfolios relied too heavily on creating portfolios which would meet the stated expectations of certification panels or prospective employers. They would not give us the kind of guidance which we needed for meaningful reflection, the starting point for authentic presentation. We would have to rely on reflection itself to guide us in producing our own texts.

We discovered that sharing self-reflection with others was a difficult process which sometimes produced a boundary conflict in which the reflector's most basic sense of public and private space (Greene 19) threatened to be violated. It became necessary to create a "safe space" in which students could explore their deepest senses of themselves as teachers/learners, and make choices about how much of what they discovered they were willing to make public. Moffett (1981) identifies meditation as a way to access the reflective inner speech from which written voice emerges. To increase the safety of the experience, and access inner speech, we began with a guided meditation in which I asked students to look back through their teaching and learning journeys, and then visualize an object which they felt represented that journey. In that session, they visualized and then wrote, but they did not discuss their reflections with each other. Instead, I asked them to go home, find this object and bring it into class the following week. I hoped that this would provide some distance from the experience, and enable them to make decisions about what they felt was private, and what they felt was public.

Anxiety at the next session was palpable as people prepared to present the objects which they had brought and begin the process of opening their reflections to others. This process which Sunstein calls the reflexive encounter proves to be critical to the process of portfolio development. In order to present the understanding gained through reflection, a student must look outside herself to understand the expectations and the contexts of others. Qualley (1996) writes of reflexivity occurring "in response to a person's critical engagement with something (or someone) else." In our case the collective "someone else's" in this class were able to provide a supportive network of "others" through whose understanding success of presentation could be judged.

As students presented their objects, they discussed their personal meanings. Sondra brought a scroll which had been presented to her by the first class of her 21 year teaching career. Ellen, a preservice student teacher, brought a sponge, Laverne, a veteran teacher, a Teacher's Prayer, and Shantanu, also a student teacher, a rocket. Each spoke of its personal meaning creating and communicating it as she went along. Finally, Jim, quiet up to this point, produced a set of keys which he related to opening the locks of the minds of his students with knowledge. Still struggling with his sense of personal and private space, Jim told us that he usually didn't discuss himself with others and had been unable to bring to class the original object which he had chosen because it was too personal. These keys provided a safe object through which he could express his self reflection comfortably. Allowing the metaphor to speak for them, students had begun to construct their teaching/learning identities.

Seeking to further access inner speech, the next activity was to create a collage which would reflect the students' teaching/learning journey. We collected odd bits of art supplies from closets, drawers, and art boxes. We bought poster board, and sat on the floor of the classroom trying to understand how random bits of wool, paper and fabric fit together. The project lasted for three sessions during which time we cut, pasted, and crayoned, until randomness began to form patterns, patterns began to intersect, and harmony grew out of chaos. To further the meta-cognitve element, I asked students to write about the experience and what they had learned once the collages were completed. We then spent two sessions talking about what we had learned.

Some students used the collage to extend the metaphor of their original object. Gina, a former graphic designer, had originally chosen a pen as her object. She had explained to us that the pen was both the tool of her former trade, and the instrument through which her thinking flowed onto the page when she wrote. It symbolized the freedom of expression which she hoped to encourage in her future students. When Gina began her collage, the pen was the central image. Strands of wool emerged from the pen and trailed off the page as she explored and transcended the "boundaries" of her own mind. The more she worked, the further her collage extended, in much the same way she sought to encourage her high school writing students to transcend their self imposed boundaries and become more expressive writers.

Other students took off in different directions. Ellen, a student teacher, created a series of steps which represented the steps which she had taken, and had yet to take to become a teacher. Each step had been labeled with a significant benchmark in her journey. College, graduate school, and student teaching all figured prominently. Brina had difficulty with her collage. She began with an amorphous black figure in the middle of a white poster board, and seemed unable to proceed from there. I knew that she was having difficulty in her teaching and suggested that she spend some time seeing what the figure she had created had to show her. It took her a few weeks longer than anyone else to finish her collage, but on a day when the rest of the class was already involved in other pursuits, she asked if she might present her completed collage. It was still small, and uncomp-licated in design, but the black figure was now a bright purple, and it was surrounded by flowerlike designs in bright colors. Brina had recently been moved to a different school where she was having more success in her teaching and was learning to decenter power and build community in her classroom. In her collage she depicted her own growth as well as the flowering of her community.

Once the collages had been completed, reflected upon, and discussed, the work on the final product began. We felt ready to create criteria which would guide portfolio development and help us to think about the kinds of artifacts which could serve as evidence of knowledge or experience. We wanted to achieve a balance between product and assessment, while avoiding constriction of thought and presentation. Initially we discarded the idea of a rubric, as we felt that it would inhibit self expression. Gina's experience with portfolio development as a graphic designer was helpful because she challenged us to think outside of the boundaries of our own teaching paradigm. She helped us to understand that a portfolio should present not only what the presenter has done, but also what she believes she can do. Our linguistic lens for portfolio creation was "Where have you been? Where are you now? Where do you want to go?"

Alan's suggestion that we look at the curriculum model which was used at the alternative high school at which he was teaching filled out our portfolio concept. We decided that evidence should fit domains which would be general enough to accommodate a variety of different artifacts, but communal enough for portfolios to reflect the shared values of our community. The domains would also serve as a framework for presentation to outsiders which we were considering as a culminating activity. Creating the domains involved serious discussion of what we value as teachers, and how we might make those values manifest in the portfolios. This process, which had not been a part of my original thinking about the course, proved to focus our thinking, and create a bridge from reflection to reflexion. Although there was much discussion and some argument about which domains would best represent their work, agreement was reached far more quickly than I would have expected. I was gratified to discover that shared experience of the program had resulted in a shared philosophy and values. The domains which we settled on as best framing our work were Community Building, Curriculum and Instruction, Our Own Voices, The Voices of Students, The Voices of Others. We now had five lenses through which to search for artifacts.

We agreed that we wanted to include artifacts that were personal and professional, that included student work, and work from graduate education courses. We wanted these artifacts to demonstrate content knowledge, knowledge of pedagogy, professional interests and contributions, field evaluations, and most of all, change. We searched closets, boxes, and attics, and found artifacts that stretched back to twenty years of teaching experience and sometimes to our childhoods. We struggled to define what these artifacts said about us, and how we could communicate what we were learning and believing about ourselves to others. We went through periods of intense anxiety, unsure that this process would work, and that ideas would become thoughts, thoughts become symbols, symbols become words, and words lead to concrete representations of our work. We worked together and played together, and worried together, and in the process built a community of learners who supported each other through doubts and celebrated each other's triumphs. And, somehow, all of the pieces fell into place. Inner speech became outer speech. Each student found his/her identity theme, and portfolio voices were established.

Alan, a third year teacher, went through his closet and found a "report card" which he had created when he was eight years old. The report card triggered memories of "teaching" other children in the neighborhood from the time he was very small, and organized his portfolio around the theme of "Evidence of Things not Seen." Bound in a brown leatherette scrapbook which he had been keeping for years, Alan's portfolio begins with a memory:

> Dolores . . . "Here!" Michael . . . "Here!" David . . . "Here!" Susan
> . . . "Here" Agonies . . . "Here!" One by one I went down the roll
> . . . Judy . . . "Here!" James . . . "Absent!" the whole class would say.
> "I would like for you to take out your homework from last night
> and pass it to the front row," I would say. "David, please go down
> the row and collect the homework." A whole class . . . a whole dia-
> logue . . . interaction.

The reflection which follows this memory continues:

> And it was all make believe. I would never have imagined becom-
> ing a teacher. Yet there I was imagining I was a teacher. Yes, I had
> roughly twenty five students. I made report cards for each student. I
> had a roll book and an attendance book. And, yes, I knew the names
> of each student in my class (first and last). My students had it all,
> from tests to homework assignments and, NO, I am sorry to say, I
> did not have a blackboard.

On the page facing this narrative Alan has placed the handwritten report
card of "Roger Whipple" which he had created so many years ago.

Continuing his work in the Our Own Voices Domain, Alan included
awards and report cards from his early school years, articles which he wrote
as editor of the college newspaper, and pictures of various graduations. The
narrative which weaves his artifacts tells the viewer that:

> There has been a constant interaction between me as the teacher and
> me as the student. It is the same as the interaction between all stu-
> dents and teachers. To me, they are one and the same. And this is
> what this portfolio is about, interactions. . . .
> Teaching is about interactions. . .
> Learning is about interactions. . . .
> Life is about interactions.

The Curriculum and Instruction section incorporated curricula which he had
developed over his three years of teaching. They were framed by domains
which are similar to the ones which he helped us to construct. In answer to
the question "How does my portfolio show growth in my pedagogy over
time?" Alan created some resonance with his introductory section. The
Curriculum and Instruction section contained portfolio development and
roundtable guidelines along with the curriculum guides. Under his eighth
grade report card in the introductory section, Alan had written the words
Authentic Assessment??? Clearly, one major area of Alan's growth has been
in assessment practices. The rest of Alan's portfolio contains pictures of him
with students, samples of student work, letters from students, and
administrators thanking him for his hard work and caring, and programs

from ceremonies at which he has been a featured speaker. Alan's portfolio is an ongoing reflection on the multiple roles of teacher which he has created in his life. From its imaginary beginnings, Alan understood that teaching was based in interactions, and his portfolio successfully represents him in interactions with his students, his colleagues, his environment and most powerfully, with himself.

Like Alan, all of us learned that we had a story to tell, and, in the end, all but one of us produced works which told this story. Much to my relief, the portfolios themselves were vastly different from those which I had seen before. Despite the fact that they all presented material which explored the agreed upon domains, each portfolio expressed the individual voice of its creator.

In reflecting on the process of creating the portfolio, Sondra said:

> Returning to teaching after a year's sabbatical was frightening for me. I knew that I wanted to use what I had learned in the program to change my methodology, and involve my students more closely in curriculum planning, but I didn't have the confidence to believe that I could really do this. The process of building the portfolio helped me to understand that I had already changed, and to construct ways to substantively bring those changes back into the classroom. I am going back with a new way of being in the classroom.

All of us felt that we were better teachers for the experience, and all of us felt that this was an experience which we could continue as we continue to construct and reconstruct the essence of who we are in this "uncertain craft" McDonald (19) called teaching.

Works Cited

Gordon, K. (Fall 1994). The quilt as metaphor for teaching portfolio. *Portfolio News* 6.

Greene, M. (1988). *The dialectic of freedom.* New York: Teachers College Press.

Mayher, J. (1990). *Uncommon sense.* Portsmouth, New Hampshire: Boynton Cook.

McDonald, J. (1992). *Teaching making sense of an uncertain craft.* New York: Teachers College Press.

Moffett, J. (1981). *Coming on center.* Montclair, New Jersey: Boynton Cook.

Qualley, D. (June 1996). "The reflective encounter: What is it and what it means for literacy and learning." Paper presented at NCTE Professional Development Conference Albuquerque, New Mexico.

Schön, D. (1987). *Educating the reflective practitioner.* San Francisco, California: Jossey Bass.

Sunstein, B. (November 1996). Assessing portfolio assessment: Three encounters of a close kind. *Voices From the Middle.* Volume 3 Number 4.

Wiggins, G. (April 1989). Teaching to the authentic test. *Educational Leadership.* Volume 46.

8 Inside the Portfolio Experience: The Student's Perspective

C. Beth Burch

Process and product synthesized: writing portfolios are, for writers and composition instructors alike, not only a product—a body of writing to be assessed—but ideally, evidence of the process by which that writing is created, shaped, revised, selected, presented. Writing portfolios have in the past ten years become immensely popular, at least with instructors and directors of writing programs. Many teachers still know little, though, about how students perceive portfolios. We like to think that portfolios present advantages for students, give them increased insight into themselves as writers, and increase their ownership in their writing. Advocates believe that students who "own" their writing are more confident and positive writers (Overbeck, 1994, p. 11-12). And writing teachers hope that more confident, positive writers produce better writing—and therefore develop better attitudes toward writing. Are portfolios, then, a means to combat students' apathy toward writing, a method for pushing students to a higher plane of rhetorical existence and awareness? What do students actually think of portfolios? How do they perceive their experiences in creating them? What are students' attitudes toward writing and the assessment of their writing? And how do these notions entwine?

In this essay, I begin to answer these questions. I examine whether first-year composition students at two state universities believe that portfolios are as effective for students as composition instructors widely assume them to be. And I investigate the assumption in composition pedagogy that portfolios are good for students' writing and that students like and appreciate the opportunity to be in a writing class using portfolios for assessment.

Reprinted from *English Education*, October 1999.

As an assistant professor of English education now at SUNY Binghamton, I teach writing and how to teach writing—and frequently combine these aims in one course. The strictly writing courses I teach are mostly undergraduate courses. But I also teach English education courses that combine writing with composition pedagogy; these are graduate courses in a Master of Arts in Teaching program. For years I have used writing portfolios in both kinds of classes. And for years I have faced persistent and inevitable questions and concerns from students about how portfolios might be created and how they will be evaluated and graded. I have also observed distinct advantages in teaching with writing portfolios, advantages often articulated by students. If we aim to use portfolios as a move toward authenticity in assessment, then students' responses to portfolios may help us use them better.

Description of This Project and Participants

Using questionnaires and interviews, I examined the attitudes of university students in first-year portfolio writing classes (hereafter called *portfolio students* or *portfolio classes*) and compared their attitudes to those of first-year students in non-portfolio classes (*non-portfolio students*). The non-portfolio classes, like the portfolio classes, incorporated invention, drafting, and revision of writing assignments—but the non-portfolio classes did not feature portfolios as pedagogy or as assessment. In non-portfolio classes, instructors read and evaluated pieces of writing shortly after they were submitted. Thus non-portfolio students had a sense of their grades throughout the course, including when they were surveyed for this study. In portfolio classes, on the other hand, grades were not assigned to individual pieces of writing throughout the course, but each piece was read and evaluated with comments and suggestions for revision. Portfolios were assessed by instructors of record, not by a review committee, and given grades near the end of the course; thus, when questionnaires for this study were administered, portfolio students did not yet formally know their portfolio or course grades.

In addition to polling students for this study, I also surveyed instructors of both groups of writers and interviewed one instructor and a sample of students from each group. All questionnaires and interviews were administered at two state universities, one in the Midwest and the other in the South. In both places, undergraduate student populations tended to come from middle-class, in-state residents, relatively inexperienced in academic discourse, and characterized by one portfolio instructor as "students who are not quite prepared to write in a mature way, who have not yet fully learned the power of words or the advantages that can be derived from writing well."

Admittedly, many factors that create differences in composition classrooms cannot be understood within this study. From one writing classroom to another—even within the same university—there are likely to be differences in the nature of instruction, experience of the instructor, writing experience of the students, the quality of peer and instructor's conferences, requirements set forth for instructors. Considering the institutional culture toward writing, institutional norms, and a host of differences could not be measured for this study. These and other variances surely apply; yet in important ways, the first-year composition programs in these universities resembled one another. In both, directors of composition managed a series of required courses taught primarily by graduate teaching assistants. At both schools, portfolios were a feature of many, but not all, first-year writing courses. All instructors were graduate teaching assistants, and at the time, both state universities had similar first-year composition programs—that is, a two-course sequence required of most first-year students, except those who "tested out" with the Advanced Placement or other examinations or those who were required to take remediation or ESL sections. Both universities offered first-year courses in basic writing, English as a second language, and honors composition as well as a two-semester sequence of expository writing taken by most first-year students. Classes in both universities were similar (with an average size of 22-23 students per section) and customarily taught by graduate teaching assistants rather than tenure-track faculty. Both universities offered mentoring sessions led by composition professors or experienced senior teaching assistants for inexperienced teaching assistants and other instructors who used portfolios.

The Student Surveys: Population and Method

A three-page questionnaire of 24 items was administered to 338 students from "regular" first-year composition classes, rather than from basic or developmental writing or from ESL classes; not using basic writers or ESL writers was part of a purposeful attempt to filter out differences that might emerge because of more complicated educational backgrounds that such writers might bring to the writing course. Of the 338 students surveyed, about two-thirds were in portfolio classes (215), and one-third were in non-portfolio classes (123). Other than the treatment—portfolios—no material differences existed between groups. In both populations, slightly more than half the students were male (51% of the portfolio and 53% of the non-portfolio group),[1] and most students were between seventeen and nineteen years old (80%); fewer than one-fifth of the students (17%) were 20 to 22, and only 3% of the students surveyed were 23 or older. All questionnaires were administered by instructors in their classes during the last two weeks of the semester, before portfolios were assessed for final grades. Students completed the questionnaires anonymously. For most students, being in a portfolio class was a new experience: 85% of them had never prepared a portfolio of any kind; for 11% of portfolio students, the current class was a second course experience with portfolios; and a small percentage, 4%, had two or more course experiences with portfolios, usually in other disciplines such as art.

Interviews with Individual Students

I also interviewed individual first-year students from both universities and from both portfolio and non-portfolio classrooms about their assessment experiences in writing classes.[2] However, not all students who were interviewed completed questionnaires. Therefore, to maintain similar proportions as in the questionnaire population, I interviewed 9 students from portfolio classes and 6 from non-portfolio classes. Students were chosen from instructors' recommendations and were split about evenly between males and females (4 males and 5 females from portfolio students, 3 and 3 from non-portfolio students). Individual interviews, lasting half an hour, were conducted from a list of ten basic questions during the last three weeks of the semester, but not always before portfolios were evaluated or students were assessed for a final grade. Interviewing students recommended by instructors may have skewed results toward a favorable rendering of experience.

Instructor Surveys: Population, University Setting, and Method

Fifteen writing instructors were surveyed. Nine were teaching with portfolios, and 6 were not. Items on instructors' questionnaires paralleled those on students' questionnaires. Instructors were self-selected; that is, I asked for volunteers to administer the student survey and to take the instructor's survey, and results were drawn from the classes of those who volunteered. One portfolio instructor who had written provocative comments on her questionnaire and identified herself was interviewed personally.

Key Results and Significance of Findings

The questionnaires and interviews revealed some differences between the attitudes of portfolio students and non-portfolio students. These are the major findings, distilled from the 24 items, the interviews, and students' and instructors' comments:

1. *Portfolio students viewed the writing task more positively than did non-portfolio students.* Given a range of possible affective responses (respondents could select more than one choice), portfolio students were more likely than their non-portfolio counterparts to select terms at the positive end of the range, like *excited* and *happy* to describe their writing experience. On the questionnaires, for instance, 23% of portfolio students claimed to be *excited* about writing for their classes, compared to 14% of non-portfolio students. More portfolio students described themselves as *happy* (21% compared to 8% of non-portfolio students). And portfolio students were less *bored* (11% vs. 19%) and *tired* of writing (7% vs. 16%). Worth noting is that fewer than half the students in each group chose terms to describe writing positively.

Interestingly, instructors of both groups perceived their students' attitudes more positively than students did; portfolio instructors characterized 30% of their students as *excited* about writing and 20% as *happy*. Non-portfolio instructors believed 28% of their students to be *excited* and 21% *happy* about writing.

Interviews supported the finding that portfolio students are happier with the act of writing than non-portfolio students—and, to some degree, this "happiness" is probably influenced by enthusiastic instructors and is a product of students' telling instructors or interviewers what students think instructors want to hear. Annie B., a portfolio student, reported that she thought portfolios were "wonderful" and that she "loved the freedom" that the portfolio gave her to create; she pointed out that the portfolio was "very much her own," that she "chose the things that went in it," and that she believed that she "made good decisions about the content." Alison H., also a portfolio student, described the portfolio experience as making her "feel more competent and certainly more comfortable" about writing. Only one portfolio student, John P., responded negatively in the interview, characterizing his writing for the semester as "hell to do." A smaller percentage of non-portfolio students reported happiness or pleasure in their writing; of the 6 interviewed, 3 expressed positive views of writing. Jack J. said that he "learned a lot" and liked to write for his teacher because she let him write about subjects he "cared about" (this would be as likely in portfolio courses as in non-portfolio courses); he wrote all his papers that semester about some aspect of baseball. Ellen B., also a non-portfolio student, wrote poems and short stories outside class; she liked "being creative with more informative assignments, like trying to figure out how to give instructions and make it interesting."

   2. *Female portfolio students were more positive about portfolios than males.* More females reported being *happy* writing for the course than males (17% of females, 10% of males). Females were less likely to feel *tired* (11%, compared to 30% of males) or *bored* (9%, compared to 14% of males). Instructors were not aware of such gender differences, but interviews with students did corroborate this finding. Female interviewees commented more positively about their portfolio experiences (4 of 5 female students interviewed) than males. Only one female student complained that her "frustration level got very high at times." On the other hand, 2 of 4 male students interviewed made negative remarks about portfolios. Differences in attitudes toward writing were apparent between non-portfolio male and female students: 40% of males reported feeling *tired* (40%); 22%, *tense* when writing. In comparison, females in the same group were less likely to be *tired* (10%) or *tense* (11%).

   These differences in male and female attitudes reflect other gender differences regarding writing reported in research about portfolios and writing in general. Laurel Black, Donald Daiker, Jeffrey Sommers, and Gail Stygall (1994) observe differences between male and female students' writing portfolios at Miami University of Ohio, especially with regard to the required reflective letter. They argue that women's letters reveal that women "position themselves in relationship to others" (p. 239), mentioning collaboration, friends, and family and emphasizing caring and connection. Black and her colleagues also find that women, generally more wary of criticism than men, explicitly seek "compassionate, responsible readers" (p. 241). In contrast, reflective letters written by men are more likely to mention accomplishments, evaluate their writing positively, refer to the letter writer as a writer, and to praise the Miami program: men's letters more frequently construe the relationship with portfolio scorers as public, whereas women's letters seek a more private audience. Other researchers note similar phenomena. Elizabeth A. Flynn (1988) describes the narratives of her female students as stories of "interaction, of connection, or of frustrated connection" and those of her male students as stories of "achievement, of separation, or of frustrated achievement" (p. 428). Sandra K. Rose (1990) finds in her reading of literacy narratives that for female students, literacy represents "a means to social participation" but for male students, "a means to achieve social autonomy" (p. 250).

Lest we become too comfortable with this interpretation of female behavior in writing classes, however, we should consider the recent work of Margaret Finders (1997), whose research into literacy practices of adolescent girls reveals that their public personas may be much different than their "backstage" lives. Finders reports that although girls appeared to cooperate and presented a "unified front" to persons of authority and in public, behind the scenes they were far less congenial, often disagreeing, blaming one another, denying allegiances, and perhaps most importantly, competing (p. 53). It is possible that women responding to my survey felt compelled to present what they perceived as socially acceptable opinions while they concealed their more aggressive behind-the-scenes behavior. It is also possible that female students saw that giving their feelings about writing a positive spin might lend them more cache' and power with the instructor—and thereby a subtle edge over other class members.

Then again, males may express more discontent than females in any kind of writing class that emphasizes process, and these findings may suggest more discomfort in dealing with process in general than with portfolios in particular. Judith K. Gardiner (1982), writing from the psychoanalytic texts of Nancy Chodorow, argues that the fundamental difference between male and female writers is illustrated in the metaphor "female identity is a process." Gardiner maintains that the "processual nature of female identity illuminates diverse traits of writing by women" (p. 179). Deborah Tannen, (1990) drawing widely on a variety of gender studies in *You Just Don't Understand: Women and Men in Conversation* and confirming the work of Carol Gilligan, describes men as perceiving social relations primarily in terms of hierarchy, women in terms of connections. Thus men are likely to position themselves above or below another person, and women to try to find points of relationship and similarity. Traditional writing classes are typically task-oriented, teacher-centered with the teacher/instructor at the top of a hierarchy, and guided by clearly defined goals and policies. The emphasis in a traditional writing class is on the completed work of writing. In contrast, process-based classes (and portfolio classes as a subset of process-based classes) rely on a more egalitarian class structure. The teacher is a facilitator; students initially must rely on themselves and one another in peer group relationships. The focus is on the process of writing and on writers' developing metacognition within the context of a small writing community. Females are more socially conditioned to feel comfortable in the process-based scenario; males, in the traditional one.

3. *Portfolios appear to enhance students' confidence for future college writing tasks.* Asked to characterize their preparation for further college writing (*excellent, adequate, insufficient,* or *other*), more portfolio students chose excellent than did non-portfolio students (54% vs. 37%). Far fewer portfolio students considered their preparation *insufficient* (8% vs. 21%). More portfolio instructors considered their students excellently prepared (64%) than did non-portfolio instructors (53%). The confidence of portfolio students may be owing to the responsibility they must assume for selecting, reflecting, commenting on, and presenting their work; they are by necessity more involved with the hard work of text production and more deeply attuned to the metacognition of writing. This increased confidence reported by portfolio students seemed apparent in interviews: Sonya D. said that she felt "ready to conquer the world" of college writing after "organizing, writing, reflecting, and pulling [her] hair out" during the creation of her portfolio. A frequently unsolicited theme emerging in interviews was appreciation of the freedom to create the portfolio: Chris C. expressed gratitude "for the freedom to figure out how to make the portfolio [his] own." And Victoria S. said she "loved the freedom" her instructor gave her to create for herself. She was afraid of so much freedom at first, she reported, because she was worried about her grade, but she thought portfolios were "wonderful" and made her a "better writer" for the rest of her college classes. Confidence, ownership, and freedom seem to be linked by-products of the portfolio experience.

4. *But ironically, portfolios may not be linked to students' notions of their writing progress.* Students in both groups had similar opinions about whether and how much their writing improved during the semester. Most felt their writing did improve; thus, portfolios likely have neglible effects in terms of students' notions of their development as writers. Among portfolio students, 39% believed that their writing skills had *improved greatly* during the semester, compared to 34% of non-portfolio students. And 45% of portfolio students believed that their writing was *somewhat better,* compared to 53% of non-portfolio students. Nearly identical percentages in each group considered their writing to have stultified during the course: 13% of portfolio

students and 12% of non-portfolio students selected *about the same as in the beginning* to describe their writing at the end of the course. Revealing a heightened sense of efficacy, instructors in both groups estimated their students' gains more highly than students did: about 60% of all instructors believed that their students had *improved greatly.* Very few instructors believed their students' skills remained *about the same,* and none believed their writing had *worsened.* Interviews were revealing; nearly all students in both groups commented positively about their writing improvement during the course (only one person in each group felt the course didn't help him write better).

5. *Portfolios made little difference in students' estimates of their possibilities for earning a good grade.* Students were asked whether the way their work was assessed made it *easier to get a good grade in the course, more difficult to get a good grade in the course,* or *made no difference.* This item did not specify what constituted a *good grade* because its purpose was to gauge students' perceptions; what actually constituted a *good grade* was in fact irrelevant. In both groups, most students believed that the assessment methods (portfolio or not) made getting a good grade easier. Instructors' questionnaires from both groups corroborated these findings: overwhelmingly, instructors believed that their assessment methods helped students earn a good grade (88% of portfolio instructors vs. 83% of non-portfolio instructors).

Students' comments during the interviews confirmed that portfolios are not relevant to students' perceptions about the difficulty of getting a good course grade. In an interesting affirmation of students' beliefs in the inherent fairness of writing teachers, students interviewed from both groups believed that they would be rewarded for their work and achievement, regardless of how the instructor measured them. Nana O., a non-portfolio student, said, "I think my instructor's revision policy makes it possible—and not that hard—to get the grade I want from the class." One portfolio student commented that portfolios "reward the lesser talented writers and are also very fair to the accelerated people."

In the interviews, though, four portfolio students commented about how the idea of the portfolio had gradually come to dominate the idea of the grade. Typical was Tammy W., who said, "When I began to work seriously on this, I couldn't see it coming together. My mind was set on pleasing my instructor, earning a grade. Then something clicked: I began to enjoy myself. Finally, I realized that I was doing this for me." No non-portfolio student made such a statement.

Portfolios or not, students in both groups were extremely sanguine about their expected course grades. Portfolio students had slightly but not significantly higher expectations for good grades, though, than did non-portfolio students. In both groups, more than half the students expected As: 64% of portfolio students and 60% of non-portfolio students. More portfolio students, however, expected Bs than did non-portfolio students: 32% vs. 26%. Only 3% of portfolio students expected a C for the course (compared to 13% of non-portfolio students), 1% of portfolio students expected Ds while no one in the non-portfolio group had this expectation. Portfolio students clearly expected grades along the upper part of the spectrum; non-portfolio students looked for grades more distributed along the range.

6. *Non-portfolio students accepted assessment better than portfolio students.* Respondents identified attitudes toward assessment by selecting either *enthusiastic, accepting, reserved, mistrustful, or antagonistic.* Similar percentages from both groups were enthusiastic about the assessment used by their instructors: 29% of portfolio students and 23% of non-portfolio students. But considerable differences existed in percentages *accepting* of their assessment: only 49% of portfolio students chose this response as opposed to 61% of non-portfolio students. Portfolios provoked a higher percentage of negative feelings, however. Among portfolio students, 12% felt *mistrustful* or *antagonistic* toward portfolio assessment compared to 4% of non-portfolio students. This antagonism toward portfolios as assessment may reflect students' unfamiliarity and discomfort with the delayed grades of the portfolio system, feelings which many respondents expressed. Perhaps students need to be taught something of the pedagogical background of portfolios to allay these concerns. Incidently, expected grades apparently had little relationship to students' antagonism: 70% of those who claimed to be *antagonistic* expected As or Bs, regardless of their group.

Curiously, interviews from portfolio students yielded overwhelmingly positive comments about portfolios vis-a-vis course grades, even though grades had not yet been assigned: Renee P. explained that "the portfolio was a wonderful learning experience. . . . It made me feel professional. . . . It contained a great deal of me and my personality in it—I definitely take pride in my work and believe my grade will show that." This theme of ownership was reiterated by Jill G., who reported, "This portfolio is me," and by Nancy P., who commented, "I expect to get an A for my portfolio: it is completely mine because I wasn't told how it had to be organized or exactly what I had to put into it; it is an expression of my personality."

7. *Portfolio students believed their instructors to be more positive toward assessment than did non-portfolio students.* But portfolio students also held more widely varying opinions of their instructors' attitudes toward assessment of writing. Seventy percent of portfolio students considered their instructors *enthusiastic,* compared to only 50% of non-portfolio students. More portfolio female students (78%) than males (62%) considered their instructors *enthusiastic.* Responses among non-portfolio students were less diverse, more centered around the neutral indicators, and about the same percentages of females (48%) and males (52%) thought their instructors *enthusiastic.* In interviews, this gender difference did not, however, emerge, nor did the results of the instructors' questionnaires suggest it.

Instructors confirmed students' perceptions. Most reported being *accepting* and *enthusiastic* about their assessment method. Indeed, *all* non-portfolio instructors characterized their attitudes toward assessment as either *enthusiastic* or *accepting.* But just as portfolios make many teachers happy, they also bring out the curmudgeon in others. Among portfolio instructors, 22% indicated *mistrust* or *antagonism* toward portfolios. It is important to recall that all instructors surveyed were graduate students teaching in composition programs where portfolios were frequently part of the required course structure and dictated by either the writing program administrator, a mentor professor, or a committee. One portfolio instructor explained that she was "told to" use portfolios, adding that they "had never been introduced" to her before and were "definitely something new." Obviously, instructors need to be taught about portfolios just as much as students do.

8. *The opportunity to revise was the clearest advantage students saw in portfolios.* Choosing from a menu of possible advantages of the method for assessing their writing (with a write-in slot to provide flexibility), portfolio students selected the opportunity for revision (79%) most frequently. Portfolio students also saw an advantage in *additional feedback* before grading (67%) and in the idea that *improvement counts* (64%). Paul W. commented in an interview that in portfolio courses, writers have "a chance to improve their writing skills instead of being docked for their mistakes." Less valuable to portfolio students were *more encouragement* (36%) and a *greater sense of accomplishment* (35%). A surprisingly small percentage perceived *fewer deadlines for assignments* as an advantage (28%).

Few differences appeared in the responses of males and females to this item. It is interesting, though, that students over twenty selected more advantages by circling multiple answers than did younger students. Indeed, 47% of students over twenty believed that *fewer deadlines* were an advantage, but only 22% of students under twenty considered this important. Perhaps younger students believe that they need the structure that frequent grading provides—or perhaps they are less aware of the number of grading deadlines they will face in their college careers. Sally M., in the 26-30 age bracket, reported that "portfolios leave a lot of open space for both students and instructor. This room to grow and time to follow your own internal (and external) schedule is a real advantage."

9. *Concern about grades was the greatest disadvantage of portfolios for students.* Seventy-five percent of portfolio students believed the greatest disadvantage to portfolio-based instruction was *uncertainty about the grade* for the course. Females and males did not differ. Megan T. claimed that the only way she could find out how she was doing was to "bug the TA [teaching assistant]." Students also saw *infrequent grading* as a disadvantage: 52% of students chose this response (56% of males, 49% of females). Charles O. said that he didn't like "writing four-or five-page papers that aren't for a grade" but "other than that, portfolios are pretty cool." A portfolio instructor hypothesized that throughout the semester "most kids *did* know what grade they were getting," but that "realistically, they wanted proof of it—and because they weren't getting proof, that was disturbing to them."

In descending order, other disadvantages of portfolios were the *emphasis on revision* (18%) and that *too many drafts of papers are required* (16%). Just 11% of portfolio students believed that the *difficulty of keeping documents* was a disadvantage, and only 4% disliked *preparing the portfolio for evaluation.* Interestingly, students reported fewer multiple responses to this item about disadvantages of portfolios than to the *advantages* item; on average, they cited about 1.75 disadvantages but over 3 advantages. This finding suggests that students view portfolios with some ambivalence.

Implications for Teaching Writing

What do these findings mean for writing instructors? First, we may expect that regardless of how excited we are by the pedagogical possibilities of portfolios, our students may be less charmed by them. We may expect male and female students to differ in their reactions to portfolios. We may expect that delaying grades until the portfolio is assessed is likely to disturb many students. Finally, we may realize that instructors and students perceive the writing course through significantly different lenses; thus instructors need to be especially aware of how students are reacting to pedagogy and assessment. Sometimes we forget that students may be less interested in writing and in thinking about writing than their instructors!

What's a writing instructor to do? To help students feel more comfortable with portfolio grading, instructors might consider being entirely open about the criteria for portfolios. In *Assessing Student Performance*, Grant Wiggins argues that to remove the mantle of secrecy from the examination process is to make it more moral (p. 91-100). To make criteria for portfolios transparent and specific, instructors might consider developing the portfolio rubric jointly with students, incorporating students' criteria for grading as well as instructors'. And instructors might offer a "dry run" in the middle of the assessment period or one or two oral grade estimates on "as is" papers throughout the grading period. Portfolio conferences, *de rigeur* in most composition programs, can (if handled well) students understand their writing, their instructor, and the demands of the course.

Certain teaching strategies also may address students' tensions and make the entire portfolio experience more manageable. Instructors can allay students' concerns by posing questions on early drafts to prompt students to address weaknesses head on. Instructors might make *specific* suggestions for revising and indicate *specific* places where changes may be useful. Most important, though, instructors might refrain from overpraising all of a student's efforts. This phenomenon seems endemic to relatively inexperienced instructors—and I am *not* arguing against genuine praise for a well-done effort. But students tend to interpret extensive comments of encouragement on a draft as endorsement of what they have already written, and vague remarks like "good job" or "I like this" written on a wobbly paper can create a false sense of grade security. Janet J., for example, felt betrayed by the grade on her portfolio because her instructor's remarks on her drafts, she thought, had been highly positive. She angrily explained to me that "the teacher's comments mean nothing without a letter grade to back them up. If the teacher says it is a 'good paper,' but it's only a C paper, that is no help." A portfolio instructor frankly explains the portfolio grading dilemma this way:

> I gave out almost all As first semester. And I felt almost trapped into it. I'm a neophyte in terms of evaluating student writing, so I would say, "OK, Student X, you have to do all these things to get an A." And by golly, she'd do them—but I'd read the paper and I'd think "This is not A work," but I'd have to give the A anyway. So I felt that I was trapping myself into giving As.

Two related dilemmas for portfolio instructors seem apparent here: how to convey progress (or lack thereof) with words rather than grades and how to help students be less concerned about grades and more concerned about writing. Instructors may simply find it necessary to steel themselves against students' complaints about the lack of grading. Students' discomfort over a dearth of grades is not, after all, necessarily entirely negative; and cognitive dissonance is a typical response to a new learning situation.[3]

Portfolio students who successfully navigated the portfolio experience offered these suggestions on their questionnaires to instructors who teach portfolio-based courses:

> I wish the grading had been more thoroughly explained; instructors should do this more than once during the course. —Jack H.

> I'm a terrible procrastinator, so I don't pace myself well. I found it harder to pace myself in the portfolio class and would like to have more specific deadlines. —Paul B.

> Portfolio guidelines must be clearly delineated or else the student may misunderstand the assignment and turn in a piece of good, but ungradeable, writing. —Patricia F.

> The student must write at all times with a portfolio theme in mind, insuring a more cohesive final product. —Ellen B.

These comments point to students' need for information and guidance through the portfolio process. Students want instructors to impose deadlines, to explain specifically how evaluation works, to provide specific responses to their writing, and to help them shape their writing to "insure a more cohesive final product." Students are inevitably, and perhaps inextricably, also connected to products: notice in these few comments the emphasis on grading, which necessitates a product, and the specific mention of a "final product." Turning students' attention to their processes will doubtlessly require instructors' active attention and perhaps Herculean efforts. And, for this reason, teaching assistants with little or no experience with portfolios should not teach portfolio courses.

Considering the large question of whether portfolios positively affect students' overall attitudes toward writing and writing instruction, this researcher found that in some respects, portfolios did not create differences. Similar percentages of students in both groups believed that the structures of their courses and the methods of assessment improved their writing skills, and similar percentages of students believed their instructors' assessment methods or course structure made it easy to earn good grades. In addition, similar numbers of students in both groups considered their instructors very helpful. Given the difficulties of implementing portfolios and of exposing students to a change in grading and evaluation, some instructors may find that portfolios produce negligible benefits *as far as students' attitudes are concerned.*

The central difficulty with implementing a portfolio approach is the uncertainty and discomfort that frequently arise when students assume increased responsibility for their learning. Creating a portfolio demands that students learn about themselves, that they trust themselves and their peers and their instructors, and that they pace and begin to evaluate themselves— and unfortunately this process of increasing metacognition, self-awareness, and responsibility for one's learning is largely anomalous in American education, where students frequently do only what they need to get by and instructors coerce them with the threat of poor grades. Jumping through academic hoops to get a grade is common. So when we dare to base writing instruction upon a portfolio pedagogy, we are truly revolutionary in our teaching and our learning.

Author's Note:

I extend special thanks to colleague Professor Lawrence Stedman, who reviewed this manuscript in an early stage and made helpful suggestions. In addition, I am grateful for summer grant-in-aid from The University of Alabama Research Grants program that supported one part of this research. Correspondence concerning this article should be addressed to C. Beth Burch, Division of Education, Academic 230, Binghamton University, SUNY, 13902-6000. The telephone number is 607.777.4697; FAXes may be directed to 607.777.6041 and electronic mail may be sent to <bburch@binghamton.edu>.

Notes

1. The figures cited in this paper were subjected to statistical analysis and were not found to be altogether significant. Nevertheless I believe them to be valuable indicators of difference and sites for future study.

2. Names of interviewees, who gave written permission for their words to be used, have been altered to maintain their anonymity.

3. Leon Festinger's (1964) theory of cognitive dissonance specifies that "the amount of dissonance that exists after a decision has been made is a direct function of the number of things the person knows that are inconsistent with that par-

ticular decision" (5). Thus a student's decision to accept a writing portfolio assign-ment (as opposed to choosing another section of composition or a different instructor or to failing a course) may be more troubling if the "number of things" the student knows about portfolios and writing is few and if the student is inex-perienced in the ways of academe.

Works Cited

Baker, N. W. (1993). The effect of portfolio-based instruction on composition stu-dents' final examination scores, course grades, and attitudes toward writing. *Research in Teaching English 27*, 2, 155–174.

Belanoff, P. & Dickson, M. (Eds.). (1991). *Portfolios: Process and product.* Portsmouth, NH: Boynton/Cook.

Belanoff, P. & Elbow, P. (1986). Using portfolios to increase collaboration and community in a writing program. *Writing Program Administrator 93*, 27–40.

Belanoff, P. & Elbow, P. (1986). Portfolios as a substitute for proficiency exami-nations. *College Composition and Communication 37*, 336–339.

Black, L., Daiker, D., Sommers, J., & Stygall, G. (Eds.). (1994). *New directions in portfolio assessment.* Portsmouth, NH: Heinemann.

Black, L., Daiker, D., Sommers, J., & Stygall, G. (1994). Writing like a woman and being rewarded for it: Gender, assessment, and reflective letters from Miami University's student portfolios. In L. Black, D. Daiker, J. Sommers, and G. Stygall, (Eds.), *New directions in portfolio assessment* (pp. 225–247). Portsmouth, NH: Heinemann.

Chodorow, N. (1978). The reproduction of mothering: *Psychoanalysis and the sociology of gender.* Berkeley: UC Press.

Festinger. L. (1964). *Conflict, decision, and dissonance.* Stanford, CA: Stanford UP.

Finders, Margaret. (1997). *Just girls: Hidden literacies and life in junior high.* New York: Teachers College Press.

Flynn, E. A. (1988). Composing as a woman. *College Composition and Com-munication 39*, 423–435.

Ford, J. E. & Larkin, G. (1978). The portfolio system: An end to backsliding writ-ing standards. *College English 39*, 950–955.

Gardiner, J. K. (1982). On female identity and writing by women. In E. Able (Ed.), *Writing and sexual difference* (pp. 177–192). Chicago: U of Chicago Press.

Gilligan, C. (1982). *In a different voice: Psychological theory and women's devel-opment.* Cambridge, MA: Harvard UP.

Graves, D. H. and B. Sunstein. (1993). *Portfolio portraits.* Portsmouth NH: Boynton/Cook.

Hamp-Lyons, L. and W. Condon. (1993). Questioning assumptions about portfo-lio-based assessment. *College Composition and Composition 44(2)*, 176–190.

Hewitt, G. (1995). *A portfolio primer: Teaching, collecting, and assessing student writing.* Portsmouth, NH: Heinemann.

Murphy, S. & Camp, R. (1996). Moving toward systemic coherence: A discussion of conflicting perspective on portfolio assessment. In R. Calfee & P. Perfumo (Eds.), *Writing portfolios in the classroom.* (pp. 103–148). Mahwah, NJ: Lawrence Erlbaum.

Overbeck, L. M. (1994). *Developing self-awareness about writing processes: The Perry model and the remedial writer.* (Report No. ED 246476). ERIC Document Reproduction Service.

Rose, S. K. (1990). Reading representative anecdotes of literacy practice; or "See Dick and Jane read and write." *Rhetoric Review 8(2),* 244–259.

Shay, S. (1997). Portfolio assessment: A catalyst for staff and curricular reform. *Assessing Writing 4(1),* 29–52.

Smit, D. W. Evaluating a portfolio system. (1990). *Writing Program Administration 14(1-2),* 51–62.

Tannen, D. (1990). *You just don't understand: Women and men in conversation.* New York: Ballantine.

Tierney, R. J., Carter, M., & Desai, L. *Portfolio assessment in the reading-writing classroom.* Norwood MA: Christopher Gordon.

Underwood, T. (1997). Portfolios on the precipice. *Assessing Writing 4(2),* 225–234.

Wiggins, G. (1993). *Assessing student performance.* San Francisco: Jossey Bass.

Yancey, K. B., (Ed.). (1992). *Portfolios in the writing classroom.* Urbana IL: National Council of Teachers of English.

III TECHNOLOGY

Articles and books on technology played a major role in postsecondary publication during 1999, with pieces on issues ranging from computers as word processors to the virtual university. As each practical technique for using digital technology is published, another one replaces it with a new adaptation incorporating more current technological advances. While it would be tempting to present articles and chapters on what seemed to be the most current technology of 1999, it is apparent that those techniques will soon be replaced with the next generation of technology, if indeed they haven't already been. But several articles raise thoughtful questions and ask us to reflect on the fundamental changes in our lives and work that are occurring because of these technological changes.

The first selection is Chris Anson's "Distant Voices: Teaching Writing in a Culture of Technology," which explores the university of the future with scenarios based on technology that is already available. Anson continually comes back to the questions and values of community, framing his essay with two personal journal entries that provoke a thoughtful understanding of technology as a human invention that embraces human values.

Those very human values that Anson asks us to reflect on are further elaborated in Cynthia Selfe's "Technology and Literacy: A Story about the Perils of Not Paying Attention." Both Anson and Selfe fully recognize that technology is a part of our lives, and Selfe extends this understanding by asking us and showing us how to pay attention to that technology. Literacy, as she aptly points out, has always been both a means of growth and a lever to control others' growth. If we are to fulfill our goals, we must pay attention to the literacy that technology permits, allows, and controls.

Lest we remain completely reflective, the next two articles point to the specifics of using technology to create a more universal literacy. In "The Shared Discourse of the Networked Computer Classroom," L. Lennie Irvin explains how to use technology to achieve interactive and personal communication through digital communication. A common litany objecting to distance education and electronic communication cites the faceless and therefore impersonal world it creates. Irvin shows how the virtual environment, used appropriately, can create a more personal world than many live classrooms.

The final offering in this section is the final chapter in *Weaving a Virtual Web: Practical Approaches to New Information Technology*. This volume is everything its title claims: a practical, inclusive compendium of current digital technology. Anyone involved in thinking about, administering, or teaching in a Web environment will find this collection indispensable. "The Craft of Teaching and the World Wide Web: A Reference Essay for Educators" by Kevin M. Leander is a great resource for finding and using Web resources.

9   Distant Voices: Teaching and Writing in a Culture of Technology

Chris M. Anson

> With the development of the Internet, and . . . networked comput-
> ers, we are in the middle of the most transforming technological event
> since the capture of fire.
>
> John Perry Barrlow, "Forum: What Are We Doing Online?" (36)

*August 3, Les Agettes, Switzerland. I am sitting on a veranda overlooking the
town of Sion some three thousand feet below, watching tiny airplanes take off
from the airstrip and disappear over the shimmering ridge of alps to the north.
Just below us is another chalet, the home of a Swiss family. At this time of day,
they gather at the large wooden table on the slate patio behind their home to
have a long, meandering lunch in the French Swiss tradition. Madame is
setting the table, opening a bottle of Valais wine, which grandpère ritually
pours out for the family and any friends who join them. As they sit to eat, the
scene becomes for me a vision of all that is most deeply social in human
affairs. They could not survive without this interconnectedness, this entwining
of selves, the stories passed around, problems discussed, identities shared and
nourished. For weeks, away from phones, TVs, computers, and electronic
mail, a dot on the rugged landscape of the southern Alps, I have a profound
sense of my own familial belonging, of how the four of us are made one by
this closeness of being. Just now Bernard, the little boy who lives on the
switchback above, has run down with his dog Sucrette to see if the kids can*

Reprinted from *College English*, January 1999.

play. He is here, standing before us, his face smudged with dirt, holding out a toy truck to entice the boys. For now, it is his only way to communicate with them, poised here in all his Bernard-ness, his whole being telling his story.

Not long after writing this journal entry and reflecting on how different my life had become during a summer without access to computers, I came across an issue of *Policy Perspectives*, a periodical issued by the Pew Higher Education Roundtable, which was intriguingly titled "To Dance with Change." When the *Policy Perspectives* began in 1988, the roundtable members believed that "the vitality of education would be defined by its ability to control costs, its capacity to promote learning, and its commitment to access and equity" (1). Less than a decade later, they had shifted their attention to forces beyond academia, realizing that they had been thinking of the institution itself without considering its connection to broader social pressures and movements. They conclude that "among the changes most important to higher education are those external to it"—economic, occupational, and technological. In particular, the electronic superhighway

> may turn out to be the most powerful external challenge facing higher education, and the one the academy is least prepared to understand. It is not that higher education institutions or their faculties have ignored technology. The academy, in fact, is one of the most important supporters and consumers of electronic technology. . . . The problem is that faculty—and hence the institutions they serve—have approached technology more as individual consumers than as collective producers. For the most part the new capacities conferred by electronic means have not enhanced the awareness that teaching might be conceived as something other than one teacher before a classroom of students. While academicians appreciate the leverage that technology has provided in the library and laboratory, they have not considered fully how the same technology might apply to the process of teaching and learning—and they have given almost no thought to how the same technologies in someone else's hands might affect their markets for student-customers. The conclusion that has escaped too many faculty is that this set of technologies is altering the market for even the most traditional goods and services, creating not only new products but new markets and, just as importantly, new providers. (3A)

In the context of our beliefs about how students best learn to write, many educators are haunted, like the Pew members, by a sense that bigger things are happening around us as we continue to refine classroom methods and tinker with our teaching styles. Theorists or researchers or just plain teachers, we spend much of our time working within the framework of certain fairly stable educational conditions. These conditions include physical spaces that define the social and interpersonal contexts of teaching: classrooms where we meet large or small groups of students, offices where we can consult with students face-to-face, and tutorial areas such as writing centers. We expect students to come to these places—even penalizing them for not doing so—and also to visit other physical spaces on campus such as libraries, where they carry out work connected with our instruction. The textual landscape of writing instruction also has a long and stable history: students write or type on white paper of a standard size and turn in their work, adhering to various admonitions about the width of their margins and the placement of periphera such as names, dates, and staples. Teachers collect the papers, respond in predictable places (in the margins or in the spaces left at the end) and return the papers at the institutional site. Innovations like portfolios are extensions of the use of this textual space, but the spaces themselves remain the same.

While the Pew Roundtable members may be concerned that faculty are not attentive to the frenzy of innovation in computer technology, it is difficult for them to make the same claim about academic administrations. Searching the horizon for signs of educational and institutional reform, administrators are often the first to introduce new campus-wide initiatives to the professoriate, who react with delight, resistance, apathy, or outrage to various proposals for change. In the climate of burgeoning developments in technology that have far-reaching consequences for teaching and learning, such changes will no doubt challenge existing ideologies of writing instruction, in part because of the assumed stability on which we have based our curricula and pedagogies.

In this essay, I will consider two of the ways in which teaching and responding to student writing are pressured by rapidly developing technologies now being introduced into our institutions. The first—the increasing replacement of face-to-face contact by "virtual" interaction—is the product of multimedia technology, email communication systems, and the recently expanded capabilities of the Word Wide Web. The second, somewhat more institutionally complex development is distance education, in which students hundreds or even thousands of miles apart are connected via interactive television systems. While these technologies offer an endless array of new and exciting possibilities for the improvement of education, they also frequently clash with some of our basic beliefs about the nature of classroom instruction, in all its communal richness and face-to-face complexity. Of even greater urgency is the need to understand the motivation for these developments. More specifically, new technologies introduced with the overriding goal of creating economic efficiencies and generating increased revenues may lead to even greater exploitation in the area of writing instruction, the historically maligned and undernourished servant of the academy. The key to sustaining our pedagogical advances in the teaching of writing, even as we are pulled by the magnetic forces of innovation, will be to take control of these technologies, using them in effective ways and not, in the urge for ever-cheaper instruction, substituting them for those contexts and methods that we hold to be essential for learning to write.

The Allure: Technology and Instructional Enhancement

Until recently, writing instruction has experienced the greatest technological impact from the personal computer, a tool that had an especially powerful effect on the teaching and practice of revision. The integration of the microcomputer into writing curricula seemed a natural outcome of our interests and prevailing ways of teaching: it offered students a screen on which they could manipulate texts, but they could still print out their writing and turn it in on paper.

Throughout the 1980s and 1990s, many writing programs experimented with labs or computerized classrooms where students could write to and with each other on local area networks. (For a historical account of computers in the teaching of writing, see Hawisher, Selfe, Moran, and LeBlanc.) Simultaneously, an array of computer-assisted instructional programs became available, allowing students to work through guided activities (typically alone) on a personal computer. Computer-generated questions could prompt students to invent ideas; style checkers could give them an index of their average sentence length or complexity; and outline programs could help them to map out the structure of their essays as they wrote. But even with all the cut-and-paste functions and floating footnotes that eased the writing process and facilitated revision, the "textuality" of academic essays remained relatively unchanged: students continued to meet in classrooms to work on their assignments, and teachers reacted to and assessed their products in conventional ways, by carrying the papers home and grading them. Personal computers offered students and teachers a new tool to practice the processes of writing, but the outcome still emerged, eventually, on paper.

In the field of composition studies, the development of more reasoned, theoretically informed methods of response to students' writing has been framed by assumptions about the perpetuation of these physical and textual spaces. Recent studies of response analyze marginal comments written on students' papers for various rhetorical or focal patterns (see, e.g., Straub; Straub and Lunsford; Smith). Studies that deliberately attend to the contextual factors that influence teachers' responses continue to do so within the traditional parameters of typed or handwritten papers turned in for (usual handwritten) response or assessment (e.g., Prior). While such work is much needed in the field, it largely ignores the sweep of change in the way that many students now create, store, retrieve, use, and arrange information (including text) in their academic work. Artificial intelligence expert Seymour Papert pictures a scenario in which a mid-nineteenth century surgeon is time-warped into a modern operating theater. Bewildered, the doctor would freeze, surrounded by unrecognizable technology and an utterly transformed profession, unsure of what to do or how to help. But if a mid-nineteenth century schoolteacher were similarly transported into a modern classroom, the teacher would feel quite at home. Recounting Papert's anecdote, Nicholas Negroponte points out that there is "little fundamental difference between the way we teach today and the way we did one hundred and fifty years ago. The use of technology is at almost at the same level. In fact, according to a recent survey by the U.S. Department of Education, 84 percent of America's teachers consider only one type of information technology absolutely 'essential' to their work—a photocopier with an adequate paper supply" (220). Yet most statistics show the use of computers, particularly by students in high school and college, increasing at lightning speed. Today, more than one-third of American homes already have a computer, and it is predicted that by 2005 Americans will spend more time on the Internet than watching TV.

That personal computers have done little to disrupt our decades-old habits of working with and responding to students' writing is partly because the channels of electronic media have been separate and discrete. Video has been kept apart from computer text, audio systems, and still pictures, requiring us to use different equipment for each technology (and allowing us to focus on computer text to the exclusion of other media). Whether teachers focus on text to the exclusion of other media is not really the point; as Pamela McCorduck points out, "knowledge of different kinds is best represented in all its complexity for different purposes by different kinds of knowledge representations. Choosing *la représentation juste* (words, images, or anything else) is not at all an obvious thing: in fact, it's magnificently delicate. But we have not had much choice until now because text, whether the best representation for certain purposes or not, has dominated our intellectual lives" (259).

The introduction of hypertext and multimedia refocused attention on the relationship between text and other forms of representation. Experimenting with new technology, teachers of literature dragged laptops and heavy projection equipment into their classrooms and displayed stored multimedia Web sites to students reading *Emma* or *King Lear;* linking such texts to their social and political contexts, revealing connections to pieces of art of the time, playing segments of music that the characters might have heard, or showing brief video clips of famous stage presentations. Early advocates of multimedia in teaching and learning clearly framed its advantages in terms that emphasized the process of absorbing information, however innovatively that information might be structured, and however freely the user might navigate through multiple, hierarchically arranged connections (see, for example, Landow). Multimedia was something *presented* and perhaps *explored*, but it was not "answerable." In all their activity as creators of their own knowledge, students remained relatively passive, now receiving deposits of knowledge from automatic teller machines that supplemented the more direct, human method.

But that situation, as Negroponte has suggested, is rapidly changing, creating potentially profound implications for the delivery and mediation of instruction in schools and colleges. Within a few years, the disparate channels of video, audio, and computerized text and graphics—channels that come to us via airwaves, TV cable, phone cable, CD-ROM and computer disks—will merge into a single set of bits sent back and forth along one electronic highway at lightning speed. Our equipment will selectively manipulate this information to produce various outputs, a process already visible in the rapidly developing multimedia capabilities of the World Wide Web. In turn, users can assemble information and send it back (or out) along the same highway. The effect on both the production and reception of writing may be quite dramatic. Modern newspapers, for example, which are already produced electronically, may largely disappear in their paper form:

> The stories are often shipped in by reporters as e-mail. The pictures are digitized and frequently transmitted by wire as well. And the page layout . . . is done with computer-aided design systems, which prepare the data for transfer to film or direct engraving onto plates. This is to say that the entire conception and construction of the newspaper is digital, from beginning to end, until the very last step, when

> ink is squeezed onto dead trees. This step is where bits become atoms.
> . . . Now imagine that the last step does not happen . . . but that the
> bits are delivered to you as bits. You may elect to print them at home
> for all the conveniences of hard copy. . . . Or you may prefer to down-
> load them into your laptop, palmtop, or someday into your perfectly
> flexible, one-hundredth-of-an-inch thick, full-color, massively high
> resolution, large-format, waterproof display. (Negroponte 56)

In the educational realm, the new capabilities emerging from multimedia
technology offer many alternatives for teaching and learning, and for
assigning and responding to writing, particularly as "papers" and "written
responses" are replaced by electronic data. Imagine, for example, a college
student (call her Jennifer) coming into the student union a few years from
now. She pulls from her backpack a full-color, multimedia computer
"tablet," just half an inch thick, plugs it into a slot on a little vending
machine, puts three quarters into the machine, and downloads the current
issue of *USA Today*. Over coffee, she reads the paper on the tablet, watching
video clips of some events and listening to various sound bites. She finds a
story of relevance to a project she is working on and decides to clip and save
it in the tablet's memory. Then she deletes the paper.

Jennifer's first class of the day is still remembered as a "lecture course" in
history, but the lecture material has been converted into multimedia
presentations stored on CD-ROM disks (which the students dutifully buy at
the bookstore or download onto massive hard drives from a server, paying
with a credit card). Students experience the lectures alone and meet
collectively only in recitation sections. Because her recitation begins in an
hour and she did not finish the assignment the night before, Jennifer heads
for one of the learning labs. There, she navigates through the rest of a
multimedia presentation while handwriting some notes on her tablet and
saving them into memory. She is impressed with the program, and justifiably:
the institution is proud to have an exclusive contract with a world-famous
historian (now living overseas) for the multimedia course.

The recitation is held in a room fully equipped for distance learning.
Cameras face the students and teacher. Enormous, high-resolution monitors
provide a view of two distant classes, each located a hundred miles away on
smaller campuses. Jennifer sits at one of seventy-five computer stations. The
first half of the class involves a discussion of some of the multimedia course
material. The recitation coordinator (a non-tenure-track education specialist)
brings the three sites together using artful techniques of questioning and
response. After raising a number of issues which appear on a computerized
screen from his control computer, the coordinator asks the three classes to

discuss the issues. Students pair off electronically, writing to each other; some students at the main site pair with students at the distant sites, selected automatically by the instructor using an electronic seating chart and a program that activates the connections for each pair.

After the recitation, Jennifer remembers that she is supposed to send a revised draft of a paper to her composition instructor. She heads for another lab, where she accesses her electronic student file and finds a multimedia message from her instructor. The instructor's face appears on her screen in a little window, to one side of Jennifer's first draft. As Jennifer clicks on various highlighted passages or words, the instructor's face becomes animated in a video clip describing certain reactions and offering suggestions for revision. After working through the multimedia commentary and revising her draft, Jennifer then sends the revision back electronically to her instructor. Jennifer has never actually met her teacher, who is one of many part-time instructor/tutors hired by the semester to "telecommute" to the institution from their homes.

Because Jennifer is a privileged, upper-middle-class student who has a paid subscription to an online service, her own high-end computer system and modem, and the money to buy whatever software she needs for her studies, she can continue her schoolwork at home. There, she uses her multimedia computer to study for a psychology course offered by a corporation. On the basis of nationally normed assessments, the corporation has shown that its multimedia course achieves educational outcomes equal to or greater than those provided by many well-ranked colleges and universities. Jennifer will be able to transfer the course into her curriculum because the corporation's educational division has been recently accredited. She also knows that, as multimedia courses go, this one is first-rate: the corporation is proud to have an exclusive contract with its teacher-author, a world-famous psychologist. As she checks the courseline via email, she notices that a midterm is coming up. She decides to schedule it for an "off" day, since she will have to go to one of the corporation's nearby satellite centers to take the test at a special computer terminal that scores her answers automatically and sends the results to her via email.

Later that day, Jennifer decides to spend an hour doing some research for her history project. From her home computer, she uses various internet search programs to find out more about the Civil War battle of Manassas. On her high-resolution, 30-inch monitor (which also doubles as a TV and video player), she reads text, looks at drawings, opens video and audio files, and locates bibliographic material on her topic. She also finds some sites where

Civil War aficionados share information and chat about what they know. She sends and receives some messages through the list, then copies various bits of information and multimedia into her computer, hoping to weave them into her report, which itself may include photos, video clips, and audio recordings. Due in less than three weeks, the report must be added (quite simply) to a privately accessed course Web site so that one of the several teaching assistants can retrieve it, grade and comment briefly on it, and send it back to Jennifer with an assessment. Just before she quits her research to watch some rock videos from the massive archives in a subscription server, Jennifer locates a Web site at another college where the students had researched the Civil War. The site includes all twenty-six projects created by the students; one focuses for several electronic pages on the battle at Manassas. Intrigued, Jennifer copies the pages into her computer, intending to look at them carefully the next day and perhaps use parts of them in her own multimedia project.

While this scenario may seem futuristic, much of the technology Jennifer experiences is already here or soon to be. The Knight-Ridder Corporation, for example, has recently developed a prototype of Jennifer's multimedia news "tablet" weighing about two pounds (Leyden). The Web now has the capability to send software to the receiver along with the actual information requested, and this software enhances the user's capacities to work with the information. Programs are currently available that allow teachers to open a student's paper onscreen and scroll through it to a point where a comment might be made to the student. At that point, an icon can be deposited that starts up a voice-recording device. The teacher then talks to the student about the paper. Further marginal or intertextual icons encase further voice comments. Opening the paper on disk at home, the student notices the icons and, activating them, listens to the teacher's response and advice. Computers with tiny videocameras are already enabling a picture-in-picture window that shows the teacher's image talking to the student as if face-to-face. The technology that now provides teleconferencing, when merged with Web-like storage and retrieval devices, will easily facilitate "one-way" tutorials that project audio and video images from a teacher, superimposed over typed text on which marks, corrections, and marginal notes can be recorded "live," like the replay analyses during televised football games.

When demonstrated, such advances may dazzle teachers because we see them as a promise to simplify our lives and streamline our work. New technologies often seem to improve our working conditions and provide better ways to help our students (seasoned teachers, as they stand at the computer-controlled reducing/collating/stapling photocopier, have only to reminisce about the old fluid-and-ink ditto machines to feel these advantages quite tangibly). Teaching, too, seems if not eased, affected in ways that enhance students' experiences. Positive accounts already show that email can help students to form study groups, interact with their teachers, or carry on academic discussions with students at other locations all over the world. In one experiment, students in an all-black freshman composition course at Howard University teamed up with a class of predominantly white students in graphic design at Montana State University to create a 32-page publication, *On the Color Line: Networking to End Racism*. Using digital scanners and email, the students and teachers were able to bring together two classes 1,600 miles apart to critique each other's work, discuss race-related views, and collaboratively produce a pamphlet (Blumenstyk). Many other accounts of networked classrooms suggest increased participation among marginalized groups (see, for example, Selfe, "Technology"; Bump).

Curiously, these and other positive accounts almost always describe adaptations of new technologies as ancillary methods within classrooms where students interact with each other and with their teacher. In a typical computerized grade-school class, for example, a student might use email to ask kids around the world to rank their favorite chocolates as part of a project focusing on *Charlie and the Chocolate Factory*; but then the entire class tallies the results and shares the conclusions (Rector). At the college level, Rich Holeton describes his highly networked electronic writing classroom and its advantages, especially in the area of electronic groups and discussions, yet still sees face-to-face interaction as the "main action" of the course and electronic techniques as "supplementary." Similarly, Tom Creed discusses the many ways he integrates computer technology into his classrooms, but finds it essential to create cooperative learning groups and build in time for students to make stand-up presentations to the class. Electronic innovations, in other words, appear to be carefully controlled, integrated into the existing curriculum in principled ways that do not erode the foundations on which the teacher-experimenters already base their instructional principles. Recognizing the importance of this configuration, some educators much prefer the term "technology-enhanced learning" to other terms that imply a radical shift in the actual delivery of education, such as "technologized instruction."

Because of improvements in educational software and hardware, however, our profession will feel increased pressure to offer technologically enhanced "independent study" courses. Some campuses are already experiencing dramatic differences in students' use of communal spaces with the introduction of dorm-room email. Clifford Stoll, a former Harvard University researcher and author of *Silicon Snake Oil: Second Thoughts on the Information Highway*, claims that by turning college into a "cubicle-directed electronic experience," we are "denying the importance of learning to work closely with other students and professors, and developing social adeptness" (qtd. in Gabriel). Students may be psychodynamiclly separated from one another even while inhibiting the same campus or dorm building; even more profound effects may be felt when students and faculty use advanced technologies to link up with each other in a course without ever meeting in person. Although many studies and testimonials affirm the ways that internet chat lines, listservs, email, and other "virtual spaces" can actually increase the social nature of communication, there is no doubt that the physical isolation of each individual from the others creates an entirely different order of interaction.

Distance, Independence, and the Transformation of Community

The teaching of writing, unlike some other disciplines, is founded on the assumption that students learn well by reading and writing with each other, responding to each other's drafts, negotiating revisions, discussing ideas, sharing perspectives, and finding some level of trust as collaborators in their mutual development. Teaching in such context is interpersonal and interactive, necessitating small class size and a positive relationship between the teacher and the students. At the largest universities, such classed taken in the first year are often the only place where students can get to know each other, creating and participating in an intimate community of learning. Large lecture courses, driven by the transmission and retrieval of information, place students in a more passive role. In her book on the effect of college entrance examinations on the teaching of English, Mary Trachel points out that the "factory" model of education, which privileges standardized testing and the "input" of discrete bits of information, is at odds with our profession's instructional ideals, which align more comfortably with those of theorists like Paulo Freire:

> The model for [authentic education] is that of a dialogue in which hierarchical divisions are broken down so that teachers become teacher-learners, and learners become learner-teachers. Educational values are thus determined not by a mandate to perpetuate an established academic tradition but by local conditions and by the emerging purposes and realizations of educators and learners in social interaction with one another. This socially situated version of

education stands in opposition to the "banking concept" of
traditionally conceived schooling. (12)

For such ideological reasons, the teaching of writing by correspondence
or "independent study" has always lived uneasily within programs that also
teach students in classrooms. Although such instruction can be found at
many institutions, few theorists strongly advocate a pedagogy in which
students write alone, a guide of lessons and assignments at their elbows to
provide the material of their "course," a remote, faceless grader hired by the
hour to read assignments the students send through the mail and mail back
responses. Next to classrooms with rich face-to-face social interaction—
fueled by active learning, busy with small groups, energized by writers
reading each other's work, powered by the forces of revision and response—
independent study in writing appears misguided.

But in the context of our convictions about writing and response, new
technologies now offer educational institutions the chance to expand on the
idea of individualized learning. Online communication with students is an
idea that seems stale by now but is by no means fully exploited; only some
teachers eagerly invite email from students, and only some students end up
using it when invited. Those faculty who value their autonomy and privacy
find that email makes them better able to control when and where students
enter their lives. Departments at many universities are requiring faculty to
use email by giving them computers, hooking them up, offering workshops
on how to use them, and then saying that faculty have no excuse for not
voting on such and such an issue or not turning in their book orders on time.
The results have already been felt on many campuses, as meetings give way
to electronic communion, turning some departments into ghost haunts. Very
few universities have developed policies that disallow the use of online
office hours in place of physical presence on campus. As teachers across the
country realize the tutorial potential of electronic media, such media may
come to substitute for direct contact with students. For faculty busy with their
own work, the gains are obvious: consultation by convenience, day or night;
freedom from physical space; copyable texts instead of ephemeral talk.

From a more curricular perspective, the concept of independent study is
rapidly changing from its roots in study manuals and the US Postal Service to
a technology-rich potential for students to learn at their own pace, in their
own style, with fingertip access to an entire world of information.
Multimedia computers using text, sound, video, and photos provide
opportunities to bring alive old-fashioned text-only materials. But it is not just
independent-study programs, usually seen as ancillary to "real" education,

that will change: multimedia could transform the very essence of classroom instruction. At many institutions, administrators are realizing that creating a state-of-the-art multimedia course out of, for example, "Introduction to Psychology," which may enroll up to five hundred students, represents a major improvement. The quality of faculty lectures is uneven; they come at a high cost; and they are often delivered in settings not conducive to learning—hot, stuffy lecture halls with poor sound systems and ailing TV monitors hung every few rows. In the converted version, a student can choose when to work through a multimedia presentation in a computer lab, can learn at her own pace, can review fundamental concepts, can download some information for later study, and can even test her developing knowledge as she learns. In such situations, as journalist Peter Leyden writes, "the time-honored role of the teacher almost certainly will change dramatically. No longer will teachers be the fonts of knowledge with all the answers that [students] seek. They can't possibly fill that role in the coming era" (2T).

In itself, multimedia technology has not directly challenged the field of composition. True, many educators are working on integrating into their research-paper units some instruction on citing electronic sources, searching the Web, or using online databases. The prospect of a teacherless and "community-less" course, however, creates much debate in the composition community, where many see computers as poor substitutes for old-fashioned forms of human interaction. In areas involving context-bound thinking, Stanley Aronowitz maintains, "knowledge of the terrain must be obtained more by intuition, memory, and specific knowledge of actors or geography than by mastering logical rules . . . Whatever its psychological and biological presuppositions, the development of thinking is profoundly shaped and frequently altered by multiple determinations, including choices made by people themselves" (130-31). In the face of the trend to increasing "indirectness" of teaching, Charles Moran argues, "we will need to be more articulate than we have yet been in describing the benefits of face-to-face teaching, or what our British colleagues call "live tuition" (208).

New technologies are also giving a strong boost to distance learning. Like the concept of independent study, distance learning too may powerfully affect the way in which we teach and respond to students. In distance learning, students actually participate in the classroom—they are just not there, physically. Beamed in by cable or broadcast, their personae are represented on TV monitors, which, as the idea expands, are becoming larger and gaining in resolution. As classrooms become better equipped, students at several sites will work in virtual classrooms, writing to and for each other at terminals. Teachers can pair students, using small cameras and monitors at their desks, and then regroup the classes at the different sites for larger discussions using the bigger screens.

Institutions are attracted to the concept of distance education for reasons obvious in times of fiscal constraint. Students register for a single course from two or more sites, generating tuition revenue for the parent institution. A course previously taught by several salaried faculty (each on location, hundreds of miles apart) now needs only one main teacher, aided by non-tenure-track staff "facilitator-graders" or teaching assistants hired inexpensively at the different locations. If small satellite sites are created, sometimes in available spaces such as public schools, community centers, or libraries, new revenue sources can be exploited in remote areas. Even after the cost of the interactive television equipment and link-up is calculated, distance education can generate profit for the institution at reduced cost, using its existing faculty resources as "lead teachers." Such an arrangement is especially attractive to institutions used to delivering instruction via the traditional "banking" model of lectures and objectively scorable tests.

Distance learning is also allowing some pairs or groups of institutions to consolidate resources by sharing programs with each other. Imagine that University A realizes that its Swahili language program does not have the resources to compete with the Swahili language program at University B; but it does have a nationally recognized Lakota language program. Unfortunately, the Lakota program is not very cost-effective, in spite of its standing, because its student cohort is so small. Likewise, University B recognizes that its own Lakota language program pales by comparison with University A's, yet it boasts a particularly strong Swahili program similarly suffering from its inability to generate profits for the school. Using sophisticated interactive television and multimedia resources, the two institutions team up to exchange programs, swapping the tuition revenues along with their instructional programs. As technology keeps expanding and becoming refined, collaborations like these will become increasingly popular, even necessary. In part, these ideas save money. In part, they also respond to growing competition from non-academic providers of education, a major threat to our present institutions. By collaborating to deliver the "best" programs possible, the institutions protect themselves against the intrusion of industry, of what the Pew Roundtable calls "high-quality, lower-cost educational programming conjoined with the rising demand for postsecondary credentials that creates the business opportunity for higher education's would-be competitors" (3). But the result is almost certain to be a continued reduction in full-time, tenure-track faculty and an increased reliance on modes of instructional delivery that physically distance students from each other and from their mentors.

Practically speaking, the idea of distance learning seems reasonable in the context of Lakota and Swahili—it saves duplication of effort, it cuts costs, it may lead to increased institutional collaboration, and it offers students at different locations the chance to be taught, in some sense of the word, by high-quality teachers. It is when the prospect of fully interactive, technologically advanced distance learning conflicts with our most principled educational theories that we feel an ideological clash. Long privileged in composition instruction, for example, is the interactive teaching style. Writing teachers arrange and participate in small groups in the classroom, talk with students before and after class, walk with them to other buildings, meet them in offices, and encourage students to respond to each other instead of through the teacher. Distance learning has yet to overcome the virtuality of its space to draw all students interpersonal relationships. Teachers often report feeling detached from the students at the distant sites, unable to carry on "extracurricular" conversations with them. The savings promised by distance education come from the elimination of trained professionals who reduce teacher-student ratios and offer meaningful consultation with students, face to face. If distance learning becomes the norm in fields where general education courses are usually delivered in large lectures with little chance for students to learn actively or interact with each other or the teacher, it will not be long before writing programs are encouraged to follow suit.

In exploring the concept of humans in cyberspace, we can find, as Anna Cicognani has found, many of the same conditions as those we experience in physical space: social interaction; logical and formal abstractions; linguistic form; corresponding organizations of time; the possibility for rhetorical action; and so on. But it is, finally, a "hybrid space, a system which is part of another but only refers to itself and its own variables." It belongs to the main system of space, but "claims independence from it at the same time." Cicognani's representation of cyberspace as a hybrid, which still allows communities to form and develop but relies for its existence on the physical space from which is has been created, offers a useful metaphor for the continued exploration of the relationships between education and computer technology, as the latter is carefully put to use in the improvement of the former. Yet to be considered, however, are broader questions about the role of teachers in technology-rich educational settings.

Response, Technology, and the Future of Teaching

The quality of faculty interaction with students is a product of our *work*—our training, the material conditions at our institutions, how much support we get for developing our teaching and keeping up on research. While to this point we have been reflecting on the possible effects of new technologies on the quality of students' learning experiences and contexts, we must also consider ways in which colleges and universities, as places of employment, may change.

Teachers of composition continue to argue that writing programs provide an important site for active and interactive learning in higher education. Our national standards have helped to keep classes small; our lobbying continues to call attention to the exploitation of part-time faculty. We argue the need for support services, such as writing centers, tutors, and ESL programs. And, in writing-across-the-curriculum programs, we have helped to integrate the process approach in various disciplines and courses with considerable success. But the current cost-cutting fervor will continue to erode these principles. Massy and Wilger argue, for example, that "most faculty have yet to internalize the full extent of the economic difficulties facing higher education institutions, both public and private. . . . [F]ew faculty take seriously the current fiscal constraints. Most believe that the problems are not as significant as administrators and others warn, or that the conditions are only temporary" (25).

As teachers, our own occupational space is clearly defined. We "belong" to a particular institution, which pays us, and the students get our instruction, consultation, expertise, and time in exchange for their tuition or, in public schooling, the revenues generated by local taxes and other local, state, and federal funds. Yet technology will soon change not only how we work within our institutions but also how "attached" we may be to an institution, particularly if we can work for several institutions at some physical (but not electronic) remove from each other. In an article in the Information Technology Annual Report of *Business Week*, Edward Baig lists by category the percentage of sites that plan additional "telecommuters"—"members of the labor force who have chosen to, or have been told to, work anywhere, anytime—as long as it's not in the office" (59). Higher education is placed at the very top of the heap, with over 90 percent of sites planning to increase telecommuting.

Universities once looked upon computer technology as an expense and a luxury; increasingly it is now seen as an investment that will lead to increased revenues and reduced expenses. The standards of work defined by the Conference on College Composition and Communication have not anticipated a new vision of writing instruction involving low-paid reader-responders, tutorial "assistants" for CD-ROM courses taken "virtually" by independent study, or coordinators at interactive television sites where students from many campuses link to a single site requiring only one "master professor." Robert Heterick, writing for Educom, predicts a major shift in resource allocation across institutions of higher education:

> The infusion of information technology into the teaching and learning domain will create shifts in the skill requirements of faculty from instructional delivery to instructional design . . . with faculty being responsible for course content and information technologists being responsible for applying information technology to the content. These changes will increase the number of students the institutions can service without corresponding increases in the need for student daily-life support facilities. (3)

In the area of composition, part-time telecommuters, supplied with the necessary equipment, could become the primary providers of instruction to many students. At some locations, private industry is already exploring the possibility of supplying writing instruction, using technology, to institutions interested in "outsourcing" this part of their curriculum. In the *Adjunct Advocate*, a newsletter for part-time and temporary writing teachers, instructors have expressed considerable concern about administrators" requests that they teach sections of introductory composition via the Internet (see Lesko; Wertner). The "profound change in work" represented by advanced technology may also further isolate women. Although the computer once promised to level gender discrimination by removing direct identity from online forums, some social critics are now seeing the potential for new inequities in the labor force. In her contribution to Susan Leigh Star's *The Cultures of Computing*, for example, Randi Markussen takes up the question of "why gender relations seem to change so little through successive waves of technological innovation" (177). Technology promises the "empowerment" of workers, but it also reinforces and more strongly imposes the measurement of work in discrete units. In her analysis of the effects of technology on practicing nurses, Markussen notes that instead of "empowering" employees by making their work more visible or supporting their demands for better staffing and pay, new computer technology actually places greater demands on nurses to account for their work in "categories of work time," decreasing the need for "interpersonal task synchronization" and cooperation with other people. "The transformation of work," Markussen writes, "puts new demands on nurses in terms of relating the formalized electronic depiction of work to caregiving activities, which may still be considered residual and subordinate" (172).

Like nursing, composition has been positively constructed through its preoccupation with the development of the individual and the creation of an engaging, student-focused classroom. Yet composition likewise suffers from higher education's continued attitude that it serves a "residual and subordinate" role, necessary for "remediation." This gross misconception of the value of writing instruction is directly linked to employment practices at hundreds of colleges and universities, where large numbers of "service professionals," a majority of them women, are hired into low-paid, non-tenurable positions with poor (or no) benefits. With the potential for the further automation of writing instruction through the use of telecommuting and other technology-supported shifts in instructional delivery, composition may be further subordinated to the interests of powerful subject-oriented disciplines where the conception of expertise creates rather different patterns of hiring and material support.

Our key roles—as those who create opportunities and contexts for students to write and who provide expert, principled response to that writing—must change in the present communications and information revolution. But we cannot let the revolution sweep over us. We need to guide it, resisting its economic allure in cases where it weakens the principles of our teaching. The processes of technology, even when they are introduced to us by administrations more mindful of balancing budgets than enhancing lives, will not threaten us as long as we, as educators, make decisions about the worth of each innovation, about ways to put it to good use, or about reasons why it should be rejected out of hand. More sustained, face-to-face discussions—at conferences and seminars, at faculty development workshops, and in routine departmental and curricular meetings—can give us hope that we can resist changes that undermine what we know about good teaching and sound ways of working. Such discussions are often difficult. They are highly political, painfully economic, and always value-laden and ideological. But as teachers of writing and communication, we have an obvious investment in considering the implications of technology for working, teaching, and learning, even as that technology is emerging.

Because technology is advancing at an unprecedented rate, we must learn to assess the impact of each new medium, method, or piece of software on our students' learning. Most of the time, such assessments will take place locally (for example, as a genetics program decides whether it is more effective for students to work with real drosophila flies or manipulate a virtual drosophila world using an interactive computer program). But we also urgently need broader, institution-wide dialogues about the effect of technology on teaching, particularly between students, faculty, and administrators. Deborah Holdstein has pointed out that as early as 1984 some compositionists were already critiquing the role of computers in writing instruction; "caveats regarding technology . . . have always been an important sub-text in computers and composition studies, the sophistication of self-analysis, one hopes, maturing with the field" (283). Among the issues she proposes for further discussion are those of access, class, race, power, and gender; she questions, for example,

> those who would assert without hesitation that email, the Net, and the Web offer us, finally, a nirvana of ultimate democracy and freedom, suggesting that even visionaries such as Tuman and Lanham beg the question of access, of the types of literacies necessary to even gain access to email, much less to the technology itself. What *other* inevitable hierarchies—in addition to the ones we know and understand . . . —will be formed to order us as we "slouch toward cyberspace"? (283)

While it is impossible to overlook not only that advanced learning technologies are here to stay but that they are in a state of frenzied innovation, Holdstein's admonishments remind us of the power of thoughtful critique and interest punctuated by caution. In addition to the issues she raises, we can profit by engaging in more discussions about the following questions:

1. What will multimedia do to alter the personae of teachers and students as they respond to each other virtually? How do new communication technologies change the relationships between teachers and students? Recent research on small-group interaction in writing classes, for example, shows labyrinthine complexity, as demonstrated in Thomas Newkirk's study of students' conversational roles. What do we really know about the linguistic, psycho-social, and pedagogical effects of online communication when it replaces traditional classroom-based interaction? (See Eldred and Hawisher's fascinating synthesis of research on how electronic networking affects various dimensions of writing practice and instruction.)

2. How might the concept of a classroom community change with the advent of new technologies? What is the future of collaborative learning in a world in which "courseware" may increasingly replace "courses"?

3. What are the consequences of increasing the distance between students and teachers? Is the motivation for distance education financial or pedagogical? Will the benefits of drawing in isolated clients outweigh the disadvantages of electronically "isolating" even those who are nearby?

4. What will be the relationship between "human" forms of response to writing and increasingly sophisticated computerized responses being developed in industry?

5. How will the conditions of our work change as a result of increasing access to students via telecommunications? Who will hire us to read students' writing? Will we work at home? Will educational institutions as physical entities disappear, as Alvin Toffler is predicting, to be replaced by a core of faculty who can be commissioned from all over the world to deliver instruction and response via the electronic highway? What new roles will teachers, as expert responders, play in an increasingly electronic world?

6. What are the implications of telecommuting for the hiring and support of teachers? Could technology reduce the need for the physical presence of instructors, opening the door to more part-time teachers hired at low wages and few benefits?

7. How will writing instruction compete with new, aggressive educational offerings from business and industry? What will be the effects of competing with such offerings for scarce student resources?

If we can engage in thoughtful discussions based on questions such as these, we will be better prepared to make principled decisions about the effect of new technologies on our students' learning and the conditions of our teaching. And we will be more likely, amid the dazzle of innovation, to reject those uses of technology that will lead to bad teaching, poor learning, unfair curricular practices, and unjust employment.

August 21, Les Agettes, Switzerland. I have met the family below. They tell me grandpère has lost some of his memory. He often spends part of the day breaking up stones, clack, clack, clack, behind the chalet. It's not disturbing, they hope. We haven't noticed, I say. We talk almost aimlessly, wandering around topics. Have we met the priest who rents an apartment below the chalet? Can they tell me what the local school is like? We talk about learning, about computers. As if scripted by the ad agency for IBM, they tell me they are interested in the Internet; their friends have computers, and they may get one too, soon. Later, gazing down toward the bustling town of Sion, I wonder how their lives will change. I imagine them ordering a part for their car over the computer without ever catching up on news with Karl, the guy at the garage near the river. Yet I'm also optimistic. They will use email someday soon, and I can get their address from my brother and write them messages in bad French, and they can share them during their long lunches on the patio, where they still gather to eat and laugh, turning my text back into talk.

Works Cited

Aronowitz, Stanley. "Looking Out: The Impact of Computers on the Lives of Professionals." Tuman 119–38.

Baig, Edward C. "Welcome to the Officeless Office." *Business Week* (Information Technology Annual Report, International Edition) 26 June 1995: 59–60.

Barlow, John Perry, Sven Birkerts, Kevin Kelly, and Mark Slouka. "Forum: What Are We Doing Online?" *Harper's Magazine* Aug. 1995: 35–46.

Blumenstyk, Goldie. "Networking to End Racism." *Chronicle of Higher Education* 22 Sept. 1995: A35–A39.

Bump, Jerome. "Radical Changes in Class Discussion Using Networked Computers." *Computers and the Humanities* 24 (1990): 49–65.

Cicognani, Anna. "On the Linguistic Nature of Cyberspace and Virtual Communities." <http://www.arch.usyd.edu.au/~anna/papers/even96.htm>

Creed, Tom. "Extending the Classroom Walls Electronically." *New Paradigms for College Teaching.* Ed. William E. Campbell and Karl A. Smith. Edina, MN: Interaction, 1997. 149–84.

Eldred, Janet Carey, and Gail E. Hawisher. "Researching Electronic Networks." *Written Communication* 12.3 (1995): 330–59.

Gabriel, Trip. "As Computers Unite Campuses, Are They Separating Students?" *Minneapolis Star Tribune* 12 Nov. 1996: A5.

Hawisher, Gail E., Cynthia L. Selfe, Charles Moran, and Paul LeBlanc. *Computers and the Teaching of Writing in American Higher Education, 1979–1994: A History.* Norwood, NJ: Ablex, 1996.

Heterick, Robert. "Operating in 90's <http:/ivory.educom.edu:70/00/educom.info/html>

Holdstein, Deborah. "Power, Genre, and Technology." *College Composition and Communication* 47. (1996): 279–84

Holteton, Rich. "The Semi-Virtual Composition Classroom: A Model for Techn-Amphibians." *Notes in the Margins* Spring 1996: 1, 14–17, 19.

Landow, George. "Hypertext, Metatext, and the Electronic Canon." Tuman 67–94.

Lesko, P. D. "Adjunct Issues in the Media." *The Adjunct Advocate* March/April 1996: 22–27.

Leyden, Peter. "The Changing Workscape." Special Report, Part III. *Minneapolis Star Tribune* 18 June 1995: 2T–6T.

Markussen, Randi. "Constructing Easiness: Historical Perspectives on Work, Computerization, and Women." *The Cultures of Computing.* Ed. Susan Leigh Star. Oxford: Blackwell, 1995. 158–80.

Massy, William F., and Andrea K. Wilger. "Hollowed Collegiality: Implications for Teaching Quality." Paper presented at the Second AAHE Annual Conference on Faculty Roles and Rewards, New Orleans, 29 Jan. 1994.

McCorduck, Pamela. "How We Knew, How We Know, How We Will Know." Tuman 245–59.

Moran, Charles. "Review: English and Emerging Technologies." *College English* 60.2 (1998): 202–9

Negroponte, Nicholas. *Being Digital.* New York: Knopf, 1995.

Newkirk, Thomas. "The Writing Conference as Performance." *Research in the Teaching of English* 29.2 (1996): 19–215.

Pew Higher Education Roundtable. "To Dance with Change." *Policy Perspectives* 5.3 (1994): 1A–12A.

Prior, Paul. "Contextualizing Writing and Response in a Graduate Seminar." *Written Communication* 8 (1991): 267–310.

———. "Tracing Authoritative and Internally Persuasive Discourses: A Case Study of Response, Revision, and Disciplinary Enculturation." *Research in the Teaching of English* 29 (1995): 288–325.

Rector, Lucinda. "Where Excellence is Electronic." *Teaching and Technology* Summer 1996: 10–14. <http://www.time.com/teach>

Selfe, Cynthia. "Literacy, Technology, and the Politics of Education in America." Chair's Address, Conference on College Composition and Communication, Chicago 2 April 1998.

———. "Technology in the English Classroom: Computers Through the Lens of Feminist Theory." *Computers and Community: Teaching Composition in the Twenty-First Century.* Ed. Carolyn Handa. Portsmouth, NH: Boynton/Cook, 1990. 118–39.

Smith, Summer. "The Genre of the End Comment: Conventions in Teacher Responses to Student Writing." *College Composition and Communication* 48.2 (1997): 249–68.

Stoll, Clifford. *Silicon Snake Oil: Second Thoughts on the Information Highway.* New York: Doubleday, 1995.

Straub, Richard. "The Concept of Control in Teacher Response: Defining the Varieties of 'Directive' and 'Facilitative' Commentary." *College Composition and Communication* 47.2 (1996): 223–51.

Straub, Richard, and Ronald F. Lunsford. *Twelve Readers Reading: Responding to College Student Writing.* Cresskill: Hampton, 1995.

Trachsel, Mary. *Institutionalizing Literacy.* Carbondale, IL: Southern Illinois UP, 1992.

Tuman, Myron C., ed. *Literacy Online: The Promise (and Peril) of Reading and Writing with Computers.* Pittsburgh: U of Pittsburgh P, 1992

Wertner, B. "The Virtual Classroom" (letter to the editor). *The Adjunct Advocate* May/June 1996: 6.

10 Technology and Literacy: A Story about the Perils of Not Paying Attention

Cynthia L. Selfe

Technological literacy—meaning computer skills and the ability to
use computers and other technology to improve learning, productivity and performance—has become as fundamental to a person's
ability to navigate through society as traditional skills like reading,
writing and arithmetic. . . . In explicit acknowledgment of the challenges facing the education community, on February 15, 1996, President Clinton and Vice President Gore announced the Technology
Literacy Challenge, envisioning a 21st century where all students are
technologically literate. The challenge was put before the nation as
a whole, with responsibility . . . shared by local communities, states,
the private sector, educators, local communities, parents, the federal
government, and others. . . .

—*Getting America's Students Ready for the 21st Century* (5)

We know, purely and simply, that every single child must have access
to a computer. . . .

—Bill Clinton, qtd. in
Getting America's Students Ready for the 21st Century (4)

A central irony shaping my experience with the CCCC as a professional
organization goes something like this: I consider it a fortunate occurrence
and a particular point of pride that many of the best ideas about teaching

Reprinted from *College Composition and Communication*, February 1999.

and learning writing, the most powerfully explanatory theoretical insights about language and discourse and literacy that inform education today, grow directly out of conversations among CCCC members. Given this situation, however, I find it compellingly unfortunate that the one topic serving as a focus for my own professional involvement—that of computer technology and its use in teaching composition—seems to be the single subject best guaranteed to inspire glazed eyes and complete indifference in that portion of the CCCC membership which does not immediately sink into snooze mode.

This irony, I am convinced, has nothing to do with collegial good will. CCCC colleagues have been unerringly polite in the 17 years of discussions we have had about technology. After all this time, however, I can spot the speech acts that follow a turn of the conversation to computers—the slightly averted gaze, the quick glance at the watch, the panicky look in the eyes when someone lapses into talk about microprocessors, or gigabytes, or ethernets. All these small potent gestures, as Michel de Certeau would say, signify pretty clearly—technology is either boring or frightening to most humanists; many teachers of English composition feel it antithetical to their primary concerns and many believe it should not be allowed to take up valuable scholarly time or the attention that could be best put to use in teaching or the study of literacy. I have, believe me, gotten the message as subtle as it is.

These attitudes toward technology issues, of course, aren't shared by everyone in this organization—there are pockets of technology studies scholars and teachers here and there among us; notable occasions when an individual CCCC leader does speak about technology; and, every now and again, a professional conversation among us about the array of challenges associated with technology. These occasions remain exceptions, however, and anybody familiar with the values of traditional humanism knows that, as a group, we tend to hold in common a general distrust of the machine, that a preference for the non-technological still characterizes our community.

Our tendency to avoid focusing on the technological means that—while we are tolerant of those colleagues interested in the "souls of machines," to use Bruno Latour's term—we assign them to a peculiar kind of professional isolation "in their own separate world" of computer sessions and computer workshops and computers and writing conferences that many CCCC members consider influenced more by the concerns of "engineers, technicians, and technocrats" (vii) than those of humanists. It is this same set of historically and professionally determined beliefs, I think, that informs our actions within our home departments, where we generally continue to allocate the responsibility of technology decisions—and oftentimes the responsibility of technology studies—to a single faculty or staff member who doesn't mind wrestling with computers or the thorny, and the unpleasant issues that can be associated with their use. In this way, we manage to have the best of both worlds—we have computers available to use for our own studies, in support of our classes and our profession—but we have also relegated these technologies into the background of our professional lives. As a result, computers are rapidly becoming invisible, which is how we like our technology to be. When we don't have to pay attention to machines, we remain free to focus on the theory and practice of language, the stuff of real intellectual and social concern.

Why We Allow Ourselves to Ignore Technology

As humanists, we prefer things to be arranged this way because computer technology, when it is too much in our face (as an unfamiliar technology generally is), can suggest a kind of cultural strangeness that is off-putting. We are much more used to dealing with older technologies like print, a technology conventional enough so that we don't have to think so much about it, old enough so that it doesn't call such immediate attention to the social or material conditions associated with its use. Books, for example, are already and always—almost anyway—there. At this point in history, books are relatively cheap, they are generally accessible to students and to us, and they are acknowledged by our peers to be the appropriate tools of teaching and learning to use. As a result, our recognition of the material conditions associated with books have faded into the background of our imagination. Thus, although we understand on a tacit level that the print technology in which we invest so readily (and in which we ask students to invest) contributes to our own tenure and promotion, to our own wallets, and to our own status in the profession and in the public eye-this understanding is woven into the background of our professional attention, and we seldom pay attention to it on a daily basis. If we did, we'd go mad.

There are other things that don't occur to us, as well. When we use the more familiar technology of books, for instance, it is mostly within a familiar ideological system that allows us to ignore, except for some occasional twinges of conscience, the persistence of print and our role in this persistence. It allows us to ignore the understanding that print literacy functions as a cultural system—as Lester Faigley noted two years ago—not only to carry and distribute enlightened ideas, but also as a seamless whole to support a pattern of continuing illiteracy in this country.

I provide this example to suggest that composition studies faculty, educated in the humanist tradition, generally prefer our technologies and the material conditions associated so closely with them to remain in the background for obvious reasons, and the belief systems we construct in connection with various technologies allow us to accomplish this comfortable process of naturalization.

In the case of computers—we have convinced ourselves that we and the students with whom we work are made of much finer stuff than the machine in our midst, and we are determined to maintain this state of affairs. This ideological position, however, has other effects, as well. As a result of the inverse value we generally assign to discussions about computers, our professional organizations continue to deal with technology in what is essentially a piecemeal fashion. We now think of computers, for instance, as a simple tool that individual faculty members can use or ignore in their classrooms as they choose, but also one that the profession, as a collective whole—and with just a few notable exceptions—need not address too systematically. And so we have paid technology issues precious little focused attention over the years.

Why Composition Specialists Need to Pay Attention to Technology Issues

Allowing ourselves the luxury of ignoring technology, however, is not only misguided at the end of the 20th century, it is dangerously shortsighted. And I do not mean, simply, that we are all—each of us—now teaching students who must know how to communicate as informed thinkers and citizens in an increasingly technological world—although this is surely so. This recognition has led composition faculty only to the point of *using* computers—or having students do so—but not to the point of *thinking* about what we are doing and understanding at least some of the important implications of our actions.

I believe composition studies faculty have a much larger and more complicated obligation to fulfill—that of trying to understand and make sense of, *to pay attention to*, how technology is now inextricably linked to literacy and literacy education in this country. As a part of this obligation, I suggest that we have some rather unpleasant facts to face about our own professional behavior and involvement. To make these points more persuasively, I offer a real-life story about what has happened in American schools and literacy instruction as a result of our unwillingness to attend to technological issues.

An honest examination of this situation, I believe, will lead composition studies professionals to recognize that these two complex cultural formations—technology and literacy—have become linked in ways that exacerbate current educational and social inequities in the United States rather than addressing them productively. The story will lead us to admit, I believe, that we are, in part, already responsible for a bad—even a shameful—situation, and, I hope, will inspire us to do something more positive in the future.

I'll provide readers the moral of this story up front so that no one misses it. *As composition teachers, deciding whether or not to use technology in our classes is simply not the point—we have to pay attention to technology.* When we fail to do so, we share in the responsibility for sustaining and reproducing a unfair system that, scholars such as Elspeth Stuckey and Mike Rose have noted in other contexts, enacts social violence and ensures continuing illiteracy under the aegis of education.

I know, however, that it is not easy for composition teachers to pay attention to technology. As Anthony Giddens would say, our tendency to ignore technology—to focus on humans rather than on machines—is "deeply sedimented" (22) in our culture, in the history of our humanist profession. And the sedimentation of this belief system is so deep that it has come to comprise a piece of what Pierre Bordieu might call doxa (166)—a position everyone takes so much for granted, is so obvious, that people no longer even feel the need to articulate it. But by subscribing to this attitude, we may also be allowing ourselves to ignore the serious social struggles that continue to characterize technology as a cultural formation in this country.

Nowhere are these struggles and debates rendered in more complex terms in the United States—and nowhere are they more influential on our own work—than they are in the link between literacy and computer technology that has been established in increasingly direct ways over the last decade. This potent linkage is sustained and reproduced by a complexly related set of cultural influences: workplaces in which approximately 70% of jobs requiring a bachelors degree or an advanced college degree now require the use of computers (*Digest of Education Statistics* 458); a corporate sector focused on exploiting the 89% of "teachers and the public" who believe that the Internet adds value to teaching and learning specifically because it "reduces the costs teachers spend on classroom activities" ("MCI Nationwide Poll"); schools in which 87% of high school students are now writing on computers by Grade 11 (Coley, Crandler, and Engle 27); and homes in which 86% of parents are convinced that a computer is the one "most beneficial and effective product that they can buy to expand their children's opportunities" for education, future success, and economic prosperity (*Getting America's Students Ready* 10).

The tendential force generated by these complexly related formations—which magnify our country's economic dependence on technology—is considerable. However, because it is always easier to ascribe responsibility for such a situation to others—to blame the greed of the corporate representatives who sell computers, or the blindness of school administrators who mandate the use of computers, or the shortsightedness of parents who consider technology a guarantor of learning for their children, I want to focus primarily on our own professional roles and responsibilities associated with this social dynamic.

It is, after all, partly a result of the involvement of English composition specialists, or lack of involvement, in some cases, that the linkage between literacy and technology has come to inform most of the official instruction that goes on within the United States' educational system, most official definitions and descriptions of literacy featured in the documents we write and read, and many of the criteria used to gauge literacy levels within this country. Few government documents about educational goals; few documents outlining national or state educational standards, including our own NCTE standards document; and few corporate job descriptions now fail to acknowledge a citizen's need to read, write, and communicate in electronic environments.

And certainly, like most Americans, we have not felt a responsibility to involve ourselves directly in some of the more public discussions about technology and educational policy because many of us unconsciously subscribe to a belief—both culturally and historically determined—that technology is a productive outgrowth of Science and Innovation (cf. Winner; Virilio; Feenberg; Johnson-Eilola). As a result, we take comfort when the linkage between literacy and computer technology is portrayed as a socially progressive movement, one that will benefit American citizens generally and without regard for their circumstances or backgrounds. Such a belief releases us from the responsibility to pay attention.

It is this last point, however, that makes the American cultural narrative about technology and literacy a particularly potent force in our lives, and that provides a jumping off point for our real-life story about technology.

An American Narrative about Computer Technology and Its Growing Links to Literacy Instruction

This story about technology and literacy could be dated by any number of historical events, but for the purposes of this paper, we turn to the June of 1996, when the Clinton-Gore administration—with direct reference to the larger cultural narrative of social-progress-through-technology that I have just identified—published a document entitled *Getting America's Children Ready for the Twenty-First Century*, which announced an official national project to expand *technological literacy*, the "ability to use computers and other technology to improve learning, productivity and performance" (5).

The purpose of this large-scale project—as outlined by Secretary of Education Richard Riley—was, and is, to help "all of our children to become technologically literate" so that each "will have the opportunity to make the most of his or her own life," to "grow and thrive" within in the "new knowledge- and information-driven economy" (3–4). By "technologically literate," this document refers to the use of computers not only for the purposes of calculating, programming, and designing, but also for the purposes of reading, writing, and communicating (15–19)—at least for the officially-sponsored academic tasks required in schools across the country.

Estimates indicate that this particular literacy project may cost up to $109 billion dollars—averaging either $11 billion annually for a decade or between $10 and $20 billion annually for five years—from a variety of sources at the national, state, and local levels (*Getting America's Students Ready* 6). Where has this money come from and where has it gone? As Todd Oppenheimer notes:

> New Jersey cut state aid to a number of school districts this past year and then spent $10 million on classroom computers. In Union City, California, a single school district is spending $27 million to buy new gear for a mere eleven schools . . . in Mansfield, Massachusetts, administrators dropped proposed teaching positions in art, music and physical education, and then spent $333,000 on computers. (46)

Secretary of Education Richard Riley, in *Getting America's Students Ready*, lists other funded projects from various states—here is a sampling:

> *California*
>
> $279 million (one time, State Board) for "instructional materials, deferred maintenance, technology . . ."
>
> $13.4 million (State Board) for educational technology.

$10 million (State budget) to "refurbish and update used or donated computers."

$100 million (current year, Governor Wilson) for "educational technology."

$35 million (Pacific Telesis) for rate overcharges. (60)

Delaware

$30 million (State, three years) to fund "infrastructure initiative." (61)

District of Columbia

$9 million for "hardware and software purchases." (61)

Idaho

$10.4 million (Idaho Educational Technology Initiative) for "technology in the classroom." (62)

Maine

$15 million (Governor) to "establish a distance learning network." (63)

Montana

$2.56 million (NSF) to support "SummitNet"

$100,000 (State) "for technology" (65)

Texas

$150 million (State, Telecommunications Infrastructure Fund)

$30/student (State) for "purchasing electronic textbooks or technological equipment . . . , training educational personnel directly involved in student learning, . . . access to technological equipment." (67)

Wisconsin

$10 million (State) for "improve[d] access to advanced telecommunications and distance education technologies." (68)

> [Telecommunications providers] have provided unidentified funds
> for Advanced Telecommunications Foundation. (68)

In comparison to the miserly federal funding this country is allocating to
other literacy and education projects, these amounts stagger the imagination.

To put these expenditures for technology into perspective, we can look at
the 1999 budget for the Department of Education that President Clinton has
recently sent to the United States Congress. In this budget, the President has
requested $721 million of direct federal funding for educational technology
but less than half of that amount, $260 million, for the America Reads
Challenge and less than one-tenth of that amount, $67 million, for teacher
recruitment and preparation (Community Update, No. 56, p. 3).

And we are already in the midst of this project—the administration's
deadline for creating such a technologically literate citizenry, one that will
think of official, school-sponsored literacy practices as occurring primarily in
technological contexts, is "early in the 21st century" (*Getting America's
Children Ready 3*).

This project, and the extensive influence it has had on our national
understanding of officially-sponsored literacy practices, is a phenomenon
that deserves close study not only because of the considerable attention that
individual teachers and school districts around the country have already paid
to its goals, but, interestingly and conversely, because of the utter lack of
systematic and considered attention that our profession as a whole and our
professional organizations have accorded it. And so I will move the story
forward a bit more.

Since 1996, although our professional standards documents now reflect
the core values of this project in that they assume the necessity of computer
use by communicators in the 21st century, they do not provide adequate
guidance about how to get teachers and students *thinking critically about
such use.* Moreover, in a curious way, neither the CCCC, nor the NCTE, nor
the MLA, nor the IRA—as far as I can tell—have ever published a single word
about our own professional stance on this particular nationwide technology
project: not one statement about how we think such literacy monies should
be spent in English composition programs; not one statement about what
kinds of literacy and technology efforts should be funded in connection with
this project or how excellence should be gauged in these efforts; not one
statement about the serious need for professional development and support
for teachers that must be addressed within the context of this particular
national literacy project.

Nor have these organizations articulated any official or direct response to the project's goals or the ways in which schools and teachers are already enacting these goals within classrooms. And this is true despite the fact that so many literacy educators in a range of situations—including all English and Language Arts teachers in primary, secondary, and college/university classrooms—have been broadly affected by the technology-literacy linkage for the past decade and will continue to be so involved well into the next century.

In other words, as members of these professional organizations, we need to do a much better job of paying critical attention to technology issues that affect us. Now why is this particular task is so important? By paying critical attention to lessons about *technology*, we can re-learn important lessons about *literacy*. It is the different perspective on literacy that technology issues provide us that can encourage such insights. In the sections that follow, I point out just a few of these lessons.

Remembering the Truth about Large-Scale Literacy Projects and the Myth of Literacy

The first lesson that the national project to expand technological literacy can teach us has to do with the efficacy of large-scale literacy projects, in general, and with the myth of literacy. One of the primary arguments for the project to expand technological literacy rests on the claim that such an effort will provide all Americans with an education enriched by technology, and, thus, equal opportunity to access high-paying, technology-rich jobs and economic prosperity after graduation. The truth of this claim, however, has not been borne out and is not likely to be so. This fact is one of the primary reasons why we need to pay attention to technology issues.

Scholars such as Brian Street, Harvey Graff, and James Paul Gee note that such claims are not unusual in connection with large-scale, national literacy projects. Indeed, our willingness to believe these claims contributes to the potency of what Graff has called the "literacy myth," a widely held belief that literacy and literacy education lead autonomously, automatically, and directly to liberation, personal success, or economic prosperity. This myth, however, is delusory in its simplicity, as Street says:

> The reality [of national literacy movements] is more complex, is harder to face politically . . . when it comes to job acquisition, the level of literacy is less important than issues of class, gender, and ethnicity;

lack of literacy is more likely to be a symptom of poverty and depri-
vation than a cause. (18)

In the specific case of the project to expand technological literacy, the
claim is that a national program will provide all citizens equal access to an
improved education and, thus, equal opportunity for upward social mobility
and economic prosperity. If we *pay attention* to the facts surrounding the
project's instantiation, however, we can remind ourselves of the much harder
lesson: in our educational system, and in the culture that this system reflects,
computers *continue to be distributed differentially along the related axes of
race and socioeconomic status* and this distribution contributes to ongoing
patterns of racism and to the continuation of poverty.

It is a fact, for instance, that schools primarily serving students of color
and poor students continue to have less access to computers, and access to
less sophisticated computer equipment than do schools primarily serving
more affluent and white students (Coley et al. 3). And it is a fact that schools
primarily serving students of color and poor students continue to have less
access to the Internet, less access to multimedia equipment, less access to
CD-ROM equipment, less access to local area networks, less access to
videodisc technology than do schools primarily serving more affluent and
white students (Coley et al. 3).

This data, which is profoundly disturbing, becomes all the more
problematic if we trace the extended effects of the technology-literacy
linkage into the country's workplaces and homes. There, too, the latest
census figures indicate, the linkage is strongly correlated to both race and
socioeconomic status. It is a fact, for instance, that Black employees or
Hispanic employees are *much* less likely than white employees to use a
range of computer applications in their workplace environments (*Digest*
458). It is also a fact that employees who have not graduated from high
school are much less likely to use a range of computer applications than
are employees who have a high school degree or have some college
experience (*Digest* 458). And it is a fact that poor families in both urban
and rural environments and Black and Hispanic Americans are much less
likely to own and use computers than individuals with higher family
incomes and white families (*Condition* 212; *Digest* 1996 458;
Getting 36).

In other words, the poorer you are and the less educated you are in this
country—both of which conditions are correlated with race—the less likely
you are to have access to computers and to high-paying, high-tech jobs in
the American workplace.

The challenges associated with the unequal distribution and use of computer technology along the related axes of socioeconomic status, education, and race have proven embarrassingly persistent for a number of related reasons. Secretary of Education Richard Riley, for example, citing a 1995 General Accounting Office Survey, notes that

> half of all schools do not have adequate wiring (such as outlets) to handle their technology needs. More than half do not have sufficient telephone lines, and 60 percent consider the number of conduits for network cable unsatisfactory. Schools that have all of these infrastructure elements are clearly the exception to the rule. Strikingly, schools in large central cities are even less equipped to meet the demands of technology than other schools; more than 40 percent do not even have enough electrical power to use computers on a regular basis. . . . Classrooms in older buildings, for example, may require expensive renovations to improve electrical systems before computers and networks can be installed, discouraging the community from making a commitment. (*Getting America's Children Ready* 34–35)

As a result of this overdetermined system, the differential distribution of technology and technological literacy continues—albeit, with some complex new variations. In a recent article published in *Science*, for example, Hoffman and Novak identified the following findings:

- Overall whites were significantly more likely than African Americans to have a home computer in their household. Whites were also slightly more likely to have access to a PC at work. (390)

- Proportionately, more than twice as many whites as African Americans had used the Web in the past week. As of January 1997, we estimate that 5.2 million (± 1.2 million) African Americans and 40.8 million whites (± 2.1 million) have ever used the Web, and that 1.4 million (± 0.5 million) African Americans and 20.3 million (± 1.6 million) whites used the Web in the past week. (390)

- As one would expect . . . increasing levels of income corresponded to an increased likelihood of owning a home computer, regardless of race. In contrast, adjusting for income did not eliminate the race differences with respect to computer access at work. . . . Notably . . . , race differences in Web use vanish at household incomes of $40,000 and higher. (390)

- 73% of white students owned a home computer, only 32% of African American students owned one. "This difference persisted when we statistically adjusted for students' reported household income." (390)

- White students were significantly more likely than African American students to have used the Web, especially in the past week. (391)
- White students lacking a home computer, but not African American students, appear to be accessing the Internet from locations such as homes of friends and relatives, libraries, and community centers. (391)

Acknowledging these facts, we might understand better why the rhetoric associated with national literacy projects serves to exacerbate the dangers that they pose. When Secretary of Education Richard Riley states, for example, that "Computers are the 'new basics' of education . . . " or that the project of technological literacy can help us give "all of our young people" an "opportunity to grow . . . and thrive" in the "new knowledge- and information-driven economy" (Getting 3), he erroneously suggests, in Brian Street's words, "that the acquisition of literacy" will by itself "lead to 'major' impacts in terms of social and cognitive skills and 'development'" within a population (14). As Street reminds us, these "simple stories" that "both politicians and the press" tell about literacy to justify and sustain the momentum of such major programs, frequently "deflect attention from the complexity and real political difficulties" (17). The ultimate effect, according to Street, is an overly narrow understanding of literacy—usually in terms of a single official literacy—and the development of accompanying "patronizing assumptions about what it means to have difficulties with reading and writing in contemporary society. Such rhetoric also serves to raise false hopes about what the acquisition of literacy means for job prospects, social mobility, and personal achievement" (17).

In the specific case of computers and literacy, these stories serve to deflect our attention from the fact that "every single child" does not now have access to technology, and some students, especially those who are poor and of color, have less access than others. And so, if access to and use of, technology in school-based settings is now a fundamental skill of literacy and if such skills do help prepare graduates for the jobs they will be asked to do, these same students can expect less opportunity to assume high-tech and high-paying jobs, not more. As Richard Ohmann described the underlying dynamic in a prescient 1985 *College English* article about the general relationship between technology, literacy, and economic conditions:

> Of course there will be more jobs in the computer field itself. But . . . the field is layered into specialties, which will be dead ends for most people in them . . . Graduates of MIT will get the challenging

jobs; community college grads will be technicians; those who do no more than acquire basic skills and computer literacy in high school will probably find their way to electronic workstations at McDonald's. I see every reason to expect that the computer revolution, like other revolutions from the top down, will indeed expand the minds and the freedom of an elite, meanwhile facilitating the degradation of labor and the stratification of the workforce that have been hallmarks of monopoly capitalism from its onset. (683)

The frustrating cycle associated with this situation is so dismally clear and sickeningly familiar because it mirrors exactly the dynamics associated with more traditional literacy efforts in our country. As Graff notes, official literacies usually function in a conservative, and reproductive, fashion—in favor of dominant groups and in support of the existing class-based system:

> Hegemonic relationships have historically involved processes of group and class formation, recruitment, indoctrination, and maintenance at all levels of society. For most of literacy's history, these functions have centered upon elite groups and their cohesion and power. For them, the uses of literacy have been diverse but have included common education, culture, and language . . . shared interests and activities; control of scarce commodities, such as wealth, power, and even literacy; and common symbols and badges, of which literacy could be one. (*Legacies* 12)

Thus, the national project to expand technological literacy has *not* served to reduce illiteracy—or the persistent social problems that exacerbate illiteracy. Rather, it has simply changed the official criteria for both "literate" and "illiterate" individuals, while retaining the basic ratio of both groups.

In sum, we have little evidence that any large-scale project focusing on a narrowly defined set of officially sanctioned literacy skills will result in fundamental changes in the ratio of people labeled as literate or illiterate. These categories are socially constructed identities which our current educational system reproduces rather than addresses. Similarly, we have no specific evidence that the current project to expand technological literacy will change the patterns of literacy and illiteracy in this country. Rather, this project is likely to support persistent patterns of economically-based literacy acquisition because citizens of color and those from low socioeconomic backgrounds continue to have less access to high-tech educational opportunities and occupy fewer positions that make multiple uses of technology than do white citizens or those from higher socioeconomic backgrounds.

Literacy Education Is a Political Act

Given the effects we have just described, the national project to expand
technological literacy can also serve to re-teach us a second lesson—that
literacy is always a political act as well as an educational effort. In this context, we can understand that the national project to expand technological
literacy is motivated as much by political and economic agenda as it is by
educational values and goals. To trace the concrete forms of political agenda, one relatively easy starting place is 1992. At that time in history, the
Clinton-Gore team was preparing to enter Washington, and this administration had already identified technology as a key factor in both its domestic
and international economic policies. At home, the Clinton-Gore team was
facing a long-standing slowdown in manufacturing and productivity, persistent poverty, and an increasing income gap between the rich and the poor.
As the 1997 *Economic Report to the President* tells the story:

> For more than two decades America has faced serious problems: pro-
> ductivity growth has been slower than in the past, income inequity
> has increased, and poverty has persisted. In addition, serious chal-
> lenges loom for the future, such as the aging of the baby boom,
> which threatens to create severe fiscal strains in the next century.
> (Council 18)

The administration knew well that its ability to address these problems and
to inject new vigor into the domestic economy—or to convince the
American public that it had done so—would be a deciding factor in the way
the effectiveness of their administration was judged. On the international
scene, the Clinton-Gore team faced three important and related changes in
the world's economic picture: the end of the Cold War and the fall of
Communism in the Soviet Union, the emergence of growing markets among
the developing countries of East Asia and Latin America that threatened to
capture an increasingly large percentages of the world's consumers, and the
threatening increase in competition due to the global scope of the
international economy.

To kill these two economic birds with one stone, the Clinton-Gore
administration focused on the idea of expanding America's technology
efforts—the design, manufacturing, and consumption of both technology
and technological expertise. On the international scene, the administration
took three steps to expand technology efforts. The first step involved defining
America's focused area of specialization in the world marketplace as
technology and information services:

> The Administration's economic policy has been an aggressive effort
> to increase exports through the opening of markets abroad. . . . The
> United States will certainly gain, both as a major exporter of infor-
> mation technology and as an importer, as American industries take
> advantage of new foreign technologies that will lower their costs and
> increase their productivity. (*Economic Report* 27)

The second and third steps involved exerting leadership in the development
of a Global Information Infrastructure (GII) built on the back of the country's
own National Information Infrastructure (NII). As part of this effort, the
United States offered other countries—especially those with emerging
markets that were hungry for technological involvement—the opportunity to
buy American goods and services exported in connection with the GII. As
Gore described the plan to the International Telecommunications Union in
Buenos Aires in 1994:

> We can use the Global information infrastructure for technical col-
> laboration between industrialized nations and developing countries.
> All agencies of the U.S. government are potential sources of infor-
> mation and knowledge that can be shared with partners across the
> globe. . . . The U.S. can help provide the technical know-how needed
> to deploy and use these new technologies. USAID and U.S. busi-
> nesses have helped the U.S. telecommunications Training Institute
> train more than 3500 telecommunications professionals from the
> developing world, including many in this room.

Such a system also set up the possibility of continued reliance on American
goods and services. Technicians trained in the deployment and use of
American technology and American-designed operating systems, and
American software, and American networks, for example, would tend to
continue to rely on—and purchase—those products and components with
which they were most familiar. Gore articulated the economic reasoning
behind this plan:

> For us in the United States, the information infrastructure already is
> to the U.S. economy of the 1990s what transportation infrastructure
> was to the economy of the mid-20th century.
>   The integration of computing and information networks into the
> economy makes U.S. manufacturing companies more productive,
> more competitive, and more adaptive to changing conditions . . .

The benefits associated with the GII expansion had political as well as
economic effects. If the GII was constructed according to the Clinton-Gore
plan, it would not only re-vitalize the American economy, it would also help
promote the spread of democracy and capitalism around the globe within

the context of a liberalized global economic system. The GII would accomplish this goal by providing forums for democratic involvement and expanded freedom of speech, by increasing privatization of technology resources, and by decreasing government regulation. As Gore noted:

> The GII will not only be a metaphor for a functioning democracy, it will in fact promote the functioning of democracy by greatly enhancing the participation of citizens in decision-making. And it will greatly promote the ability of nations to cooperate with each other. I see a new Athcnian age of democracy forged in the fora the GII will create. . . .
> The integration of computing and information networks into the economy makes U.S. manufacturing companies more productive, more competitive, and more adaptive to changing conditions and it will do the same for the economies of other nations. . . .
> To promote; to protect, to preserve freedom and democracy, we must make telecommunications development an integral part of every nation's development. Each link we create strengthens the bonds of liberty and democracy around the world. By opening markets to stimulate the development of the global information infrastructure, we open lines of communication.
> By opening lines of communication, we open minds.

The international effort to expand technology, however, was only one part of the Clinton-Gore agenda. The other—and, in some ways, the more important—effort occurred in the domestic arena and focused on the revitalization of the American domestic economy through the expansion of the American computer industry. The Clinton-Gore team saw this particular industry as an economic "engine" (*Global Information* 3) that would, by increasing technological efforts at home, in turn, jump-start the international effort: providing the resources—the additional technology and the technological expertise—required to exploit emerging world markets.

To carry out this complex plan, the domestic engine of technology had to be cranked up and, to accomplish this goal, the Clinton-Gore administration knew that it had to accomplish two tasks:

- educate a pool of technologically sophisticated workers and technology specialists who could assist in the effort to reach new global markets and export more American manufactured equipment and specialized technology services to the rest of the world; and

- provide an influx of resources into the domestic computer industry so that it could simultaneously support the international effort and assume an increasingly important role in re-vitalizing the domestic economy.

And it was in response to these complexly related economic and political agenda that the national project to expand technological literacy was born. The dynamics that underlie this project were ideally and specifically suited to the economic and political goals we have just sketched out. Touted as an educational effort designed to improve citizens' literacy levels and, thus, their opportunities for future prosperity, the project was targeted at producing a continuing supply of educated workers who both had the skills necessary to design and manufacture increasingly sophisticated technological goods at home, and could offer sophisticated and specialized technological services in international arenas. Central to the task of achieving these targeted goals, the Clinton-Gore team recognized, was its ability to levy the power of the national educational system to reach large numbers of Americans in relatively short order. It was only within such a national system, they recognized, that an appropriately large proportion of the country's population could quickly acquire the training necessary to boost high-tech industries.

Importantly, such a plan was pretty close to self-fueling—citizens who learned the habits of reading, writing, and communicating on computers early in their lives within high-tech schools, would tend to demand and consume such goods later in life when they graduated, thus injecting an increasingly continuous flow of money into the computer industry. And the plan's effects in the public sector promised to resonate effectively with its effects in the private sector: when citizens used, or were exposed to, cutting-edge technologies in their workplaces, or in school settings, they would desire them, as well, in their homes—and they would purchase updated technologies more frequently. Further, to ensure the continuation of the same high-tech careers and industries that have served them so well, such citizens would also tend to vote in support of political and economic programs that involved the further expansion of technology markets both domestically and internationally. Such citizens, moreover, would recognize the key role that technological literacy plays in their own success, and, so, demand a similar education for their children.

From our perspective today, of course, we can see a darker side of this dynamic. The economic engine of technology must be fueled by—and produce—not only a continuing supply of individuals who are highly literate in terms of technological knowledge, but also an ongoing supply of individuals who fail to acquire technological literacy, those who are termed *"illiterate"* according to the official definition. These latter individuals provide the unskilled, low-paid labor necessary to sustain the system I have described—their work generates the surplus labor that must be continually re-invested in capital projects to produce more sophisticated technologies.

The people labeled as "illiterate" in connection with technology—as expected—are those with the least power to effect a change in this system. They come from families who attend the poorest schools in this country and they attend schools with the highest populations of students of color. In part because of such facts, these students have less access to technology, in general, and less access to more sophisticated technology during their educational years. Partially as a result of their educational backgrounds, such individuals are hired into less desirable, lower-paid positions that demand fewer official technological literacy skills.

Moreover, because skills in *technological* communication environments are so closely linked with literacy instruction *in general*, and because students who come from such backgrounds are afforded the poorest efforts of the educational system and the lowest expectations of many teachers, the label of "illiterate" has broader implications for these individuals' ability to acquire other skills through their formal schooling years.

Remembering Our Own Role in the Literacy/Illiteracy Cycle

The danger associated with such an extensive ideological system, as Terry Eagleton points out, is the effective processes of naturalization that it engenders. Successful ideological systems "render their beliefs natural and self evident" by so closely identifying them with "common sense" of a society so that nobody could imagine how they might ever be different (58). More importantly, as Eagleton continues,

> This process, which Pierre Bordieu calls *doxa*, involves the ideology in creating as tight a fit as possible between itself and social reality, thereby closing the gap into which the leverage of critique could be inserted. Social reality is redefined by the ideology to become coextensive with itself, in a way which occludes the truth that the reality in fact generated the ideology. . . . The result, politically speaking, is an apparently vicious circle: the ideology could only become transformed if the reality was such as to allow it to become objectified; but the ideology processes reality in ways which forestall this possibility. The two are thus mutually self-confirming. On this view, a ruling ideology does not so much combat alternative ideas as thrust them beyond the very bounds of the thinkable. (58)

It is within this effectively naturalized matrix of interests, I would argue, that English teachers all over this country have become the unwitting purveyors of technology and technological literacy—even as we try to avoid a technological focus by attending to more traditionally conceived topics within the humanities.

The paradoxical dynamics at the heart of this situation are difficult to wrap our minds around especially because they function at so many different levels. Because we fail to address the project to expand technological literacy in focused, systematic, and critical ways within the professional arenas available to us, English composition teachers have come to understand technology as "just another instructional tool" that they can choose either to use or ignore. And, working from this context, we divide ourselves into two perfectly meaningless camps—those who use computers to teach classes and those who don't. Both groups feel virtuous about their choices, and both manage to lose sight of the real issue. Computer-using teachers instruct students in how to *use* technology—but, all too often, they neglect to teach students how *to pay critical attention* to the issues generated by technology use. Teachers who choose *not* to use technology in their classes content themselves with the mistaken belief that their choice to avoid technology use absolves them and the students in their classes from *paying critical attention* to technology issues. In other words, both groups contribute to the very same end. And when such things happen, when we allow ourselves to ignore technological issues, when we take technology for granted, when it becomes invisible to us, when we forget technology's material bases—regardless of whether or not we use technology—we participate unwittingly in the inequitable literacy system I have just described.

Paying Attention to Action

So can composition teachers address the complex linkages among technology, literacy, poverty, and race? The primary factors determining any individual's involvement, of course, must necessarily start with the local and specific—with social agents' own deep and penetrating knowledge of the specific colleges and universities in which they work; the particular families, communities, cultures within which we live and form our own understanding of the world; the individual students, teachers, administrators, board members, politicians, and parents whose lives touch ours.

As Donna Haraway reminds us, this kind of "situated knowledges-approach" (175) leads to a kind of "coyote" (189) way of knowing—one different from the traditional perspective of Science, but in that difference, capable of offering a "more adequate, richer, better account of the world" that makes it possible to "live in it well and in critical, reflexive relation to our own as well as others' practices" (178). Such an approach may provide "only partial perspective" (181), Haraway cautions, but it allows us to avoid the trap of claiming a scientific objectivity that invites a false sense of closure and overly simple answers.

This kind of paying attention can serve as a collective effort to construct a "larger vision" of our responsibilities as a profession, one that depends on a strong sense of many *somewheres* (e.g., schools, classrooms, districts, communities) "in particular" (187)—especially when such a project is undertaken with a critical understanding of what we are trying to accomplish with such work and a collective commitment to seeing social problems "faithfully from another's point of view" (181) and even when it is clear that such a vision must remain partial, distorted, and incomplete. In this way, our profession can assemble, from many local understandings "stitched together imperfectly" (183), a picture of technological literacy—as it now functions within our culture—that might allow us to act with more strategic effectiveness and force, both collectively and individually.

A situated knowledges-approach to paying attention also honors a multiplicity of responses to technological literacy. Given the constraints of local and specific contexts, and a commitment to engaging with the lives of individual students, for example, some teachers will find their best avenue of involvement to reside in individual agency, others will find increasing effectiveness when they work with other colleagues. Some educators will find work within their own classroom to be the most immediately pressing and others will find the action in local communities to offer the most immediate and successful venue for their work. Indeed, the appreciation of local situations and variations may help composition studies professionals understand the power of large-scale projects when they are built on the critical understandings and active participation of a diverse group of educators.

Operating from this understanding of the local and particular, suggestions for critical engagement with technological literacy issues must allow for wide variations in social, political, economic, and ideological positionings, and wide variations in teachers, students, administrators, citizens, and communities. In deference to this approach, the suggestions that follow focus on the typical sites for critically informed action on technological literacy (and on general areas of attention within such sites) rather than on specific projects that should be undertaken within these sites. Individual teachers and groups of teachers, students, parents, and school administrators must determine within such sites how best to pay increased and critical attention to the linkage between technology and literacy—recognizing as fully as possible the local conditions affecting the work they do.

In Curriculum Committees, Standards Documents, and Assessment Programs

We need to pursue opportunities for resisting projects and systems that serve to establish an overly narrow, official version of literacy practices or skills. Such projects and systems simply serve to reward the literacy practices of dominant groups and punish the practices of others. They serve to reproduce a continuing and oppressive cycle of illiteracy, racism, and poverty in this country and in others.

Within these venues, composition specialists can lead the way in insisting on a diverse range of literacy practices and values, rather than one narrow and official form of literacy. We have made a start at this effort in the 1996 NCTE *Standards for the English Language Arts*, but CCCC needs to go much further in helping both future teachers and those already in classrooms understand why this work is so important and what implications their successes and failures may have.

In Our Professional Organizations

We need to recognize that if written language and literacy practices are our professional business, so is technology. This recognition demands a series of carefully considered and very visible professional stands on a variety of technological issues now under debate in this country: for example, on the access issues we have discussed, on the issue of technology funding for schools, on the issue of multiple venues for students' literacy practices, on the national project to expand technological literacy, and so on. We need to engage in much more of this kind of professional activism, and more consistently.

In Scholarship and Research

We also need to recognize that technological literacy is our responsibility. We need not only additional examinations of the ideological systems and cultural formations currently informing the literacy-technology link, but also the historical patterns established by other literacy technologies. And we need research like that Regina Copeland has just completed in West Virginia that takes a hard look at the access that individuals in various population groups—students of color, poor students, women—have to computer-supported literacy instruction, and of the expenditure of government and schools and family funds in support of technology and literacy. We also need additional research on how various technologies influence literacy values and practices and research on how teachers might better use technologies to support a wide range of literacy goals for different populations. We need work like that Nancy Guerra Barron has completed in LA to examine the bilingual online discussions of Latino students in a Chicano studies class and trace the ways in which these students manage to shape and use electronic environments productively to mirror the linguistic richness of their lives outside the classroom. These projects represent only some of the many that we can encourage.

In Language Arts and English Studies Classrooms, and in First-Year and Advanced English Composition Courses

We need to recognize that we can no longer simply educate students to become technology users—and consumers—without also helping them learn how to become critical thinkers about technology and the social issues surrounding its use. When English/language arts faculty require students to use computers in completing a range of assignments—without also providing them the time and opportunity to explore the complex issues that surround technology and technology use in substantive ways—we may, without realizing it, be contributing to the education of citizens who are habituated to technology use but who have little critical awareness about, or understanding of, the complex relationships between humans, machines, and the cultural contexts within which the two interact.

Composition teachers, language arts teachers, and other literacy specialists need to recognize that the relevance of technology in the English studies disciplines is not simply a matter of helping students work effectively with communication software and hardware, but, rather, also a matter of helping them to understand and to be able to assess—to pay attention to—the social, economic, and pedagogical implications of new communication technologies and technological initiatives that affect their lives. Knowledgeable literacy specialists at all levels need to develop age-appropriate and level-appropriate reading and writing activities aimed at this goal. This approach—which recognizes the complex links that now exist between literacy and technology at the end of the twentieth century—constitutes a *critical technological literacy* that will serve students well.

In Computer-Based Communication Facilities

We have to put scholarship and research to work as praxis. These technology-rich facilities can serve not only as teaching environments for students completing literacy assignments—as sites within which both faculty and students can develop their own critical technological literacy—but also as sites within which students and faculty can formulate guidelines and policies for critically informed practices that put these understandings to work in complicated social situations. Feenberg offers the possibility of considering such sites in terms of their *underdetermined* potential, a potential which can be exploited by interested and knowledgeable social agents determined to make a difference in their own and others' lives. Technology-rich communication facilities are already replete with such interested agents—the English/language arts teachers involved in designing and teaching within them, the students involved in using them and learning within them, the staff members (often students) responsible for keeping them operational, and the administrators who help to fund them.

In technology-rich communication facilities, students and teachers can develop a more critically-informed sense of technology by actively confronting and addressing technology issues in contexts that matter—contexts that involve real people (peers, faculty, community members, staff members) engaged in a range of daily practices (making decisions about software and hardware purchases, hiring individuals who can help teachers and students deal more effectively with technology, setting lab fee levels for students, deciding on etiquette and use guidelines, identifying access problems) within their various lived experiences and in light of their own goals. When confronted and addressed in these complicated and often contradictory contexts, technology and technological issues become connected with social issues, human values, and material conditions—rather than naturalized and separated from such experiences.

These sets of issues and others are all part of the process of managing technology-rich environments, and each is a component of the critical technological literacy we believe students must develop as they become effective social agents and citizens. Our culture will need these activists—in school board and PTO meetings, in small businesses, on corporate boards, and in government agencies where decisions about communication technologies will influence the personal and professional lives of citizens.

In Districts and Systems and States That Have Poor Schools, Rural Schools, and Schools with Large Populations of Students of Color

We need to resist the tendential forces that continue to link technological literacy with patterns of racism and poverty. We need to insist on and support more equitable distributions of technology.

In Our Voting for School Board Elections, in Committee Meetings, in Public Hearings, at National Conventions, in the Public Relations Statements of Our Professional Organizations

We have to argue—at every chance that we can get—that poor students and students of color get more access to computers and to more sophisticated computers, that teachers in schools with high populations of such students be given more support.

In Pre-Service and In-Service Educational Programs and Curricula

We need to help all English composition teachers get more education on both technology use and technology criticism. In the curricula comprising our own graduate programs and the educational programs that prepare teachers for careers in our profession, we need to make sure these programs don't simply teach young professionals to *use* computers—but rather, that we teach them how to pay attention to technology and the issues that result from, and contribute to, the technology-literacy linkage. It is no longer enough, for instance, simply to ask graduate students or colleagues to use computers in composition classes. Instead, we need to help them read in the areas of technology criticism, social theories, and computer studies and, then, provide them important opportunities to participate in making hard decisions about how to pay attention to technology issues in departments, colleges, and local communities; how to address the existing links between literacy and technology in undergraduate curricula; how to provide more access to technology for more people and how to help individuals develop their own critical consciousness about technology.

In Libraries, Community Centers, and Other Non-Traditional Public Places

We need to provide free access to computers for citizens at the poverty level and citizens of color—not only so that such individuals have access to computers and, thus, can become proficient in computer use for communication tasks, but also so that these citizens have access to the Internet and to online sites for collective political action (Oppel; Hoffman and Novak).

Toward an End . . .

The lessons I have outlined in the preceding pages, as I am sure readers understand, are as much about literacy as they are about technology. But, as Bruno Latour notes, real-life stories always lack richness and accuracy when they are told from a single perspective. We require multiple perspectives if we hope to construct a robust and accurate understanding of the ways in which technology functions in our culture. Our profession's occasional respectful attention to technology and the social issues that surround technology may allow us to see things from a slightly different point of view, even if for only a moment in time. And from such a perspective, as Latour reminds us, our interpretations of issues "take on added density" (viii).

I might add that this occasional merging of the technological and the humanist perspectives—into a vision that is more robustly informed—has as much value for scientists and engineers as it does for humanists. Margaret Boden, an early pioneer in artificial intelligence, notes in the introduction to her landmark 1977 book, that she was drawn to the study of artificial intelligence for its potential in "counteracting the dehumanizing influence of natural science" and for its ability to "clarify the nature of human purpose, freedom, and moral choice," those "hidden complexities of human thinking" (4) that machines cannot replicate, that have always concerned us most within this profession.

One technology writer, Mark Weiser, has said that "The most profound technologies are those that disappear," that "weave themselves into the fabric of everyday life until they are indistinguishable from it" (94). I agree, but with a slightly different interpretation—these technologies may be the most *profound* when they disappear, but—it is exactly when this happens that they also develop the most potential for being *dangerous*. We have, as a culture, watched the twin strands of technology and literacy become woven into the fabric of our lives—they are now inscribed in legislation, in the law—in the warp and woof of our culture. But, recognizing this context, we cannot allow ourselves to lose sight of either formation. We must remind ourselves that laws write the texts of people's lives, that they constantly inscribe their intent and power on individuals—as Michel de Certeau says, "making its book out of them" (140).

It is our responsibility, as educators, to commit ourselves every day that we teach to reading and analyzing these texts, these lives of students—honestly, with respect, and to the very best of our collective and personal abilities. The alternative—of ignoring them, of perceiving students only in terms of their numbers in our schools or as members of undifferentiated groups—is simply unacceptable. As Elspeth Stuckey, Mike Rose, Harvey Graff, Brian Street, James Paul Gee, and many others have told us, when we participate in unthinking ways in political agendas, legislative initiatives, or educational systems that support an overly narrow version of official literacy, we all lose, and we are all implicated in the guilt that accrues to a system of violence through literacy.

It is my hope that by paying some attention to technology, we may learn lessons about becoming better humanists, as well.

Works Cited

Barron, Nancy Guerra. "Egalitarian Moments: Computer Mediated Communications in a Chicano Studies (ChS 111) Course." MA Thesis. California State U at Los Angeles, 1998.

Boden, Margaret. *Artificial Intelligence and Natural Man.* New York: Basic, 1977.

Bordieu, Pierre. *Outline of a Theory of Practice.* New York: Cambridge UP, 1977.

Coley, R. J., J. Crandler, and P. Engle. *Computers and Classrooms: The Status of Technology in U.S. Schools.* Princeton: ETS, 1997.

Copeland, Regina. "Identifying Barriers to Computer-Supported Instruction." Diss. West Virginia U, 1997.

Council of Economic Advisors. *Economic Report of the President.* Washington, DC: US Government Printing Office, 1997.

de Certeau, Michel. *The Practice of Everyday Life.* Trans. Steven Randall. Berkeley: U of California P, 1984.

Digest of Education Statistics 1996. Washington, DC: National Center for Education Statistics, Office of Educational Research and Improvement, 1996.

Eagleton, Terry. *Ideology: An Introduction.* London: Verso, 1991.

Faigley, Lester. "Literacy after the Revolution." *CCC* 48 (1987): 30–43.

Feenberg, Andrew. *The Critical Theory of Technology.* New York: Oxford UP, 1991.

Gee, James. *Social Linguistics and Literacies: Ideology in Discourses.* New York: Falmer, 1990.

Getting America's Students Ready for the 21ˢᵗ Century: Meeting the Technology Literacy Challenge: A Report to the Nation on Technology and Education. Washington, DC: US Dept. of Education, 1996.

Giddens, Anthony. *The Constitution of Society: Outline of the Theory of Structuration.* Berkeley: U of California P, 1985.

Gore, Albert Jr. "VP Remarks—International Telecommunications Union." Buenos Aires, Argentina, 21 March 1994. <http://www.whitehouse.gov/WH/EOP/OVP/html/telunion.html>.

Gore, Albert Jr. *Global Information Infrastructure: Agency for Cooperation.* Washington, DC: Government Printing Office, 1995.

Graff, Harvey J. *The Legacies of Literacy: Continuities and Contradictions in Western Culture and Society.* Bloomington: Indiana UP, 1987.

———.*The Literacy Myth: Cultural Integration and Social Structure in the Nineteenth Century.* New Brunswick: Transaction, 1991.

Green, Kenneth C. "The Campus Computing Project: The 1995 National Survey of Desk-top Computing in Higher Education." 1996. <http://ericir.syr.edu/Projects/Campus_computing/1995/index.html>.

Haraway, Donna. "Situated Knowledges: The Science Question in Feminism and the Privilege of Partial Perspective." *Technology and The Politics of Knowledge.* Ed. Andrew Feenberg and Alastair Hannay. Bloomington: Indiana UP, 1995. 175–94.

Hoffman, Donna L., and Thomas P. Novak, "Bridging the Racial Divide on the Internet." *Science* 17 April 1998: 390–91.

Johnson-Eilola, Johndan. *Nostalgic Angels: Rearticulating Hypertext Writing.* Norwood: Ablex, 1997.

Latour, Bruno. *Aramis or the Love of Technology.* Trans. C. Porter. Cambridge: Harvard UP, 1996.

"MCI Nationwide Poll on Internet in Education." National Press Club. Washington, DC, 3 March 1998.

Michigan Curriculum Framework: Content Standards and Benchmarks. Lansing: Michigan Dept. of Education, 1995.

Ohmann, Richard. "Literacy, Technology, and Monopoly Capital." *College English* 47 (1985): 675–89.

Oppel, Shelby. "Computer Lab Offers Escape from Poverty." *St. Petersburg Times* 17 Sept. 1997: 3B.

Oppenheimer, Todd. "The Computer Delusion." *Atlantic Monthly,* July 1997: 45–62.

"Public Law 102–73, the National Literacy Act of 1991." House of Representatives Bill 751, 25 July 1991. <http://novel.nifl.gov/ public-law.html>.

Rose, Mike. *Lives on the Boundary: The Struggles and Achievements of America's Underprepared.* New York: Free P, 1989.

Smith, Thomas M. *Condition of Education, 1997.* Washington, DC: National Center for Education Statistics, U.S. Government Printing Office, 1997. NCES 97–388.

Standards for the English Language Arts. Urbana: NCTE, 1996.

Street, Brian V. *Social Literacies: Critical Approaches to Literacy Development, Ethnography, and Education.* London: Longman, 1995.

Stuckey, J. Elspeth. *The Violence of Literacy.* Portsmouth: Boynton, 1990.

US Dept. of Education. Community Update, No. 56. "President Clinton Sends 1999 Budget to Congress." Office of Intergovernmental and Interagency Affairs, 1998.

Virilio, Paul. *Speed and Politics: An Essay on Dromology.* Trans. Mark Polizzotti. New York: Semiotext(e), 1986.

Weiser, Mark. "The Computer for the 21st Century." *Scientific American* 265.3 (Sept. 1991): 94-104.

Winner, Langdon. *The Whale and the Reactor: A Search for Limits in an Age of High Technology.* Chicago: U of Chicago P, 1986.

11 The Shared Discourse of the Networked Computer Classroom

L. Lennie Irvin

Introduction

"It's the network," I recall Fred Kemp stressing at a workshop for computer classroom teachers at my college. To demonstrate what computer networks facilitate, Kemp (a pioneer in the theory and practice of teaching writing in the computer classroom) showed us two diagrams depicting what he called "the discourse authority" in a classroom. By "discourse authority," he meant the control and possession of truth and knowledge for the communication in a learning setting.

The diagram for the "traditional classroom" (or as he called it, "the proscenium classroom") presented the teacher in front and the students in neat rows below. Each of the lines representing this discourse authority went through the teacher. In contrast, the diagram for the computer classroom showed a room with computers around the outer walls, and these lines formed a complex maze of interconnections resembling an airline's route map. Lines of discourse no longer went through just the teacher, but zipped between students. Kemp was trying to demonstrate the increased interactivity, or shared discourse, in a networked computer classroom environment, as well as the decentered nature of the environment.

Reprinted from *Teaching English in the Two-Year College*, May 1999.

I assumed that the discourse Kemp described was the discourse of real-time synchronous electronic conferencing. The "achieved utopia of the networked classroom," as Lester Faigley refers to it, I believed was a synchronous conferencing utopia where students communicate with each other in dynamic ways. Indeed, much of the hype and literature about the computer classroom has focused on synchronous writing (in The Daedalus Writing Environment, this activity is called "Interchange"; in Norton Connect, it is called "Group Discussion"; and for Web-based software, it is called "chat" or MOOs).

However, I recently had a revelation which expanded my understanding of the dynamics of the "talk" and learning that occur in the networked computer classroom. I began to look closely at the assignments I had the students do, and I realized that shared discourse in the networked computer classroom has three levels, one of which is synchronous writing. These levels form a continuum of interactivity from students sending messages "AT" each other, to students sending messages "TO" each other, to students sending messages "BETWEEN" each other. I believe it is helpful as teachers in the networked computer classroom environment to understand the distinct characteristics of these three levels so that we are better able to manage this discourse and extend it.

The "AT" Level of Shared Discourse

In the first level, students send a message "at" the whole group. In the traditional classroom, this sharing of text is equivalent to arranging the class in a circle and having each student read aloud his or her writing to the group. This type of discourse is usually accomplished by sending an e-mail message to the group (asynchronous writing), but students could send messages "at" each other by putting a document in a common class file accessible to all or within a synchronous electronic conference. Everyone reads aloud; everyone listens (or in the case of the computer classroom, everyone writes and everyone reads). The greatest value in this type of discourse for the student is comparability. Students learn as they read not only through exposure to new bits of knowledge, but by comparing their message with the other messages in the group. Students assemble the knowledge by their own action and at their own pace, which gives them more ownership of the knowledge, Also, they can open (read) the message as often as they wish. As a result, the socialization to knowledge and to the norms of discourse happens more easily and more readily by this means than any other.

In addition, the "at" level of shared discourse takes advantage of some of the strengths of the networked computer classroom, while avoiding some of the negatives. Faigley uses some of Bakhtin's ideas to describe the dynamics of the computer classroom. Faigley describes the traditional classroom as "monologic" and possessing the "centripetal forces of unity, authority and truth" (183). What he means is that the teacher is the sole arbiter, possessor, and communicator of knowledge—the teacher's "narrative" is preeminent. In contrast, the computer classroom is "dialogic" and contains "centrifugal forces of multiplicity, equality, and uncertainty" (183). These dialogic characteristics are what get so many people excited about the computer classroom—everyone talks (or writes), everyone has an equal voice, and the infallible authority of the teacher is decentered because students learn from each other, not just the teacher.

However, when teachers experience what Faigley describes as the lack of closure, the breakdown of the teacher's metanarrative which gives coherence to the learning environment and the confrontational dynamic inherent in real-time synchronous conferences, they may agree with him that it is "post-modern," but they may not see its pedagogical value. The "at" level of discourse allows more easily for the traditional classroom discourse of "initiation-reply-evaluation." The teacher can still initiate the discussion to which the students send an e-mail response. All the students read each other's messages (thereby taking advantage of the capacity for multiplicity, equality, and comparability), and then the teacher can select some responses to go over together with the group if he or she wishes (thereby reaching evaluation and some sense of closure).

As a hybrid between the "monologic" and the "dialogic," this "at" discourse enables the teacher to maintain more control of the learning goals and standards of the course (unity, authority, and truth). Although less glamorous, less dynamic, and less "post-modern," the "at" level of discourse is pedagogically very useful and does not deserve the little attention it has gotten.

Examples of "AT" Level Shared Discourse

Early in the semester in Composition I classes, I have the students write a ten-minute freewriting journal entry dealing with their attitudes about writing. They are to imagine the figure which embodies what makes writing difficult for them, describe this figure (called the Watcher), and write it a letter. Students do a quick edit and send the entry via e-mail to the whole class. They then read the entries of their peers (in Daedalus which we use, all mail messages show up on a common mail conference, something like a Newsgroup). This exercise contributes a lot to the shared knowledge and experience of the group. Students see that having difficulties with writing is not uncommon and that others may experience the same problems they do. As a creative piece of writing, the students also see examples of creative expressions and approaches to this topic.

I also have the students work on descriptive techniques early in the course. As they try out some of these techniques (such as using more descriptive verbs, using comparisons, or incorporating sensory images), the "at" level of discourse can be a valuable tool for helping them learn this style of writing. For instance, the students practice "showing and not telling" by taking a "telling" phrase that is general and opening it up with "showing." They take a sentence like, "The child was upset" and send a mail message with their expanded version of that sentence. Students also learn how to make judgments through such sharing: in this case, they distinguish between those who have done well at opening up with description and those who haven't. Commonly, I will also have the class open one message at a time, have the author read it aloud, and then ask all the students to point out good examples of descriptive techniques. This same approach for using the mail would work for teaching other writing features or techniques as well.

I have also used the "at" level of discourse in the early stages of a synchronous conference. For one of my classes, we had an assignment on the topic of stereotypes, and before class students read two essays which dealt with this general theme. For their initial message, students included one or two quotes from the reading which they felt were significant and related to the theme. For the second message, students shared one experience they had confronting a stereotype, These "at" messages highlighted significant points from the text and helped to generate some "between" discourse in the group. After this synchronous discussion, I introduced students to the paper topic on stereotypes, so this exercise broadened their understanding of the topic and the texts and helped them see possibilities for the specific topic of their paper.

The "TO" Level of Shared Discourse

In this level of discourse, students direct a message to a specific person in the group. It is like a letter which is addressed and sent by regular mail. Usually, this type of discourse has a clearer purpose and a more defined audience. In this way, the "to" level is rhetorically more sophisticated. E-mail is the most obvious place for this "to" discourse, but it also occurs in peer review (called "Respond" in Daedalus) and can be in synchronous conferences. With the "to" act of discourse, students many times—but not always—implement judgments and knowledge they have gained, since these messages may contain peer comments or evaluations.

One other characteristic of discourse in the networked computer classroom in general, but which seems to express itself more in the "to" level of discourse, is objectivity for the students. Since the students are not facing their audience in person, and they are not even sure when the addressee will read their message, they experience a kind of distance from their audience which allows them to be more objective and honest in their discourse. Linda Adler-Kassner and Thomas Reynolds in an article about using the computer classroom to enhance students' reading ability called this environment a "safe place": "We've found that students tend to disclose more about their interaction with reading over e-mail than they do in the classroom" (174).

Their observation confirms my own assessment of peer response in the computer classroom. Comparing peer response in the traditional classroom to that in the computer classroom, I found that students in the computer environment put 32% more content into their responses. In addition, I noted a qualitative superiority to the responses from the computer classroom (Irvin 3). Kassner and Reynolds state that "the anonymity of e-mail (although students are aware that their names are attached to their posts) seems to provide this student with the kind of distance from instructor and classmates that she needed to write an honest assessment of her reading" (174). This distance, coupled with the power and confidence computers encourage in students, seems to help students write more and better responses "to" each other.

Examples of "TO" Level of Shared Discourse

Peer response represents the most prevalent "to" discourse in the computer composition class. However this peer response is done (and in Daedalus there are at least five different ways), students most often answer a number of prepared questions which call on them to put into practice knowledge they have learned in the course by making observations, judgments, and recommendations about their peers' writing. These comments are then sent to the authors via e-mail or other means.

Another example of "to" discourse I have used (with the Daedalus software) involves students refining a tentative thesis. Before this exercise, the class should have studied some characteristics of a good thesis statement, and students should arrive at class with a tentative thesis in mind. Using the mail, students send their thesis statement in an initial message. Working in groups of five to seven, students respond "to" each peer by critiquing the thesis and then offering a revised version. This revised version can simply be a restatement of the thesis using different language from the original or a refining of the ideas expressed. After this first flurry of "to" messages, each author reads his or her mail and sends a new mail message with a revised version of the thesis. If more refining is needed, and time allows, this same sequence can be repeated. I have used this exercise with developmental students and been amazed at how good they are at responding to each other and how well this exercise gets across the idea of what makes a good thesis.

One of the great values of the computer is its ability to enhance role playing for students. In another exercise, I pair students on separate sides of an issue (one smokes and the other doesn't, one believes same sex marriages are OK and one doesn't) and then ask them to write a persuasive piece to sway their peer to their point of view. This exercise requires students to put on a "rhetorical mask" to explore aspects of audience and purpose. The point is to make the rhetorical situation of audience and purpose as defined and immediate as possible (even if the rhetorical situation is fictitious—i.e., students put on a pose). The exercise can involve a single mail message "to" each other, or it can become a back and forth debate.

The "BETWEEN" Level of Shared Discourse

The "between" level of discourse most excites students who have gotten involved in the networked computer classroom. Real-time synchronous electronic conferencing (called Interchange in Daedalus) is the primary place for this type of discourse, in which students dialogue back and forth among themselves. Out of the crucible of discourse, meaning forms, explodes, and takes shape again. It is at once "at" discourse because students send messages which are read by all the group, and it is "to" discourse because frequently students direct comments to each other, but the dynamic is continued into exchange. Students feel a real sense of audience in this environment because the rest of the class is reading and can respond immediately.

In addition, synchronous discussions have received a lot of positive attention for their qualities of "multiplicity" and "equality": more students get involved in the discussion and each has an equal "voice" since all messages appear in the same way on the computer screen. I always think of synchronous electronic conferences as a class discussion (in the traditional classroom sense), except that every student can speak at once; they tend to write more; and I cannot lead and orchestrate the discussion like in the traditional classroom (i.e. initiation-reply- evaluation). Students also engage more with each other rather than direct their discourse toward the teacher, as in the traditional classroom.

While some of the features of this type of discourse noted earlier may be negatives (such as the lack of closure, the decentering of authority away from the teacher, the confrontational dynamics, and the movement away from "truth" to uncertainty), they are also this discourse's strengths. As Faigley points out after his students finished a synchronous discussion: "By the end of this section we see a reversal of roles, with the teacher replying and students making evaluative comments. . . . The paradox is that the class discussion has gone much farther and much faster than it could have with [the teacher] standing in front" (181). Students make conclusions and evaluations on their own, rather than the teacher making them for the students. The "between" discourse may be the most glamorous and interesting to teachers, but it is also the one which teachers need to enter into with the most care and intent so that the conversation does not descend into trivialities or name calling.

Examples of "BETWEEN" Level of Discourse

Synchronous electronic conferencing is excellent for class discussion over readings or over a general subject which can be used for a paper topic. In a literature class, students can debate various interpretations of a piece of literature. In a more creative vein, students can assume pseudonyms and take on the persona of various characters in a story and then debate interpretations of the literature. Most often, I use synchronous discussions as a form of prewriting to broaden the students' understanding of a general topic for a paper assignment. The students share their perspectives on the topic and then dialogue and debate back and forth.

Synchronous writing and the "between" discourse can be used by small groups also to negotiate meaning. One of my colleagues frequently has his classes work in small groups to construct collaborative essays in competition. These groups figure out how they will work and what they will write by dialoguing in a synchronous conference. Creating these multiple synchronous conferences is easily done in Daedalus and Norton, but without these software packages a teacher could accomplish the same thing by taking students to a MOO and letting each group dialogue in different rooms.

I have also used synchronous conferencing for peer response to try to simulate the kind of discussion that happens in small peer groups in traditional classrooms. Usually, students first send an "at" message which is an initial response to the essay, and then they discuss the essay via mail among themselves.

Extending the Shared Discourse

What becomes exciting is when the shared discourse, and thus the social knowledge of the group, gets extended. This extension occurs as a repeated sequence of *invention, reflection,* and *reinvention.*

In the case of the Watcher example (where students imagined the being that makes writing difficult), the students at this point have done two of these acts—invention, the initial expression in the mail message, and reflection, reading all the messages of their peers. The act of reading and reflecting upon the multiplicity of views inevitably causes the students to expand their ideas. Next, I have students work in groups to reformulate their ideas by creating a collage on the Watcher from pieces of their peers' mail messages (which is easily done by cutting and pasting from the e-mail messages). This new expression—this reinvention—in turn can be posted for all the students in the class to read for a second act of reflection. The students can then be asked to reinvent their ideas again by writing a letter to prospective students about the most common anxieties and difficulties experienced by novice writers.

Extending the shared discourse is like a house of mirrors, with each act of reflection leading to a new act of invention and learning that leads to more reflection. For example, a typical way of extending the shared discourse might come after a synchronous conferencing session. To coalesce some points of meaning and importance, the teacher can ask the students to review the transcript of a synchronous discussion they have just completed and then pick out three important points or write some conclusion they have discovered from the discussion. These new pieces of writing can then, in turn, be posted as e-mail messages or messages in a synchronous conference and read by the class.

Paolo Freire suggests the possibilities when such shared discourse is extended: "Knowledge emerges only through invention and reinvention, through the restless impatient, continuing, hopeful inquiry men pursue in the world, with the world, and with each other" (213). Students' learning and expression grows as the discourse is extended; however, managing this extended discourse, encouraging it, fostering it, setting it in motion takes a great deal of preparation, as well as tasks and topics which move the students naturally through interacting with and learning from each other.

The Last Word

How a teacher uses a networked computer classroom is inextricably connected to his or her notions of how people learn to write. David McConnell expresses the main premise for teachers using the collaborative or constructivist approach: "The major message . . . is that people learn best when they have the opportunity to work with other people, through processes of cooperation and collaboration." And he warns that

> without an underlying educational philosophy which emphasizes the importance of cooperation, no Computer Supported Cooperative Learning system will in itself be effective. CSCL media offer an environment for such activities. It is the people using them that have to believe in the activities and ensure that they occur. (158)

Especially in many community colleges, a significant number of teachers are not using the unique capabilities that computer networks enable for teaching writing—text sharing and collaboration—because they have not adopted new approaches to teaching writing. Todd Oppenheimer points to what we might even call a crisis in "constructivist" computer use in English education today:

> . . . as successive rounds of new [educational] technology failed their promoters' expectations, a pattern emerged. The cycle began with big promises backed by the technology developers' research. In the classroom, however, teachers never really embraced the new tools, and no significant academic improvement occurred. (46)

In many schools, the majority of teachers still use the computer classrooms predominantly for word processing. With the advent of the Internet, the computer classroom can be used as a surrogate library. Most teachers haven't embraced pedagogies which fully put these new tools to good use. In 1992, Fred Kemp described the problem we still face today:

> . . . a room full of computer can do an awful lot more for instruc-
> tors and students than simply provide high-powered writing tools. The
> problem is the effective computer-based pedagogies often require a
> considerable shift in thinking from traditional thinking, a shift so great
> that most instructors cannot, intuitively, imagine useful instructional
> purposes for computers aside from word processing. . . . But to use
> . . . computers only for word processing wastes money and equip-
> ment and instructional possibilities. (15)

A close examination of the shared discourse (AT, TO, and BETWEEN) in
the networked computer classroom reveals many of the possibilities of an
electronic teaching environment. Understanding the characteristics of the
"talk" in the networked computer classroom can help teachers design and
fuel this complex and exciting learning environment.

Works Cited

Adler-Kassner, Linda, and Thomas Reynolds. "Computers, Reading, and Basic
    Writers: Online Strategies for Helping Students with Academic Texts." *Teach-
    ing English in the Two-Year College* 23 (1996): 170–76.

Faigley, Lester. *Fragments of Rationality: Postmodernity and the Subject of Com-
    position.* Pittsburgh: U Pittsburgh P, 1992.

Freire, Paolo. "The Banking Concept of Education." *Ways of Reading.* Ed. David
    Bartholomae and Anthony Petrosky. 4th ed. Boston: Bedford, 1996. 212–27.

Irvin, Lennie. *the Mouse & Key: A Newsletter Devoted to Helping Teachers Teach
    in the Computer Classroom* 1 (1996): 3.

Kemp, Fred. "Who Programmed This? Examining the Instructional Attitudes of
    Writing-Support Software." *Computers and Composition* 10.1 (1992): 9–24.

McConnell, David. *Implementing Computer Supported Cooperative Learning.*
    London: Kogan Page, 1994.

Oppenheimer, Todd. "The Computer Delusion." *The Atlantic Monthly* July 1997:
    45–62.

12 The Craft of Teaching and the World Wide Web: A Reference Essay for Educators

Kevin M. Leander

Like others represented in this volume, I believe that particular educational practices with the Web have tremendous potential to shape how we engage in the processes of learning. At the same time, we often describe the Web with metaphors of the "sea," or as a vast outer "space," and many teachers who set out to work on the Web describe their experiences in terms of being adrift or disoriented. Other educators, through initial experiences with the Web, separate "real work" from the relatively purposeless wandering or "surfing" that the Web appears to encourage. It is my hope that this essay will help narrow the distance between the educator who is a novice Web-user and the loosely structured, ever-becoming nature of the Web—that it can be a mediating tool to scaffold and inspire further discovery.

Overview of Goals

Teaching is a type of craftwork, in which one has a range of tools with which to work, a particular vision of this work, and a set of dispositions and goals. The advent of the Web marks a significant historical shift in the availability of teaching and learning tools. Yet, as noted above, because of the dramatic growth of the Web, as well as its loose, nonhierarchical structure, sifting

Reprinted from Chapter 20 of *Weaving a Virtual Web*, edited by Sibylle Gruber.

through and accessing relevant tools is a major problem for novice and experienced educators alike. Thus, the first goal of this chapter is to serve as an introductory reference to the Web, pointing educators in the direction of useful Web resources, as well as building productive relations between them. For instance, the first three parts of the essay refer to exemplary Web sites that offer perspectives from the classroom, from large-scale projects, and from student work, portraying teaching craftwork-in-action on different scales. In sum, my first goal is that this essay would serve as a manageable starting point—a home base for educators who are seeking to explore the Web as a teaching and learning resource.

Of course, in any process of selection a particular vision and set of values becomes evident, a critical purpose comes into play. In the following I have foregrounded this critical purpose by reviewing select Web sites. In these reviews I hope to venture beyond the generalized critical frames currently popularized by programs ("engines") that search the Web, which award Web sites four stars or three mice for vague categories such as "presentation" and "content." Rather, in the literal sense of "re-viewing," or seeing again, I deliberately examine a group of Web sites not merely as technological constructions, but as noteworthy sites of teaching and learning. In these reviews, my goal is to discuss educational practices that are enhanced or made possible through the World Wide Web, as well as to indicate emerging and largely unrealized potentials. Together, the reviews function as an illustrative essay, building a multistrand argument through repeated examples. As such, I have termed this chapter a "reference essay," in order to highlight both its practical, reference-based function and its critical, value-based function.

Pedagogical Values That Inform My Selections and Reviews

Despite the "Education" subject groupings necessary for search engines, it becomes rapidly clear that on the Web there is not A World of Education, but many such worlds, with radically different conceptions of teaching and learning. In producing this guide, I have become more aware of the lenses through which I am selecting and reviewing, values which are more or less implicit in my work. These values, which I share with many other educators, frame the essay's vision of the Web as an educational medium:

- student and teacher inquiry and constructivist practices
- student and teacher production and publication through diverse media

- communication and interaction with diverse communities located out-side of schools and universities
- the use of multimedia to assist different types of learners, better repre-sent experience with the world, and motivate learners
- a belief that virtual communities, resources, and activities can and should enhance their off-line counterparts, and develop complex rela-tions with them
- the Web not as a stable tool or resource to be "mined," but as a medi-um for which a new range of tools and practices can and should be developed

My hope is that this reference essay will promote dialogue on pedagogical values and the World Wide Web, and that such dialogue will promote greater self-reflexivity within and around the medium of the Web. Reflective engagement is already latent within the everyday functioning of technological tools. These moments find us when technology calls us up short, when computers and networks crash, when demos dissolve—in general when we are urged by our tools to reconsider why we picked them up in the first place. In addition to these spontaneous moments, with respect to the Web in particular there is an increasing need for deliberate, reflective critique as the medium expands and develops a history and identity as a particular set of educational tools. In turn, such reflections on technologies can provide a mirror to our larger practices and beliefs, making more explicit, and sometimes more troublesome, our educational purposes and ideologies, and the histories to which they belong.

Additionally, I hope that the following reviews and references assist you in imagining and planning for your own craftwork. Because this guide may be read hypertextually or linearly, I have listed the sections below. Within each section, you will find Web addresses ("links" or "URLs") to exemplary educational Web sites—some reviewed, others briefly described—as well as links to "Jump Stations," or Web sites that index many other valuable links. In all cases, I have avoided simply presenting long lists of links.

  I.   Classrooms Using the Web

 II.   Large-Scale Educational Projects

III.   Student Work on the Web

IV.   Discipline-Specific Sites

 V.   Journals and Magazines

I. Classrooms Using the Web

Currently, to speak of putting courses on the Web—especially courses that are not structured primarily for distance learning—means generally giving access to course descriptions and syllabi, and less often making lecture notes and assignments available online. This present state of affairs is understandable for a number of reasons: first, these Web texts represent paper documents traditionally handed out to students; second, these ready-to-hand documents are easily transferred to a digital medium; and finally, indexed by these documents is a style of teacher-centered learning that is prevalent at the secondary and university levels. In sum, a predominant "vision" is to use Web technology to make public or broadly accessible the practices we have always performed. The course development work of Jane Leuthold and Michael Hinton are refreshing examples of challenging such norms.

Dr. Jane Leuthold
University of Illinois at Urbana-Champaign
     Microeconomic Principles
     http://www.cba.uiuc.edu/college/econ/econ102/Webproj.html

     Introduction to Public Finance
     http://www.cba.uiuc.edu/college/econ/econ214/e214hmpg. html

     Taxation in Developing Economies
     http://www.cba.uiuc.edu/college/econ/econ415/e415hmpg. html

Review

Leuthold's work in various courses pushes in several innovative directions, among them student ownership and publication, ongoing dialogues among all participants, and interactivity. In an introductory course to

Microeconomic Principles, Leuthold has developed a traditional assignment—the short term paper—into what she is calling a Web Paper. In this case the assignment is writing a descriptive analysis of a market, which seems ideal for the Web as a medium. Through their links, the students take advantage of the large commercial presence on the Web, and use the market's own tools—images and graphs—to reflect back upon it. The papers represent a high sense of student ownership, audience, and meaning beyond the course that surpasses many writing assignments within general education courses.

Leuthold gives a good deal of thought to a particular use of the Web with various course goals and student groups. In the site for Introduction to Public Finance, we get a sense of the interactivity and dialogue that Leuthold is moving toward and shaping for an audience that is much larger than that of the microeconomics course. Here, Leuthold has created Powerpoint slides of lectures, and a "lab" each week consisting of readings, images, links, a computer-checked self-quiz, and student contributions to a class chat line. For still another contrast, consider how Leuthold has used the Web in a graduate-level seminar most often taken by international students: Taxation in Developing Economies. In the context of this course, Leuthold's students have created Web pages concerning taxation in their home countries. Additionally, Leuthold has constructed an "Econ. 415 Alumni Guestbook," where former and current participants can keep in touch with one another, and the international community that the course aims to foster can continue beyond its formal, temporal structure.

Michael Hinton
Urbana High School, Urbana, Illinois
    Advanced Placement Physics
    http://cyber.ccsr.uiuc.edu/cyberprof/ap-physics/Urbana-High

Review

CyberProf(http://cyber.ccsr.uiuc.edu/cyberprof/general/homepage/Newpage/first.html) is a Web-based learning and communication utility that has been developed under the direction of Alfred W. Hubler at the Center for Complex Systems Research at the University of Illinois, Urbana-Champaign. CyberProf is a valuable utility that could potentially motivate and guide students in the solving of complex problems across a range of mathematical and scientific disciplines. The utility has several functions, including the posting of lecture notes, online conferencing, and a grade book. The most developed and unique tools of the suite allow users to construct problems with intelligent feedback—the software permits the problem-writer to build in hints, suggestions, and final feedback; in effect, to construct online tutoring into the problems. These problems follow a number of different formats, and make use of a range of media, including video and graphics.

Currently, a most exciting pedagogical use of CyberProf is under way in AP Physics at Urbana High School, where Michael Hinton's students actually write Web-based problems for one another in their study of mechanics, electricity, and magnetism. Hinton writes that as authors, students interact with the problems at a higher cognitive level than they would if they were only working textbook or teacher-generated problems. Additionally, Hinton notes that the students are more capable than textbook authors in developing motivating problems. Clearly, a student's sense of identifying with a discipline could be highly enhanced through constructing careful problems, predicting and responding to potential difficulties in solving them, using powerful technological tools for this work, and receiving feedback from a wide audience of peer problem solvers.

Valuable Links and Jump Stations: Classrooms Using the Web

- Large institutional projects often give one a sense of vision for what might be possible with the Web as a medium and resource in K–12 education, but a vision of what the activity looks like at the level of the classroom is often missing. An effective yet time-consuming way to capture such a vision is to visit classroom sites that have a Web presence and are indexed by directories such as Web 66 (http://Web66.coled. umn.edu/schools.html). One institutional project that bridges classroom and broader visions in its Web representation is LDAPS (http://ldaps. ivv.nasa.gov/index.html), a constructivist approach to science and engineering through Lego projects.

- Perhaps the largest single collection of university courses with at least some material on the Web can be found at the World Lecture Hall (http://www.utexas.edu/world/lecture). This is the place to go to find course syllabi, assignments, lecture notes, exams, class calendars, etc. The unfortunate name captures a bit of the spirit of the site, but there are some innovative pedagogical uses of the Web embedded within the hundreds of courses, lectures, and syllabi indexed therein.

II. Large-Scale Educational Projects

There are a number of large-scale research and development projects that have made use of the Web to network students, researchers, scientists, and new technological tools. Such projects are often in the sciences, and are often funded by groups from the government or private industry. However, it is also possible to begin a large-scale project by way of the Web through a single person's efforts to bring widely distributed participants together around common goals, as the first exemplar highlights.

News Web
http://www.nvnet.k12.nj.us/newsWeb/index.html
Created by Brian Hanson-Harding

Review

News Web, created by Brian Hanson-Harding, a New Jersey English and journalism teacher, describes itself as "a free, on-line newswire and resource center designed for high school journalists and their advisers." The initiative takes advantage of the nature of the Web to bring multiple functions together in one location: student writers can publish and share stories, graphics, and valuable links; advisors and editors can discuss publishing problems and solutions in a weekly live round-table discussion; and through a clickable map, any user can access current Web-based student newspapers across the country. These features and others hold promise for building community among student journalists and their advisers, who are often isolated, work with few resources, and have limited readerships.

This site is clearly based upon principles of dialogue: not only is student writing centrally published and disseminated, but co-developed interviews are produced and made widely available through a feature dubbed "On-Line Press Conferences," where national experts are interviewed by student journalists and advisers. The potential of News Web extends beyond newspaper production and high schools. Rather, the site serves as a model for how we might imagine the Web educationally: a medium that permits us to co-construct widely distributed dialogues, resources, audiences, and communities that were previously thinly formed or altogether absent.

CoVis
http://www.covis.nwu.edu/
Learning through Collaborative Visualization

Review

CoVis brings together "thousands of students, hundreds of teachers, and dozens of researchers and scientists" in its efforts to develop inquiry-based learning in the geosciences at the middle and high school levels. The CoVis site gives a rich background of the project's goals, philosophies, and tools (although currently lacking much representation of student work). The key goal behind CoVis is to create "communities of practice": "Hopefully, by supplying students with some of the tools and data used by scientists in the field, engaging them in the practice of scientific inquiry, and facilitating interactions between them and members of the scientific community, they can become 'legitimate peripheral participants' of that community."

There are a number of Web-based student-to-expert communication projects that are built around the format of "Ask Dr. X" which have value in their own right. CoVis, however, is designed to reach beyond such one-shot encounters by developing project-length "telementoring" relationships, where scientists can play a number of roles, such as helping students develop research questions, locate Web-based resources, and analyze data. Mentoring and student research are facilitated by technological tools created by CoVis, such as the Weather Visualizer, which is a graphical interface that represents real-time weather data and allows students to create weather maps customized around their inquiries. Collected data, notes, and dialogues with scientific mentors can then be recorded within the online Collaboratory Notebook, a multimedia and multiuser tool that has been developed to scaffold the inquiry process. Even a quick comparison between the traditional school laboratory notebook and the Collaboratory Notebook suggests the potential richness of this project and its creation of tools for new visions of participatory learning.

Jump Stations: Large-Scale Educational Projects

- In ChickScope (http://vizlab.beckman.uiuc.edu/chickscope/homepage. html), students in grades 2 through high school have been able to operate an MRI (Magnetic Resonance Imaging) microscope over the Web to observe the development of a chick embryo. The site demonstrates how the Web can virtually place advanced scientific instruments into the hands of students.

- Global SchoolNet's Internet Project Registry (http://www. gsn.org/pr/) is a central location where you can find K–12 classroom projects carried out in collaboration with organizations such as GSN, I*EARN, IECC, NASA, GLOBE, Academy One, TIES, Tenet, and TERC. Teacher-initiated projects are indexed as well. Keyword searchable.
- Many large-scale projects are in the sciences, and NASA's On-line Educational Resources (http://quest.arc.nasa.gov/OER/edures.html) is a good place to explore some of this work.

III. Student Work on the Web

The relation between new tools and their possible social meanings is uncertain; at times the changes that technologies permit us escape us, or occur years after the creation of the tools themselves. Although there is currently a very large educational presence on the Web, much of this material reproduces our traditions in education to celebrate the educator's or institution's experience over the student's. The examples that follow, however, foreground student experience and knowledge constructions, exemplifying the ways in which the Web can be used not simply to reproduce tradition, but to produce progressive, student-centered pedagogies.

Blackburn High School
http://www.ozemail.com.au/~bhs56/index.html
Blackburn, Australia

Review

After looking at many school and university homepages, my general sense about them from a pedagogical standpoint is that they are not very interesting. Rather, such pages are often overtaken by marketing and public relations purposes, and as such the sense of the lived experiences of students and teachers gets buried under a clickable map of the campus, a picture of the front statue or main building, a generalized and puzzling mission statement, and a long list of courses or degree programs. The homepage of Blackburn High School in Blackburn, Australia, is a potent and wonderful exception to this trend, demonstrating how the multimedia functionality of the Web is capable of representing a vast range of student work and expanding its everyday audiences. The Web audience can view a photo of the "Year 9 boys" soccer team, read copies of student poems and short stories (and write back to the authors), and review student drawings and paintings.

But the real feature of this Web site is the music of the students. The site is a virtual concert of student-produced music, including the Symphony Orchestra performing Antonín Dvořák, the Senior Singers performing Cy Coleman, or some of my favorites, the Stage Band playing Matt Harris and George Shering. Midi files of student arrangements and compositions are also available. While the Blackburn High School homepage may not win awards for glitzy design, it places the experiences and accomplishments of the students at its very center, and hence decenters the idea so often conveyed in school and university homepages that educational institutions would keep moving along just fine without students.

Sundial Project, Urbana High School
http://www.cmi.k12.il.us/Urbana/projects/UHSArt/mic3/gallery. html

Review

An integrated art-science project developed at Urbana High School, in Urbana, Illinois (my former hometown), is a wonderful example of using the Web as an expressive medium. The project involved students researching sundials (which itself made use of the Web and e-mail communication with distant authorities) and then creating their own sundials out of clay, which were glazed and fired. Pictures of these beautiful sundials (one is in the shape of a "sun god," another shaped as a pair of hands) were then imported into the Web page, which also includes student journal entries about their work, a few video clips of the project, and scientific information on the sun's rotation and the functioning of sundials. Thus, this final virtual display integrates not simply science and art, but student sculpture, reflective writing, photography, film, research, layout and design, as well as technical knowledge. Additionally, the project, like Blackburn High School's Web page above, is an excellent example of how Web page design projects can be collaborative efforts by large groups and do not have to follow the one-person, one-computer model of some technology efforts (characteristic of the "create your own homepage" assignment commonly given). For both projects, while many students likely planned and gave feedback, the final Web page itself could have been created with only a computer or two accessible to the classroom.

Job Search and Employment Opportunities: Best Bets from the Net
http://asa.ugl.lib.umich.edu/chdocs/employment/job-guide.toc.html

Review

Best Bets is a Web site that indexes and reviews job search and career information. The site was created by Phillip Ray and Bradley Taylor while they were graduate students in the University of Michigan's School of Information and Library Studies. The authors state that their intent is to "save you the trouble and frustration of following up on leads that are narrowly focused; are not updated regularly; or are not organized in a way that leads one to use the material easily." Best Bets also practices what it preaches. Its own material is very accessible and is scaffolded with the user in mind, from the most general to more specific searching tools.

Perhaps most significantly, Best Bets represents an important shift in student work—learning—audience relations. The Web is often and rightly imagined as expanding the audience of student work to include a broad range of public. Through Web publication, student products and performances that were once enclosed in classroom walls can be appreciated, and even responded to, by distant audience members. As rich as this vision of interacting with a public is, it still is a fairly unidirectional exchange, relying upon a public to participate (and respond) out of good will, general interest, or commitment to educational values. Rather than presenting "school work" to a broader audience, Best Bets sheds the nature of work qua school work and becomes a resource that carries out a life of its own by providing a service for a highly motivated audience. This is not to suggest that all Web-based educational work ought to be based upon a model of production and consumption; however, such goals of public utility may often, in practice, enhance educational goals. In Best Bets, for instance, there is clearly a sense of technological savvy displayed, but much more so the work represents a vast amount of research, the creation and use of a framework for critical review, and the development of a strategy and forum for meaningful communication.

Jump Stations: Student Work on the Web

- Harnessing the Power of the Web (http://www.gsn.org/Web/index.html) gives links to exemplary student projects on the Web at the elementary, middle school, and high school levels.

- Jim Levin (http://www.ed.uiuc.edu/People/Jim-Levin/), a professor in the educational psychology department of the University of Illinois, has undergraduate and graduate students create major Web-based projects in a number of courses he teaches. Other valuable resources for project development can be accessed through his course pages.

- Kids Did This! (http://www.fi.edu/tfi/hotlists/kids.html) is a subject-based index of links to student projects, part of the Educational Hotlists (http://www.fi.edu/tfi/hotlists/hotlists.html) produced by the Franklin Institute.

IV. Discipline-Specific Sites

While it is beyond the scope and purpose of this chapter to offer a broad range of disciplinary sites, I hope you will find that the sites below, and others reviewed in Craft, will suggest ideas and visions that transcend disciplinary and age-level boundaries. The three reviewed sites represent new forms of disciplinary resources on the Web; respectively, a Web-based filing cabinet, a hyper-textbook, and a multimedia demonstration.

English Composition ("Filing Cabinet")
    On-line Writing Lab (OWL)
    http://owl.english.purdue.edu/
    Purdue University

As teachers it is tempting to think of the Web as a means by which we can access esoteric or difficult-to-find material. However, sites such as the On-line Writing Lab at Purdue demonstrate that the Web is also useful as a means of gathering together materials that have become common tools of a trade, serving as a virtual filing cabinet for needed resources. One of the main features of the OWL is an extensive library of brief guides to common writing problems and issues, covering topics as broad as comma splices and "avoiding wordiness," which are often accompanied by exercises. From my perspective as a writing teacher and former writing lab consultant, the available guides and the problems they address look both very familiar and highly useful. For the student working in an online writing environment, OWL captures the value of many reference guides that one might find in a writing lab, and could readily become an essential part of the "writer's desktop" of resources. Finally, for both student and teacher the site helps to situate writing well beyond issues of technique through its pointers to a wealthy range of locations, including indices, professional journals and associations, and search tools and directories.

History (Textbook)
　　Exploring Ancient World Cultures
　　http://eawc.evansville.edu/index.htm

Exploring Ancient World Cultures, under the direction of Anthony F. Beavers at the University of Evansville, Indiana, considers itself to be an "introductory, on-line, college-level 'textbook' of ancient world cultures." The project is in its early stages of development, but it already prompts us to imagine the possibilities for the transformation of textbooks within the environment of the World Wide Web. Currently available is a highly accessible Chronology of the Ancient World, based upon a search engine ("Argos") also under development at Evansville. The chronology, as a hypertextual timeline, permits one to consider a point in time within a culture, situate this point within a broader spectrum of history, or cross multiple cultures for any given period. As a Limited Area Search Engine, Argos is also worth further note. While many Web-based resources direct scholars and students off into the sea of resources on the Web through links, Argos is being constructed through selection and quality control. Thus, in reading chapters and essays, or using the array of maps and other resources, students and scholars alike will be able to access a preselected library of materials to pursue their inquiries. Web-based resources such as EAWC locate and construct themselves within a productive tension of resource openness and closure, and as such hold promise to represent scholarly dialogue much more actively than do traditional print textbooks.

Science (Demonstration)
　　San Francisco Exploratorium
　　http://www.exploratorium.edu
　　Cow's Eye Dissection
　　http://www.exploratorium.edu/learning_studio/cow_eye/index.html

"Yeah, it's a real cow's eye . . . no bull." (Exploratorium
"Explainer"/Dissector)

There are a vast number of resources on the Web for science education,
which is not too surprising given the history of the Web and Web authoring
as embedded in scientific and technical communities. What I find most
impressive about the Cow's Eye Dissection site is its valuing of on- and off-
line experience in the learning of science. Rather than pretending to replace
hands-on science with Web-based representations, the site celebrates both
worlds and their rich intersections. At one level, virtual activity and learning
can occur; at another level, learners are motivated and guided to further
explore the natural world. Through text and images, and especially sound
files, the stepwise group experience of the dissection is brought to life,
complete with the "ooh's" and "aah's" of the students, and even the
"crunch" of the splitting cornea, which the instructor compares to the sound
of Rice Krispies. From a pedagogical perspective, the site provides multiple
representations of the material through multimedia, through a linked
glossary of technical terms, through "Hints and Tips" from Exploratorium
"Explainers," and through links to other sites. Also within the Cow's Eye
Dissection site is a small downloadable application, a "Cow's Eye Primer,"
which is a simple vocabulary-image matching game that could function well
to both scaffold the learning, guide the dissection, and review important
concepts.

Jump Stations: Discipline-Specific Sites

- For K–12 lesson plans in a variety of subjects, try the AskERIC Virtual
  Library (http://ericir.syr.edu/About/virtual.html). The library also provides
  access to ERIC databases of interest to both teachers and researchers in
  education. Also from the AskERIC homepage, among other resources is
  a Q & A Service (http://ericir.syr.edu/Qa/), permitting teachers and
  researchers to e-mail their questions and issues of interest and receive
  information back from information specialists in the vast ERIC system
  (http://www.aspensys.com/eric/). The ERIC system also has a trove of
  resources for higher education (http://www. gwu.edu/~eriche/).

- Educational Hot Lists (http://www.fi.edu/tfi/hotlists/hotlists.html) is a master list of pointers to K–12 education resources that "stimulate creative
  thinking and learning about science." The resource categories, including "Africa," "Composition & Writing," and "Insects," are eclectic and
  clearly extend beyond science subjects.

- Education World (http://www.education-world.com/) is a key-word searchable database of links to over 20,000 sites of potential interest to educators of students at all levels. For discipline-based resources, check especially the Subject Index and Teacher's Resources sections.

- The Learning Resource Server (http://www.ed.uiuc.edu/) of the University of Illinois at Urbana-Champaign provides links to resources for K–12 education, teacher education, and other areas of higher education. The site is designed to promote a movement from "accessing knowledge" via the Web to "creating knowledge."

- The Subject Area Reference Pages (http://www.wcsu. ctstateu.edu/sarp/homepage.html) is a list of links to very general and specific resources for K–12 and higher education; there's everything from Kurt Vonnegut to the U.S. Department of Education.

V. Journals and Magazines

If you have never looked at a journal or magazine ("e-zine") on the Web, here are a few education general interest examples to get you started:

- The Chronicle of Higher Education: Academe this Week (http://chronicle. merit.edu/). The best-known weekly in higher education. After you find a job, check out their feature "This Week's Internet Resources."

- CyberSchool Magazine (http://www.cyberschoolmag.com:/csm/in0. htm). An interesting general interest magazine for students and K–12 educators and much more. Don't miss the Surfin' Librarian, which indexes a tremendous number of useful links to all types of educational resources.

- Education Week on the Web (http://www.edweek.org/). A rich resource. Includes current issues in education with background information, a separate Teachers' Magazine, a job search engine for K–12 and higher education, and a very nice archival database of all of their published articles since 1989.

- Harvard Educational Review (http://hugse1.harvard.edu/~hepg/her.html). Predates the Web by over sixty years, but here it is, or at least part of it. Article abstracts only, but full text on book reviews.

Jump Stations: Journals and Magazines

- From the University of Tennessee, the *Daily Beacon* lists campus newspapers accessible by the Web, sorted by circulation schedule (http://beacon-www.asa.utk.edu/resources/papers.html).

- e-journal (http://www.edoc.com/ejournal/). A major resource for finding online academic journals. Peer-reviewed, student-reviewed, and non-reviewed journals comprise separate categories. Journal preprint services are also indexed. For a well-organized and up-to-date general list of journals and newsletters on the Web, try NewJour (http://gort.ucsd.edu/newjour/).

- John Milam Jr. has created a valuable list of Higher Education Publications available in electronic format (http://apollo.gmu.edu/~jmilam/air95/higherpu.html).

- Education Journal Annotations (http://www.soemadison.wisc.edu/IMC/journals/anno_AB.html). A richly annotated list of both research journals and children's magazines, with a focus on K–12 education. A selective and unusual mix that evidences some good educator souls behind the project.

VI. Digital Museums and Libraries

In his 1996 election night acceptance speech, Vice President Al Gore enthusiastically reminded us that national Internet connections for education are essential to progress, as this would permit all students to "absorb" the vast "world of knowledge" contained in the Web. Through exemplars, I have been arguing that "absorption" is a misdirected way of thinking about the Web. But we also need to give thought to the metaphoric or actual "world of knowledge." Museums and libraries are significant constructions of our knowledge worlds, yet simply translating major museums and libraries into digital form seems only an elementary view of how new technologies might permit us to reshape geographical and social spaces for learning. Among other qualities, the following exemplars demonstrate careful design, selection, and movement between digital "objects" and texts, and the creation of new spaces for dialogue.

WebMuseum
http://sunsite.unc.edu/wm/

WebMuseum was created by Nicolas Pioch, a computer science teacher at Ecole Polytechnique in Paris, France. WebMuseum's popularity (currently over 200,000 visitors a week) and critical acclaim is likely due to a number of factors: high quality images; written documentation of the works, artists, and historical contexts; and a linked glossary of terms to clarify specialized vocabulary. Perhaps the most impressive feature of WebMuseum, however, is that it has digitally created a space to present art treasures unlike any physical space that existed previously; it is a virtual "traveling" exhibit that draws from many permanent collections and is always available. In the Famous Paintings Collection (http://sunsite.unc.edu/wm/paint/), for instance, one can view and read about works ranging from Botticelli's *Madonna of the Pomegranate* to over a dozen impressionist works each by Edouard Manet and Mary Cassatt to David Hockney's pop art rendition of *A Lawn Being Sprinkled*. While students can and should visit the Louvre's collections online (http://mistral.culture.fr/louvre/), WebMuseum's eclectic assemblage of significant works from many collections permits the art novice to cross periods, genres, and geographical locations with relative ease, with no expense, and without sore feet. Be sure and see the site's unique exhibit of *Les Tres Riches Heures* (http://sunsite.unc.edu/wm/rh/), a wonderful series of illuminated manuscripts.

Perseus
http://www.perseus.tufts.edu/

Perseus was developed through the Department of Classics of Tufts University and is under the direction of Gregory Crane. Originally developed (and currently available in most complete form) as a CD-ROM stack, Perseus is described by its creators as an "interactive multimedia digital library of Archaic and Classical Greece." More recently, the project has expanded to include an array of resources for study of the Roman Empire as well. The project is a fine example of how distinctions between libraries and museums tend to break down in Web environments. Like a library, the site features texts in Greek and in translation, secondary sources, and its own searching tools. However, like a museum, Perseus also contains 14,000 images of vases, coins, sculpture, architecture, and archeological sites in the ancient world, and is expanding to include panoramic photos and the rotation of objects in space through Quicktime technologies. As exciting as its vast size and breadth is the kind of interactivity that Perseus permits. All entries are extensively cross-indexed, and a powerful "Perseus Lookup Tool" provides sophisticated interaction between different types of information. One could be reading an English translation of the *Odyssey*, and in becoming interested in Poseidon, follow links not only to other texts, but to representations of Poseidon on ancient vases and in sculpture. Alternatively, one could move from the text or vase to explore temples to Poseidon through an online atlas, and view satellite pictures of the current state of these archeological sites. Significantly, the project is also committed to thinking about how such digital collections and tools might be best used in teaching. Be sure to follow the site links from "Teaching" and browse the syllabi and class notes from diverse subjects, the evaluation materials, teachers' help guides for students, and professors' reflections on their classroom experiences.

Other Valuable Links and Jump Stations

- The Electronic Text Center of the University of Virginia (http://etext.lib. virginia.edu/) is a valuable and easy-to-use repository of a large number of digitized texts in five different languages. Especially valuable is the Modern English Collection (http://etext.lib.virginia.edu/modeng. browse.html).

- Internet Public Library (http://www.ipl.org/) calls itself "the first public library of and for the Internet community" and has its own MOO space (Multi-User Object Oriented Environment) for interactions between people and objects.

- LibWeb's List of Library Webservers (http://sunsite.berkeley.edu/LibWeb/) is an easy way to quickly link to academic, public, regional, and national libraries.

- The Science Learning Network's list of science museums (http://www. sln.org/museums/index.html) is a good jumping-off point for Web-oriented museums.

- The Science Teaching and Learning Project (http://www. si.umich.edu/ UMDL/HomePage.html), developed by Eliot Soloway's research group at the University of Michigan, relates digital library development with a framework for inquiry-based pedagogy.

- The World Wide Web Virtual Library (http://vlib.stanford.edu/overview. html) has a stunning number of links to available libraries and resources by way of a "distributed subject catalogue." It also includes a directory of international digital museums and exhibitions that you can search by topic or browse by geographical location.

VII. Professional Development

"Professional Development" has widely varying meanings among different groups of educators. University educators may not think about their own professional development as an activity apart from the professional organizations, conferences, and networks in which they participate. K–12 educators, in contrast, typically have fewer valuable opportunities and resources for development within their normal work practices, overtaxed teaching schedules, and day-to-day contacts. In this sense, the Web could be a major medium of professional development for K–12 educators. The subsections below reflect a range of audience goals and needs among secondary, junior college, and university educators.

Research and Funding

- Internet Resources for Institutional Research (http://apollo.gmu.edu/~jmilam/air95.html), developed by John H. Milam Jr. of George Mason University, discusses and provides links for Web-based institutional research. The site is also informative for a general orientation to Internet-based research through its review of types of available resources, and through case studies of how the Web has been used for actual work projects.
- For research grants of all kinds, including dissertation research, consult the Illinois Researcher Information Service (IRIS) (http://www.grainger.uiuc.edu/iris). Includes links to international funding sources.
- GrantsWeb, the Research Administrator's Resources site (http://sra.rams.com/cws/sra/resource.htm), contains information on government and private funding in the United States, Canada, and the United Kingdom, as well as a whole host of other resource information of interest to researchers and administrators.

International Scholarship and Study

- The Digital Education Network (http://www.edunet.com/index.html) gives information on international conferences, seminars, distance education, and study abroad, with an emphasis upon Teaching English as a Foreign Language (TEFL).

- NAFSA (http://www.nafsa.org/) provides information on opportunities for international study and scholarship, including an online version of their *International Educator.*

Continuing Education Courses

- In many respects, the boundaries between "distance education" and locally situated education are becoming blurred as resources and practices of both forms are shared. An interesting example of such hybridization, for those interested in graduate study in library and information science, is the LEEP3 program (http://alexia.lis.uiuc.edu/gslis/tmp/leep3/) at the University of Illinois at Urbana-Champaign. The program involves initial face-to-face community construction and the subsequent development of this learning community online.
- The College Guide by Lycos (http://lycos.com/resources/college/index.html) is a well-organized resource for finding out about traditional and distance education programs at the undergraduate and graduate levels.
- Global SchoolNet (http://www.gsn.org/teach/pd/index.html) offers a number of different ways to earn graduate credit through learning about the Web and developing student-centered projects.
- For Web-based continuing education courses on literacy issues, try the Indiana University School of Education Distance Education Program (http://www.indiana.edu/~eric_rec/disted/menu.html).
- For graduate-credit science and mathematics study, NTEN (http://www.montana.edu/~wwwxs/index.html#Topics), the National Teachers' Enhancement Network, offers a highly interesting range of courses taught by university scientists, engineers, and mathematicians.

Other Development Resources: K–12

- Staff Room/Professional Development (http://www. schoolnet.ca/adm/staff/pd.html) is a site of links to professional development resources for K–12 educators maintained by Canada's SchoolNet.
- Teachers Helping Teachers (http://www.pacificnet.net/~mandel/). Created by Scott Mandel, this project exemplifies the professional development

philosophy held for many years by programs such as the National Writing Project; namely, that teachers are their own best teachers and have a wealth of expertise and resources to share with one another when given the opportunity.

- TEN, the Teacher Educator's Network (http://www. exploratorium.edu/isen/ten/index.html), has a host of different development resources for K–12 science teachers and trainers. See especially the "Resources" section for a wealth of links to information on inquiry-based learning, including professional development materials for workshops.

- TENET (http://www.tenet.edu/professional/profdev.html) has a unique annotated list of links, including categories for Action Research, Learning Communities, and Staff Development Models.

Professional Organizations

- Scholarly Societies Project (http://www.lib.uwaterloo.ca/society/overview .html). Produced by the University of Waterloo in Ontario, Canada. Users can browse forty-four different subject areas or search alphabetically for international organizations. Also includes lists of upcoming meetings, conferences, and archives of society serial publications.

- Societies, Associations, and Non-Profit Organizations (http://info.lib. uh.edu/societies/orgssocs.htm). Provided by the University of Houston Libraries. Several categories of organizations of value to educators, including business, computer science, education, humanities, sciences, and social sciences.

- Yahoo!'s searchable database of Education Organizations (http://www. yahoo.com/Education/Organizations/), divided by various categories, is also an excellent place to find a particular site or just browse. The Yahoo! section on Education Conferences (http://www.yahoo.com/Education/ Conferences/) is also a good, general, up-to-date source for international conference information.

- American Council of Learned Societies (http://www.acls.org/welcome. htm). Valuable as a source of links to a number of prominent (member) scholarly societies in the humanities and social sciences, for information on its own programs and grants, and for its carefully selected list of links to other fellowship programs, archives, and research libraries.

VIII. Tools and Strategies for Searching the Web

Directories

Directories are Web sites that contain links toward tens, hundreds, or thousands of other Web sites. Directories are put together by humans and thus involve some process of selection. Large directories sometimes contain their own databases, allowing users to enter keywords for searching within them. Directories are the best places for users who are relatively new to the Web and who do not have specific, burning issues and questions to begin searching (see "Search Engines"). Further, an effective way to investigate such a terrain is to "mine" a chosen directory for resources. Return to the directory again and again until you have exhausted its best resources, exhausted yourself, or have been led to a more interesting directory.

- Global SchoolNet Foundation's wealth of resources (http://www.gsn.org/ index.html) includes a project registry where educators can find out information about Web-based education projects. For another index of projects, check CNIDR (http://k12.cnidr.org/k12-lists/lists.html).

- Kathy Schrock's guide (http://www.capecod.net/schrock guide/). A great initial one-stop shopping location for K–12 educators interested in using and learning about the Web, including slide shows on searching and creating homepages, as well as directories for a range of subjects from arts to world cultures and regions.

- NASA's On-line Educational Resources (http://quest.arc.nasa.gov/ OER/edures.html) is much more than space-shuttle updates. Categories of resources include "Subject Trees on Education," museums, libraries, resources specific to colleges and universities, and others focused on collaborative technologies.

- My Virtual Reference Desk (http://www.refdesk.com/edusrch.html) brings together a number of major directories for education and a range of subjects in one location. The Reference Shelf (http://www.tech.prsa. org/refshelf.html) is another useful collection of desktop resources for educators.

For that classic directory—the phone book—try Four11 (http://WWW.FOUR11. COM). Also useful for finding the e-mail address of your long-lost friend in Boise.

Directories That Review and Award

Some directories (and search engines) review and rate sites. Such awards and ratings can help you avoid irrelevant, poorly designed, or very thin sites and find some of the best. On the other hand, some sites are awarded again and again simply because they have been made more visible, or have powerful budgets and flashy graphics, and the popularity of these featured sites can help hide some lesser-known treasures. Be sure to read, if you can find it, the information on how the sites were rated and awarded.

- CyberSchool Magazine Editor's Choice Awards (http://www.cyberschool mag.com:/csm/eca.htm) is an excellent resource for finding a handful of choice sites for general education purposes. Includes brief education-focused reviews.

- Education World Awards (http://www.education-world.com/awards/) lists monthly about twenty sites of choice and gives "grades" for the categories of content, aesthetics, and organization. The reviews give a good deal of useful and well-written content information about the sites.

- For search engines with rating and review capabilities, try the Lycos Top 5% site (http://www.pointcom.com/categories/), with categories in Education and many other fields, or Magellan (http://www.mckinley.com/).

- Most important, to help you teach students how to critically review, try Teaching Critical Evaluation Skills for World Wide Web Resources (http://www.science.widener.edu/%7 Ewithers/Webeval.htm). Another good evaluation tool is at (http://www.mwc.edu/ernie/search/search-Web12.html).

Search Engines

Unlike directories, which are built by hard-slogging individuals, search engines are computer programs whose job is to locate and categorize Web pages, and not make selections. These programs, sometimes called "spiders" or "robots," continually traverse the Web and index pages according to various criteria, such as document titles or even text within document bodies. Search engines are readily accessible through most Web browsers (the program you use to access the Web, such as Netscape) and their numbers are growing rapidly. It would be tempting to say that the best search engines are those which index the largest number of pages, but you will likely determine personal criteria, such as search speed, available help, types of searching supported, etc., which will help you select your own favorites.

- Ross Tyner offers a much more complete discussion of search engines and subject guides (directories) as part of a workshop entitled "Sink or Swim: Internet Search Tools & Techniques" (http://oksw01.okanagan. bc.ca/libr/connect96/search.htm).
- Search.com (http://www.search.com/) is a meta–search engine that will permit you to search via several search engines at the same time.
- Ted Slater's Search Engine Collection (http://www.regent.edu/~tedslat/tools.html) permits one-stop searching, including many major search engines on one page, as well as a dictionary, a Bible, Shakespeare, CNN news, and street-level map making.

Searching for Schools and Universities

- A key place to look for K–12 schools on the Web is Web 66 (http://Web66.coled.umn.edu/schools.html), where you'll find a terrific clickable map. Another easily searchable database is the ClassroomWeb (http://ftp.wentworth.com/classroom/classWeb/) of Classroom Connect.
- Christina DeMello has created a directory to over three thousand colleges and universities in more than eighty countries (http://www.mit.edu:8001/people/cdemello/univ.html).

IX. Technical Help for Web Projects

If there is one way in which the Web is self-reflexive, it is in offering an enormous number of resources on technical help for working within it. Below is an initial sampling; you will find that technical help is ever present within the medium as you begin project development and authoring. The need for expensive workshops, training sessions, and even books for general technical help seems slim indeed given the abundance of Web-based resources.

Understanding the World Wide Web Historically and Conceptually

- An entire workshop on the Internet developed by Patrick Crispen called Internet Roadmap 96 (http://rs.internic.net/nicsupport/roadmap96) is good for someone wanting more background on the Internet and the

WWW (lessons 23 and 24). There is also a whole range of accessible lessons on other aspects of the Internet, including e-mail, FTP, listservs, and Gopher.

- Learn the Net (http://www.learnthenet.com/english/index.html) is an excellent introduction to the history and structure of the Internet and the World Wide Web, with plenty of links for those desiring further study. Note also the useful overview of Understanding Web Addresses, which helps to demystify who it is you're communicating with on the Web.

Introductions to Creating Web Pages

These resources include information on hypertext markup language (HTML), the standard language used to produce Web pages. There is little that is mysterious about basic HTML codes, and through new software such authoring is getting easier all the time. Some of these sources also situate the creation of Web pages within the entire process of project design and within broader educational purposes.

- For a no-nonsense Beginner's Guide to HTML, go to the site produced by the National Center for Supercomputing Applications (NCSA) at the University of Illinois at Urbana-Champaign (http://www.ncsa. uiuc.edu/ General/Internet/WWW/HTMLPrimer.html).

- Another useful guide for authoring and troubleshooting is the Help Desk (http://Web.canlink.com/helpdesk/), which also discusses more sophisticated Web-weaving with Java, CGI scripts, etc., and offers a large collection of editors.

- Building a Website That Works (http://www.tenet.edu/education/ online.html), from the Texas Education Network (TENET), offers tips on the development process, links to style guides and exemplary sites, and a template. A good home base for beginning development.

- Harnessing the Power of the Web (http://www.gsn.org/Web/index.html), from the Global SchoolNet Foundation, is intended to help support work on the Web from "an old-fashioned, student-centered, project-based learning point of view." This site situates the entire process of pedagogy on the Web in a particular educational vision and offers background on the Web, examples of student projects, and a step-by-step tutorial on planning, implementing, and reviewing Web work.

- The Interactive HTML Crash Course (http://edWeb.gsn.org/resource. cntnts.html) by Andy Carvin at EdWeb is a great little introduction to

Web authoring, complete with self-quizzes. The entire EdWeb site is unique and well worth exploring in that it includes discussions of the history of the Web, its role in education, its relation to educational reform, and competing visions of its future.

- For Web page design, consult Nan Goggin's short guide (http://gertrude .art.uiuc.edu/Webdesign/design.html) from the School of Art at UIUC, or the Web Style Manual by Patrick Lynch at Yale (http://info.med.yale. edu/caim/manual/index.html).

X. Final Reflections

While it is impossible to "conclude" a reference essay on the Web in the sense of reaching closure, I would like to end with a few thoughts, reflections that are directed toward interrupting two dichotomies. First, it is tempting to imagine the Web as either an entirely old space or an entirely new space, and critiques of the Web in education often play at the extremes of this dichotomy—arguing that in the relationship between the Web and education either nothing or everything has changed. An important, related dichotomy is often constructed between the technophobic, Web-shunning naysayer (old teacher) and the technophilic Web-developing wonder educator (new teacher). As we become more familiar with the Web and both absorb and develop it into the everyday work of teaching and learning, we need also to imagine the variable and broad relations that it, and other technologies, can have to our work.

Old Space/New Space

It is important to reflect upon the ways in which the Web is historically related to teaching and learning practices that have developed over long periods of time. In many ways, the Web is an old space, a familiar space. We can and should critique constructions of education on the Web that look like more of the same—more lectures, more course notes and syllabi, more talking teachers and few talking students. At the same time, within our critiques we should recognize and reflect upon our expectations for change as well. The expectation that everything will change with the development of new media is closely related to the expectation that nothing will change: both extremes of the dichotomy express something of the non-relation of technology to other parts of the educational world. In the "old space" view, technology is seen as operating beyond educational life, with no impact upon it, while in the "new space" view, it is tempting to celebrate technology as determining the direction of educational change, rather than being deeply related to other players, including durable and evolving teaching practices, student orientations to learning, and institutional and commercial movements.

Which is to say, in the end, that the Web always confronts us with the old and the new complexly related, and that for understanding, appreciating, and participating in the Web environment it seems important to enter into the dialogue between history and innovation. As the Web moves toward becoming a new(er) space for teaching and learning, this reference essay highlights some developing potentials that are particularly encouraging. Many of the sources indexed and reviewed represent how multimedia can help motivate and enhance student learning, and how such media can also permit students to produce and represent their learning in diverse ways. Related to student construction are the potentials of interaction with diverse communities of practice, which can loosen the boundaries of "schooling," including those of "student" and "teacher" identities. Further, the Web offers avenues of engagement with museums, libraries, and other learning spaces that were formerly much more distant to the student's desk. While all of these issues have been discussed within educational practice and theory for some time, the development of the World Wide Web offers a stimulating space in which to further develop these values as practices, building productive theory-practice relations.

Old Teacher/New Teacher

In many ways the old teacher/new teacher dichotomy is a personalization of old space/new space. It is tempting to group ourselves and others as either technophobes or technophiles, and tempting as well to map these groupings onto "regressive" versus "progressive" teacher identities and pedagogies. Once again, those who are primarily critical of the Web as a learning environment will find plenty of evidence for nonprogressive education with it, and those dubbed "true believers" will find plenty of support for their position as well. In this essay, in exploring a range of Web-based resources as well as a range of pedagogies, I have tried to suggest that the spectrum of engagements with the Web is very broad. This is simply to say in closing that as educators all of us develop complex and unique identities with developing technologies, relations that change over time and that are likely not located on one end of a false dichotomy.

While for some educators complete courses as well as student projects are Web-dependent, for others the Web is merely a reference for students to consult among many. For still other educators, the Web is a personal and not a classroom learning space—a space for professional development courses and reading online journals. As the Web becomes more integrated as a learning space and tool into the daily practice of education, it is likely that individually and collectively we will make fewer distinctions between non-Web-based and Web-based learning and identities, that these worlds will intersect in complex ways. And, at this crossroads, hopefully we will develop a productively broad range of teaching and learning practices that move beyond education as we experience it today.

Note

A version of this chapter also appears online at http://www.ed.uiuc.edu/students/k-leand/craft/crafthome.html.

This book was set in Optima and Trajan by
City Desktop Productions.
The typeface used on the cover was Trajan.
The book was printed by IPC Communication Services.